DALY
LIFE

DALY LIFE

"Every Step a Struggle":
Memoirs of a World-
Champion Coach

CHUCK DALY with *Joe Falls*

MASTERS PRESS

Published by Masters Press, 5025 28th Street, S.E., Grand Rapids, Michigan 49512

Photo credits: page 48, Five-Star Basketball Camp; pages 49, 56, *Herald-Sun,* Harold Moore, photographer; page 58, Jet Commercial Photographers, Courtesy of Boston College; page 63, University of Pennsylvania Sports Information Department; chapters 5–13, Einstein Photo, except page 75, Philadelphia 76ers.

Printed in the United States of America

Library of Congress Cataloging-in-Publication Data

Daly, Chuck, 1930 –
    Daly life : every step a struggle : memoirs of a world-champion coach / Chuck Daly with Joe Falls. — 1st ed.
        p.   cm.
    ISBN 0-940279-34-7
    1. Daly, Chuck, 1930 –   . 2. Basketball—United States—Coaches—Biography. 3. National Basketball Association. I. Falls, Joe. II. Title.
    GV884.D34A3   1990
    796.323'092'2—dc20
    [B]   90-46381
                                                                                      CIP

To my parents, Earl and Geraldine,
for showing me how
to love and hope.

To my wife, Terry,
for putting up with my being away
and for just being there,
along with Koko.

To my daughter, Cydney,
for all the love and beauty
she brought into our lives.

To my exceptional players, associates, and friends,
for taking the time to teach
and support me as I am.

CONTENTS

PART 1
TIPOFF

1 WHO ARE WE PLAYING TONIGHT?

I WOKE UP WITH MY MIND RACING. Who are we playing tonight? What time is the game? Is the shoot-around at 11 or 11:30? Did we look at enough film? How is Rodman's ankle?

And then I remembered. *Relax*, I told myself. *It's over, and we did it. We really did it. We won the world championship. Again.*

I don't know how to explain my feelings as that thought washed over me the day after the playoffs ended in Portland. I thought of my team, and how hard we had worked together for the last eight months. The long, grueling, sixteen-hour days. I thought of the other teams and the other coaches in the league, many of whom had worked just as hard toward the same goal, but had been eliminated at some point along the way. I felt immense pride and satisfaction in what we had just achieved, and I felt privileged to be a part of it all.

Sometimes when I'm alone in my car I can't keep from smiling. I might be running an errand, on my way to meet a friend, or just going to work; it doesn't matter. Suddenly, and without warning, I'll break into a wide, silly, ear-to-ear grin. I must look pretty foolish, but I don't care. It's a wonderful feeling. Perhaps the most wonderful feeling in the world.

That's why I'm coming back. I just can't give up this life. I would never forgive myself if I didn't take the challenge to make it three in a row. Five years down the line I would be wondering, "What if . . . ?" I have to find out if we can do it.

When I came to Detroit in the summer of 1983 I stayed at the Ramada Inn on Telegraph Road and 12-Mile. A nearby movie theater was showing the film *To Begin Again.* I went to see it because it seemed appropriate at the time—that was exactly what I was doing. I was starting over with a new team, in a new city. The memory of the film has stayed with me. I am always wanting to begin again. And now, after seven years as coach of the Pistons, I still want to begin again.

The TV offers were tempting, and I nearly went for them. But always in the back of my mind were the thoughts of not being with my team, not getting on and off the planes, not going to practice, not watching basketball films. I'm sixty years old, and all I have ever been is a basketball coach. It's been my life, and I've loved every minute of it. I couldn't bear the thought of not coaching anymore.

Maybe I actually made my decision during the parade in our honor in downtown Detroit after our second championship. As we neared the river, I looked across to Windsor and saw the Hilton Hotel, where we stay during training camp. My stomach tightened, and I asked myself, "How can I not be with my guys on the first day of camp?"

The process of making the decision, however, was not easy. I was never as sure of what I would do as everyone else seemed to be. A lot of people considered my coaching days history, my move to television inevitable.

My name started surfacing as a future NBC analyst and color commentator as early as the middle of the season. I was amused by the media reports because I had not heard a thing from NBC. I'd had some talks with CBS in the past and nearly went to work for them once, but NBC had never expressed any interest.

Near the end of the season we played the Knicks in New York, and I met with Terry O'Neil of NBC in an out-of-the-way hotel where no one would see us. We discussed the job in general terms only. I told them I wanted to finish the season before thinking about it. I didn't want to confuse the situation. I wanted to keep my priorities in order. They understood and did not make an offer.

I had also been contacted indirectly by the Charlotte Hornets, who wanted to know if I was interested in becoming their general manager. I wasn't.

Denver also called and asked if I would be interested in the GM job before they went after John Thompson of Georgetown. I told them the same thing. I wasn't interested in becoming a GM at the time, and I didn't want want to use them as leverage against the Pistons or NBC.

I don't like to decide things until I have to, so I kept putting off the decision. Besides, we were trying to win a championship, and I didn't want to be distracted.

A week after the playoffs ended, I flew to New York to meet with O'Neil and Ebersol again. I felt I needed help, so I hired Sandy Montag and Barry Frank, who worked for IMG, the company that once represented Jack Nicklaus and Arnold Palmer. O'Neil and Ebersol were engaging, charming, and open. I enjoyed talking to them because they spoke so plainly. They told me about the job and offered me a four-year deal: $400,000, $450,000, $500,000, and $550,000. The first two years were guaranteed; the second two were at their option. And that was it. The offer was on the table.

Television is a wide-open profession with a lot of room for criticism, so the option years made me a little uneasy. I could be gone quickly if they didn't like me. But the network also had plans for an NBA entertainment show twenty-six weeks a year that I might host or contribute to in some way. That idea excited me, and the two salaries together would put me where I wanted to be financially.

At the same time, TNT offered me a four-year, $1.5 million contract, all guaranteed, to work on their NBA telecasts.

13

Chapter One

After looking at both offers, I determined I would be better off staying in Detroit, providing the Pistons would give me what I wanted.

If I stayed, the next season would be the hardest one of my life, and I didn't want to go to manager Jack McCloskey and owner Bill Davidson to talk about money until I knew how they felt about our team and the 1990–91 season. So I decided to buy some time and let things drag for a while longer.

But the indecision took its toll. I couldn't sleep or eat, and I lost ten pounds (which I needed to do anyway!). I spent every day arguing with myself. At breakfast, I'd be going one way, at lunch, the other way. And by dinner I'd be staying put.

Thirty days from the end of the season I had to tell the Pistons my decision. But how could I when I didn't know what it was?

I began calling around for advice. When I asked John Madden how he had known when it was time to quit coaching, he said, "I knew it was time when I did not want to go through another practice session or put on one more film." He walked away with no other job to go to. He'd just had enough.

Al Davis, owner of the Los Angeles Raiders, told me to be sure I was completely finished with coaching before moving on and advised me not to rule out general manager jobs that might include part ownership.

Next I turned to Billy Cunningham, with whom I had been close since coaching with him in Philadelphia. He knows basketball from every angle. He was a great player, a great coach, and is now a part owner of the Miami Heat. Billy told me I had to be selfish this time. I had to make the best decision for myself and do what I really wanted to do.

And then I heard from Dick Motta, who is now coaching the Sacramento team. I got to know him last season when he

14

was a telecaster for the Pistons. He said something entirely new, which really complicated things for me.

"Do you realize the position you'll put them in if you leave, Chuck? It may not be fair for you to walk out when they're on top. Think of the spot that will put the next coach in. If he doesn't win it all, he's going to be in trouble right away. If you stay around, you might be able to get them through the period when they don't win it all. And that time is coming."

He was talking about my responsibility to my team, and he was right. I had an obligation to the Pistons, and it was an important one. His words helped me make my decision.

Two weeks after the season, Detroit owner Bill Davidson invited the team to the Bahamas for a vacation to thank everyone for their hard work all year. The relaxed setting gave me an opportunity to talk informally to some of the players and management about the future. I wanted to know how they felt about the team and what they might be thinking of to improve it. I even asked Jack McCloskey, our current GM and a former coach, how he felt about leaving coaching. He said he did it too soon and had a hard time getting over it.

I also talked specifically with Isiah Thomas and Bill Laimbeer. One day Bill and I teamed up with a golf pro for a round of golf. As we finished the round and rode back in the cart, something I said made Bill comment, "It sounds like you're coming back." I didn't respond.

Near the end of our stay in the Bahamas, my agent and friend Albert Linder called Jack McCloskey from Philadelphia to talk about my contract. The Pistons had found out the details of the NBC offer, so we were at a disadvantage. The Pistons weren't anywhere near what I wanted, but they knew I hadn't been offered anything substantially better. I probably would have been better off if I had made an on-the-spot deal in Portland the night we won the championship. But I had my mind on so many other things, I needed time to sort the whole thing out. It was, I admit, a nice problem to have.

I knew what some of the top coaches were making. Larry Brown was getting $750,000 at San Antonio, and Pat Riley's salary was up there and would have gone up if he had stayed with the Lakers. The Pistons were paying me $400,000, with bonuses taking it to $475,000. And the Pistons had always made me fight for every dollar. It was good business for them, but now I had to think of myself.

Time was closing in on me, and I was still poised to go either way. When we got back from the Bahamas, Albert Linder talked to Jack McCloskey again, but the Pistons had not changed their figures. It was a Monday in early July, 1990, and I had told NBC I would give them my decision on Tuesday night.

I set up a conference call with Sandy Montag and Barry Frank for 9 P.M. on Tuesday to go over it one more time. While waiting, I called Albert Linder and suggested that he call McCloskey one more time and tell him where I was in my decision-making process. I wanted the Pistons to know I had reached my deadline.

A half hour later, Linder called back and said the Pistons had accepted our terms, a two-year deal, guaranteed.

I can't tell you the relief I felt. I realized then that coaching was what I wanted all along.

The next morning I called Isiah, who was vacationing at Hilton Head, to tell him my decision. I've leaned on this young man in the past, and I knew I would be leaning on him even more. I would need his help more than ever if we were going to win three in a row. He indicated that he was glad I was coming back.

I'm excited about trying for another championship, but I'm also apprehensive, because I know how difficult it will be.

The length of our last three seasons has required us to work together longer than any other NBA team. To win a third championship, we will need more tolerance than ever, not just between coaches and players, but between the owner, general manager, trainer, all of us. We've got to stay together. The odds will be against us. How many years can we go without a major injury? How long before age will become a significant factor? How long can we hold up emotionally and mentally?

Obviously, no one knows, but it became increasingly important for me to find out. The thought of someone else coaching the team, someone who didn't know the personnel as I did, really bothered me.

All I know is that for right now, the game is too exciting for me to leave, and that is something I started learning a long time ago in a little town called Kane, Pennsylvania.

2 THE KID FROM KANE

COLD. THAT'S THE FIRST WORD THAT COMES TO MIND WHEN I THINK OF KANE, PENNSYLVANIA, THE PLACE WHERE I GREW UP. It's about a hundred miles northeast of Pittsburgh, and it was called the "Ice Box" of western Pennsylvania. Snow, ice, sleet, slush. We had it all. And I loved it.

I was born during the Depression, on July 20, 1930, and grew up during some of the darkest days of our nation's history. Some of my earliest childhood memories were of haunting scenes of people in poverty.

Old photographs taken during the Depression show the gaunt faces of people in bread lines. I saw those same faces at my own back door, and I've never forgotten them. I saw men desperate to work who couldn't find jobs. Some of them came to our house asking for food, and my mother always fed them because they had no place else to eat.

They weren't beggars. They were simply down on their luck—victims of the times. They were riding the rails, traveling around the country looking for work, but there wasn't any. They had a vacant look in their eyes, and I've often thought how difficult it must have been for them to knock at our door and ask for a handout.

My mother never asked them to do anything, but she always gave them a good meal. Sometimes they would do some chores to show their appreciation, but they didn't have

Me, my brother, Bud, and our mother, the saintliest person I ever knew

to. My mother never expected it. I saw more charity at the back door of my house than I've ever seen anywhere else.

My mother was a saint, and she never turned anyone down. If there was a stray dog or cat in the neighborhood, she took it in.

Geraldine Emma Daly was a very special woman. She believed in the Bible, and she had a very strong faith. We had one Catholic church in Kane, probably three Protestant churches, and a synagogue. She went to all of them. Saturday night. Sunday morning. Sunday night. She could find God anywhere.

My father was a salesman, a neat sort of guy who always wore a suit and a hat. I suppose my love of clothes started with him because I was always impressed by how he looked. He had a car, which was uncommon in those days, but he couldn't do his job without it. He sold produce and canned goods throughout western Pennsylvania.

I acquired an early appreciation for clothes from my father, who always dressed well.

Although I was a year and a half older than my brother, Bud, he was my arch-rival in everything I did. You couldn't name a game we didn't play. We'd usually end up wrestling on the floor, throwing ping pong paddles at each other, or just punching each other. Bud was a great brother. We were always, and still are, very close.

We went to school at St. Callistus, and the school gym was so small it had padding on all the walls so nobody would get hurt running into them. We were taught by the nuns, who taught two grades at the same time. One grade on one side of the room, the next grade on the other side. They'd go back and forth.

If you had to go to the bathroom, you raised your hand, and the nun gave you permission. The boys' room was in the basement, down by the gym. I'd go down there and look at those rims and get an overwhelming urge to throw something through them. I didn't have a ball, so I'd shoot my jacket, a book, or anything else that was handy. I imagined myself making last-second, game-winning shots, and it was very exciting. I could hear the noise of the crowd. I'd stay as long as I dared and then promise myself, "OK, just one more shot." I sweated all the way back up, hoping the nuns hadn't realized how long I was gone. They must have thought I had the smallest and slowest bladder in the whole school.

I wonder if that's how Bob Cousy got started.

On the way to school we stopped at the corner store where everyone bought candy. Licorice. Gum drops. Chocolate bars. But not me. I bought olives, a ten-cent jar. I loved the taste of the olive juice. I'd put the bottle under my desk and sneak the olives out one by one. I'd suck out the pimientos, eat the olives, and, when the nuns weren't looking, drink the juice. That was about the extent of my trouble making. The sisters didn't whip us, but we were still afraid of them, so nobody really misbehaved.

Our whole life revolved around the YMCA. Somehow we always scrounged up the five or ten bucks annual membership fee. The Y had the only indoor pool in town, and the basketball court even had a running track around the top. It must have been just like the one Dr. James Naismith used in Springfield, Massachusetts, where he invented basketball in 1891 by nailing some peach baskets to the wall.

Eventually the white ball lost its luster, then its color, then its leather. It was very sad to see it go. We loved that ball. It made Bud and me—well, special. Nobody in Kane had ever seen a white ball before.

Bud and I found out that the Y needed somebody to clean the pool on Sundays, so we went to Mr. Hazzard and asked for the job. He offered to pay us fifty cents apiece to drain the pool, clean it, and refill it. We were so excited we could hardly wait to begin. We probably would have done it for nothing.

Every Sunday was like going to a party. We had the whole place to ourselves and couldn't believe our luck.

We went in early, before church, and pulled the plug to start draining the water. Then we'd go to mass. If the water was still draining after church, we'd go to the restaurant next door and get a roll and glass of milk. That was the extent of really "living it up" in our childhood.

Then the Sunday Olympics would start. We'd play everything. Checkers. Chess. Ping pong. Basketball. We could be brawling on the floor and nobody would know. It was wonderful. At about four o'clock, we'd let some guys in the back door and choose up sides to play basketball. We didn't dare turn on the lights for fear Mr. Hazzard would come back and find us. Why he never caught us, I can't imagine, although I'm pretty sure he knew.

Life's pleasures were simple in those days. Nobody had heard of TV, so we listened to the radio. I'd get enraptured listening to the Joe Louis fights and the Friday-Night fights from Madison Square Garden. I listened to the Lone Ranger and the Green Hornet on the radio, but I can't remember ever listening to a basketball game.

From my earliest days, I had a love affair with newspapers. *The Philadelphia Inquirer* was distributed in western Pennsylvania on Sundays, and I was at the store first thing every Sunday to get my copy for fifteen cents. Reds Bagnell played football at Penn, and he was one of my sports heros. I was intrigued by the way the papers drew the routes of his long passes and runs. I imagined my man, Reds, zigging and zagging all over the place.

And then I discovered girls.

In seventh grade, Mary Francis Mather made me forget Reds temporarily. She was a little blonde, and so pretty I was afraid to talk to her. I was like Charlie Brown with the little red-haired girl. I don't know how I ever got up the nerve to ask her out, but I went on my first date with her, and Bud went along with another girl. The only thing to do on a Friday night date in Kane was go to the movies, so that's what we did. They were showing a cowboy picture, which I loved, but it didn't matter. I was so frightened at being out with a girl that I never did figure out what the movie was about. I even had trouble speaking. I can't remember ever feeling more relieved than when we got home—quite a young Lothario!

It was a long time before I tried that again.

When I was twelve years old, our two cousins, Guy and Kenny Mayo, came to our house for Christmas. They knew Bud and I were crazy about sports, especially basketball, so they gave us a pure white leather basketball. When you don't have much materially in life and suddenly you own such a treasure, you think you've died and gone to heaven. Bud and I couldn't believe it. Nobody in the world had a white basketball except the Daly brothers. The problem was, Kane had no outdoor courts and no baskets in the parks or the school yards, so we took the ball to the school gym and the Y and guarded it with our lives.

Bud and I were really taken by the game. When my parents were listening to the radio in the living room, we'd be playing our championship games in the kitchen. We had a nail over the back door for the basket and used an orange for the ball. We took turns trying to squash the orange on the nail. First I was on offense and Bud was on defense, then we'd switch. You can imagine the racket we made trying to put the orange on the nail. Mom would hear the noise and come in after us. She had a switch, which we were afraid of, but after taking a couple of licks from her, we'd go right back to our game, maybe using a hat instead of an orange, which was a little quieter.

Bud and I were always doing something. Neither of us could sit still. I still can't, as a matter of fact. I like to read, but that's the only time I quiet down. If I don't have a book in my hands or my dog, Koko, on my lap when I'm watching TV, I've got to get up and move around.

To work on our jumping, Bud and I went to the main street in Kane every night to jump up and try to touch things—the trees, the street lamps, the signs in front of the stores. We were always trying to outdo each other. We'd try to beat each other kicking a football. We'd line up in the street, and one of us would try to kick the ball over the other's head. Then the other guy would get his turn. We went back and forth, back and forth. And it seemed like we always wound up in a fight.

I got a few jobs mowing lawns around town at a buck apiece, and when I turned fourteen, I took a job in Dolan's Furniture store on Main Street. I had to drive the truck, which I wasn't legally old enough to do, and handle the refrigerators, couches, or whatever else we were delivering. I wasn't very strong physically, and I probably could have hurt myself lifting those heavy things, but I never gave it a thought. All I thought about was the fourteen dollars a week I was earning. The worst part of the job was dusting. I had to dust every piece of furniture every day and I hated it. To this day, dusting is one of the most irksome chores I can think of.

Starting in ninth grade, I went to Kane High School. I was one of the few guys who was always taking books out of the library, and that's where I learned to appreciate reading. John R. Tunis came into my life about that time. He wrote about high school basketball in Indiana, and I could see Kane High School in all his works. It was as if he were writing just for me. Our coach was like the coach in the movie *Hoosiers*, except ours didn't drink. His name was C. Stuart Edwards, and he became a very strong role model for me. He was a good coach, a fine dresser, and a quiet but strong person. He later became an outstanding academician.

I wasn't a very good player, but at six-feet, two-inches, I had some height, so they used me at forward or center. All we knew was what our coach told us. We had no TV, no films, no books about basketball. We watched the other teams and tried to learn from them. Mr. Edwards was also our algebra teacher, and he coached as an extracurricular activity simply because he loved kids and loved the game. I was very impressed with him; he always acted like a real gentleman. He never got excited or yelled at us. When I was in the tenth grade, I told my mother, "I'm going to be a college basketball coach and make $10,000 a year." It took a while, but I finally made it.

I played junior varsity ball and nearly got cut from the team, but I hung in there and finally got to the point where I played both JV and varsity ball—sometimes on the same night. One night I was the leading scorer in both games. Don't think I didn't brag about that to Bud!

I loved the game, and I really worked at it. Mr. Edwards had a lot of dedicated kids, and the whole town got behind his team. High school basketball was about all the excitement there was in Kane.

We heard about training rules in high school, but none of us knew what they were. We would eat a certain number of hours before each game, but we never knew why. We were told to be careful about what we ate, but that was silly, too. We ate whatever our moms put on the table. Still, we thought about these rules, and that was something. It made things seem "official."

My brother and I had one rule in our house: whoever got to the food first could eat everything in sight. If there was a

Working on my shot at the YMCA as a high school junior in Kane, Pennsylvania.

pie on the table and I got home ahead of Bud, I could eat it all. If he got there first, it was his. We both understood how things worked and neither of us ever complained.

Friday nights were big events, especially if we had an away game. I loved to travel. It was exciting to get on the team bus and drive to another town to play a game. It brought us all together, and I liked the away games better than the home games.

Traveling was difficult in western Pennsylvania, but no one considered it an inconvenience. We drove through the mountains on two-lane roads that were often covered with snow, and it wasn't unusual for a bus ride to take a couple of hours to get to a town twenty-five miles away. I'd look out the window and feel nervous and excited about the prospect of playing in another town.

I had a teammate whose father had access to a hotel, and we spent the night there before some of our big home games. That was exciting even if it was four or five kids to a room. We thought we were major league stuff.

I started thinking that basketball could take me somewhere in life. I wasn't a great student, and I wasn't a singer, a dancer, or an artist. I had some interest in drama, but never

26

did anything with it. What I knew was basketball, and it was what I liked to do. Even though I loved my home town, I knew it held no future for me.

I found a copy of *Scholastic Coach* in our school library and devoured it. Some guys read comic books, but not me. I waited for the next issue of *Scholastic Coach*. I was so taken by the magazine that years later I did an article for them and when they paid me thirty dollars, I made a photostat of the check and put it in a scrapbook. Herman Masin never did pay well!

I also played football at Kane High School. We played the single wing, shifting out of the "T" formation, and I was the fullback, which made me the "quarterback" in the single wing. I'd catch the ball, turn around, and hand it off, or else keep it and run or throw a pass to one of my teammates. I wasn't a good football player, though I had fairly good size. I always felt I was out of position. I always thought I should have been an end.

The first year I played football I broke my collarbone, and when I came back the next year, I sprained my ankle. It was a bad sprain, and they didn't know much about such injuries in those days. They didn't even know about taping. I'd limp on it all week long and then re-sprain it in the game on Friday night. I never got over it the entire season.

Football was larger than life in Kane. There were girls, bands, people in the stands, and a big party after the game. I have never quite understood why there is so much more small-town glory in football than in basketball, but that was life in western Pennsylvania.

Track was another of my sports, and my best event was the high jump. I didn't have great lift, but I liked jumping and studied the form. The U.S. Olympic Committee never called, but I didn't care. It was something else to do—something with a challenge to it. We didn't have a track in Kane, nor did we have a jumping pit. It was strictly sawdust thrown into a hole. We didn't have a true bar, or even a decent takeoff area. It didn't matter, though, because we didn't know any different. My brother was an outstanding runner and became the state champion in the mile, running 4.30 without a track. He'd do it in the streets. He simply loved to run and was a great competitor.

Every spring we went to Penn State for a big track meet. I got a fifth or sixth in the Class B high jump, which made me tremendously proud because we were competing against the best athletes from Philadelphia and the eastern side of the state. They had smart uniforms and looked as if they knew what they were doing. They probably weren't any better than we were, but by looking better they gave us an inferiority complex, which put us at a disadvantage.

A certain wanderlust has always been a part of my make-up. I always feel there is something special or exciting over the next hill or around the next corner. I hitchhiked to Florida and Washington, D.C., and thought it was the most exciting thing in the world. My mother didn't like it, but she let me go. Nobody was too concerned about crime in those days, and there were no drugs. The worst thing you could do was have a beer or a cigarette, which was out of the question if you were an athlete.

I spent several summers working on road crews, and then in my junior year I had the worst job of my life. I worked in a tannery in Mt. Jewett, a town near Kane. The tannery brought in carloads of animal hides from South America with rock salt and blood still on them. Guess whose job it was to unload them? Then the hides were put into a lime pit to have the hair removed, and who went into the pits to do that? Right again. I did it because it was part of the job and they paid me extra money for it.

One of my best friends, Don Magnuson, was working in Mt. Jewett at the time and I'd frequently go over to see him at lunchtime. Years later he told me that nobody could stand to have me around because I smelled so bad.

I learned in a hurry that lime pits didn't figure into my plans for the future. There had to be a better way to make a living, but there weren't a whole lot of choices in Kane. Either you worked in the toy factory or got a job in lumber.

Not long before high school graduation, the basketball coach at Clarion State College called and said he was interested in having me attend his school. That sounded pretty good. I knew what summer jobs and hard work were all about, and I knew I didn't want to do that type of work for the rest of my life. I wanted to do something that I enjoyed. I figured college was a requirement for that, so the Clarion State offer sounded very appealing.

Graduation from high school in Kane.

Before I made up my mind, however, St. Bonaventure called, and I decided to go there because they offered a scholarship.

It was 1948, and a lot of players were still coming back from service. Most of them were older and much better players from New York City. The coach was Eddie Milkovich, who later changed his named to Eddie Melvin and coached at Toledo. He was an outstanding coach, and he impressed me because he had a system. I was on the freshman team, and I just wasn't good enough. I liked school and had a good time, but I couldn't cut it on the basketball court. I was a pretty good shooter on the freshman team, but I wasn't big enough to compete with the other guys.

Chapter Two

Bloomsburg State and Lock Haven State were both interested in me, and I decided to transfer to Bloomsburg State starting my sophomore year. I didn't have a car and couldn't afford the bus fare, so when I went home, I hitchhiked, a distance of about 150 miles. It was a tough trip, especially in the winter, because it was through the mountains, just like our old high school away games. As it turned out, three or four other guys from Kane went to Bloomsburg, so it was almost like old home week for us. We played LaSalle, one of the big schools in Philadelphia, but basically we were a state school and played much smaller schools. I really had fun in my collegiate career at Bloomsburg.

Even though I wanted to coach, I decided not to major in physical education. With all the guys coming out of service, I thought there wouldn't be enough jobs to go around, so I decided I'd have a better chance with a background in speech. I was scared to death because I had never done any speaking in my life, but I knew it was something I was going to have to learn if I was going to advance in my profession. I went into speech correction and studied for my Bachelor of Science degree.

I didn't have any money to buy books, so I paid attention in class and borrowed the books later or got them from the school library. I worked with children who had speaking disabilities—the kids in the public school system who had "S" problems, "T" problems, stuttering, or other impediments. I learned how to help them and I enjoyed it.

The school didn't give any scholarships, so I had to take on a lot of jobs to survive. My roommate, Danny Boychuck, and I collected dry cleaning one or two nights a week. We'd go to the dorms and to private homes and pick up dirty clothes, then return them after they'd been cleaned and pressed. We got paid for it, and we got our own dry cleaning done free. I also had a job in the school kitchen cleaning pots and pans. Two or three of us did this, and we earned three meals a day. Sometimes we'd sneak some ice cream, too. They probably knew we were doing it and let us get away with it. They were only paying us about ten cents an hour, so maybe they figured they owed us a bit more.

Everyone hung out at night and played cards in an old gym. It had a small snack bar where you could get pop, pretzels, and ice cream. It was a good place to meet girls, but I was more interested in collecting the bottles people left so I could return them for the deposit and have money to pay for my pop and pretzels. I got no money from home, so I had to hustle to keep body and soul together.

I went to summer school, and I still needed money. The head of the speech department was a woman named Alice Johnstone. She let me do her lawn and I also took care of the school tennis courts, grading them and liming them down. I became a night watchman on weekends at a Ford garage, where I worked all night Saturday and Sunday, from six o'clock in the evening until six o'clock in the morning. I also took a job as a waiter at the local vet club.

I did a lot of heavy construction work in the summers, the kind with jackhammers and sledgehammers. I tried to pile up enough money to get through the school year, but could never quite make it. My brother worked with me, and we both loved our jobs. It never got too hard for us. We were out in the fresh air all day long, and when the day was done, we'd go straight to the Y and take a swim and play basketball. We'd be home by seven o'clock for dinner, and Mom always had a great meal for us.

G I Chuck.

31

Chapter Two

We were heavy-duty eaters. My nickname was "Hungry." I could eat an entire pie at one sitting. I would buy it for myself, along with a quart of milk, and go straight to heaven. I could eat seven or eight sandwiches for lunch. Obviously, my appetite was enormous.

I finished school in 1952; and then, like a lot of people before and after me, I got a call from my uncle. In October I was drafted into the army, and my basketball career was benched for the foreseeable future.

3 ME AND THE GROUNDHOG

BASKETBALL WASN'T ALLOWED DURING BASIC TRAINING AT CAMP PICKETT, VIRGINIA. The recruits had sixteen weeks to learn to be soldiers, and dribbling and passing weren't part of the training.

In the middle of basic training I got word that my father had been taken to a veterans' hospital, and I never saw him alive again. He died of cancer at the age of fifty-eight. I hitchhiked to Washington, where I met my brother, and we hitchhiked home together for the funeral.

My dad's death left my mother with no income, so most of my army paycheck, ninety dollars a month, went to her. I kept ten dollars for myself.

When I got back to the army I was shipped to Seattle, then put on a boat to Tokyo. I had no idea what the future held for me.

I started out in Camp Drake, a processing center outside Tokyo. Every morning at roll call they announced who would be going where, so every morning I held my breath. As a medical corpsman, I was sure I was going to see combat in the Korean War. I had seen plenty of war movies in which guys with my job rushed heroically onto the battlefield and dragged wounded comrades to safety. If things had worked out differently, I might have been assigned to a M*A*S*H* unit in Korea and become the prototype for Radar in the TV

33

series. As it turned out, however, my assignment was more prosaic. One morning they called my name and said I was being assigned to Tokyo General Dispensary. I didn't know whether to be happy or angry.

Tokyo General was the largest and most important medical facility for military personnel in Tokyo. All the celebrities stopped there to get their shots before going to Korea to entertain the troops. I saw Xavier Cugat and Abbe Lane, who put on concerts, along with some good jazz musicians. I worked with a nurse, Capt. Jeffries, who took a liking to me. She had been assigned to Tokyo General Headquarters, where Gen. Mark Clark was stationed, and you couldn't do much better than that. They had a little medical establishment over there, and Capt. Jeffries offered to take me with her. She was a beautiful person, and I guess she liked my manners and the way I handled myself. The two of us took care of all the people who came through for their shots. I got to know her and her husband, an army colonel, pretty well. She found out about my financial plight and got me a job working nights at the largest enlisted men's club in the world, right in Tokyo, where the enlisted men from Korea came for R&R.

The club had one ballroom with a complete aquarium around the wall, and another with real palm trees growing inside. It had a water wheel at one bar, restaurants all over the place, and even its own tailor shop, which interested me because I was so fond of clothes. I made an extra ninety dollars a month, working every third night. Every night I worked, I was allowed to have a free meal, so I ate the same thing every third night for eighteen months—steak, french fries, lemon pie, and chocolate ice cream. Five of us worked there. We weren't bouncers, exactly, just peace officers who tried to keep things orderly.

Every month, I went to a certain tailor shop in Tokyo and had a piece of clothing made, either a suit, a jacket, or a sport coat. I bought the material in Yokohama and designed the clothes myself.

I gained a reputation as a man about town on the American scene in Tokyo. I was single, and when I went into one particular club, a Japanese girl would sing "Stranger in Paradise." I can't say I didn't enjoy the attention.

I played a little basketball on one of the medical teams and was asked to go back to Camp Drake and play. I didn't go, though, because it would have meant giving up my job at the club, and I needed the extra income.

I also went to my first basketball clinic in Tokyo. The speakers were Ray Oosting of Trinity College in New England and Bruce Drake, the man who invented "The Drake Shuffle," a famous offense that I had never heard of. I was completely taken in by the whole atmosphere and the teaching aspect of the game. After hearing those coaches speak, I had an incredible desire to go to every clinic and listen to every coach.

I got out of the army in October, 1954, and went looking for a teaching job, but there were none available. I decided to go to Washington, D.C., mostly to see Terry, a girl I had met at Bloomsburg State. I had seen her in the cafeteria line one day, and we had dated during the school year. It didn't come as any surprise when I later found out she had been runner-up for Miss Pennsylvania. By the time I got out of the service, we had decided to get married.

I had come a long way since Mary Francis Mather.

Terry worked for the CIA in Allen W. Dulles' office. She had Top Secret clearance in her job, and to this day I still don't know what she did.

In Washington, I worked part-time at a clothing store on Connecticut Avenue. When a job opened up at Takoma Park Junior High School I wasn't even thinking about basketball; I just wanted the job so I'd have enough money to live on. In January, 1955, I began teaching high school social studies and English and also taking courses at American University, which had one of the first television schools in the country. I enrolled in education administration, working toward a graduate degree. I worked through June and the last thing on my mind was basketball.

Since Terry was working for the CIA, I decided to apply for a job there. I filled out all kinds of forms and applications and finally was called in for an interview. The man who interviewed me asked every kind of question you can imagine. At the end of the interview, he said, "I think you ought to go into coaching because that would make you happier than anything else."

Smart man.

During the summer I was working on my Master's degree, taking six hours of studies while working part-time at the clothing store. I decided that if nothing opened up in basketball by fall, I would enroll full-time in the American University television school and complete my Master's degree.

In the middle of the summer I got a call from Stuart Edwards, my former high school coach, who had become the principal at Ridgeway High School in the town where my mother was raised. The basketball coaching job was open at Punxsutawney Area Joint High School in Pennsylvania, and he wondered if I was interested. Was I!

"I certainly am," I told him, and he said he would support me in my attempt to land it.

I drove all night to Punxsutawney, a five-hour drive, and stopped at a service station on the edge of town to change clothes. I was nervous when I went into the superintendent's office because I really wanted the job. James Downey interviewed me for teaching speech correction, speech, English, and coaching the basketball team, with maybe a little golf instruction on the side. The salary was $3,600—$3,000 for teaching and $600 for coaching.

"Would you be willing to take the assistant's job?" the superintendent asked me.

I told him no.

He also interviewed a man named Melvin (Molly) Dry, who had a lot more experience than I did and had already done some coaching. The superintendent asked him the same question he'd asked me, and Dry said yes, he'd take the assistant's job.

So that is how I became head coach and Molly Dry became my assistant.

Our team was called the "Chucks," after the celebrated groundhog in Punxsutawney. Every town needs a gimmick to promote itself, and ours was the groundhog. If he came out on February 2 and saw his shadow, the nation could expect six more weeks of winter, or winter would be over, or there would never be another winter, or something. I never could get it straight. But it was a very big deal. They took the groundhog to a special place at a nearby mountain and put him under the ground. All the TV stations showed up, along with the radio stations, the newspapers, and wire services. They waited for him to come out so they could flash the word around the country.

Once in a while during my first year in Punxsutawney, I hitchhiked to Washington or Terry came to see me. We couldn't afford any phone calls, so we wrote letters. While on a scouting trip to my old home town of Kane I saw a diamond ring in the window of a jewelry store. I bought it, and Terry and I became formally engaged at Christmas and were married a year later.

The priest who happened to marry us was a good-looking man, and I was taken by the fact he wore custom-made clerical clothes. He looked very sharp. Terry came from Hometown, Pennsylvania, so I guess I can say I married a Hometown girl.

The 1956–57 Punxsutawney high school team, which finished with a 13–8 record.

We lived in an apartment off the park in Punxsutawney and paid sixty dollars a month for rent. The guy who fired up the building's furnace every morning called it "honey." Maybe it was the only object he'd been successful at heating up. In a town that gains nationwide attention one day every year for a weather-predicting groundhog, I probably shouldn't have been surprised to find a person having a relationship with a furnace.

Sometimes we go back to Punxsutawney for a visit. Guess who's living in our old apartment? The groundhog. They've made a kind of museum of the place, and you can see him sitting in the window. I may be the only man in America who has been replaced by a groundhog—successfully too, I might add.

Once I became a high school coach, I couldn't get enough of the clinics. I'd go anywhere within reason, and sometimes I stretched "within reason" to include some pretty long distances. When I went to Buffalo to watch the Big Three games—St. Bonaventure, Niagara, and Canisius—sometimes the snow was higher than the car. Sometimes I'd go up for the weekend, and sometimes I'd drive up, stay overnight, and come back in the morning. I couldn't get enough basketball. One of the joys of the game is the challenge of learning something new.

One of the best clinics I attended in those early years was at Kutsher's Country Club in the Catskill Mountains in Monticello, New York. The clinic, sponsored by Spalding, had speakers like Clair Bee, Frank McGuire, and Pete Newell. There I was, a high school coach from Punxsutawney, Pennsylvania, who didn't know the difference between the Catskills and the Poconos, consorting with some of the greatest coaches in history.

These clinics were designed for hardcore basketball addicts. There were several sessions lasting a couple hours each, and then we'd all stay up and talk basketball late into the night. I sat and listened, trying to absorb as much as I could. The first year I was there, Wilt Chamberlain took part in the games and was one of the busboys. Imagine, all the basketball you wanted and corned beef sandwiches on top of it. And they think I have a good job in Detroit!

The whole thing just blew my mind.

They went over man-to-man defenses, man-to-man offenses, the New York game, the give-and-go game. All the while I kept trying to figure out how I could pass on this information to the kids on my team back in Punxsutawney.

We had a fairly well-known high school coach in Pennsylvania named Ed McCluskey of Farrell High School, who won the state championship many, many years because his teams played a great game of man-to-man defense. It was the best I have ever seen at the high school level. He ran a clinic every spring that everyone in the state attended, and we all worshiped at his basketball altar.

I started going to Pittsburgh to see some of the high school games, making the five-hour round trip at night after teaching school all day. Chuck Knox was there for the football clinics, and Pete Maravich's father, Press, spoke at the basketball clinics. Again, it was heaven-on-earth because you could always go home with something new to try with your kids.

One year they had a holiday tournament at Madison Square Garden, and I was especially excited because I had never been to New York City. My team was practicing that day, so I asked my wife to run the practice for me. I wrote down everything for her and took the train from Altoona to New York.

My school paid for some of the expenses for these clinics, but I paid for a lot of them out of my own pocket. I believed I had to educate myself properly to get the job done.

In 1955 I instituted a summer basketball and weight-lifting program at Punxsutawney High School.

We used leather basketballs filled with sawdust to help teach ball-handling. We used eyeglasses taped at the bottom to teach players to dribble without looking at the ball. These and many other teaching aides were later developed and successfully marketed by large companies.

We ran a three-man, rather than a five-man, league. I decided on that because usually no more than three players are involved in any offensive play. I wanted them to play that way over the full court so they could develop their stamina as well as their style. That was one reason I got into weight-lifting.

When my wife, Terry, took over practice for me one day in Punxsutawney, the kids called it "the best practice we ever had."

Nobody knew anything about weight-lifting then, including myself. We had to use pipes with cement on the ends of them, but I figured if we could gain some strength our team would be better.

I went through the whole process with my kids, and when they saw me lifting, they had to lift. I did it every day, and they had to do it every third day. I also found ways to monitor my kids even when they weren't around.

I had a player named David Long whose family had a place in New Hampshire. They vacationed there each summer, so he was beyond my control for three months. I said to myself, "How can I monitor him if he's up there?" I made up some mimeographed sheets and gave them to David before he went away for the summer. I told him, "I want you to write down everything you are supposed to do in practice and everything you really do." I didn't care if it was 100 jumpers, 200 free throws, 30 minutes of dribbling—I wanted to know what he was supposed to do and what he actually did. "Don't lie to me," I said. "Write down the exact figure. I won't get mad." I had to know where he was when he came back to school.

Coaches weren't allowed to practice with kids in the off season, but if a kid came into my office and said, "I want to work on my game," I'd give him a ball and watch him work. He'd go out, throw the ball up, screw around, and come back in and say, "I worked out an hour and a half and got a good workout." I would say, "No, I watched you. You probably got fifteen or twenty minutes."

I was a tough coach and a strict disciplinarian. I even insisted on a dress code, and was probably one of the first coaches in the country to have every one of his players wear uniform blazers when traveling. The town raised the money, and our kids really looked sharp. When we went on a bus trip, I'd feed them at a nice restaurant and take care of other amenities they appreciated. I made sure they looked and felt like a basketball team, and I loved being their coach.

I wanted my players to be as absorbed in the game as I was. A lot of parents didn't like some of the things I did, and some of the girls didn't either because they couldn't spend as much time with their boyfriends. I gave the guys a hard time about dating girls because I knew dating took their minds off basketball. I got upset when they were involved in other sports, but I understood. I too had been a two-sport athlete in school.

My practices were totally organized, and before a player could begin he had to go through a whole series of drills. He had to do dribbling exercises with the taped glasses, ball-handling drills with the weighted ball, and a tipping drill against the wall. I had two guys assigned to each basket and they had to run the offensive drills. I felt I had the same responsibility to every player I coached as I had to each student I taught in the classroom. The objective for students was to get them to learn, and if they wanted to advance with their studies, it was up to them. I felt the same way about basketball. It didn't matter if we played a straight zone or a match-up zone. I wanted them to understand all aspects of it so they could make themselves better players if they chose to do so, and I held long and demanding practices.

Nobody quit, but not everyone was always happy. The players absorbed a lot and we became successful. We won the district championship, and that success helped us.

I used to get so nervous and excited at games that I started eating oyster crackers to calm my churning stomach. They were dry and I figured if I munched them during the games my stomach wouldn't get so upset. It soon became a ritual with me, and it got into the papers. Our major rival in District 9 was Dubois High School, which was coached by Steve Black. He observed me eating oyster crackers, so he countered with black licorice, and the papers loved it. It was a gimmick, and it was fun, and truthfully, probably an attention-getting device. One night I had a mouthful of oyster crackers when the other team called a timeout I wasn't expecting. When my players came over to the bench, I spit oyster crackers all over them trying to get my words out. That was the end of that.

A radio station came to me in Punxsutawney and was interested in doing an interview about our team. I had no experience, but I was intrigued. It lasted no more than five minutes, and I just spoke off the top of my head about our prospects. I was a little shy, but I was interested in the media, and I knew if I wanted to be successful in my profession I'd have to deal with them. The more my team knew about man-to-man defenses, the better we'd be offensively, and the more I knew about the media, the more effective I'd be in

43

dealing with them. It was another opportunity to learn more about the sport.

A coach's wife has to be a saint, and Terry certainly is no exception. If I wasn't on the golf course, I was involved with the kids in basketball or I was off somewhere at a clinic. I was still playing, too, at the YMCA, and I wasn't ready to quit. I wanted to keep my weight down and that was hard because I loved to eat.

I was teaching a lot of subjects, including speech correction and English, and started thinking about moving up the job ladder. I still have letters of application I sent out when I heard about job openings. I liked Punxsutawney, but I was getting frustrated because I wanted to move on and nothing was happening. I started to think I'd be there forever.

I had been offered a great high school job at Mt. Lebanon, a wealthy suburb of Pittsburgh, but it came in October, just before our new season was to start in Punxsutawney. I was apprehensive about going to Pittsburgh because it would mean a whole new way of life and a lot of additional pressure. The school had already won some championships and had always had a strong program. I said no because I didn't think I was ready. I was still dedicated to clinics, learning, and growing.

In the summers, I went to camps all over the country. "If I can make my players better, I'm going," I said.

I established a relationship with some people from the Everett Case Basketball Camp at North Carolina State and took two or three of my players there for a couple of weeks to work at the camp. It was legal, but it was unheard of in those days. There weren't many summer camps in the East and none near our school.

The camp at North Carolina State started me thinking again about moving on in my career. But what were my chances? I had been reasonably successful, but my biggest player was only six-feet, six-inches, and there just wasn't much talent to choose from in Punxsutawney; the entire population was only about 10,000 people. Yet we had to play against Pittsburgh schools in the playoffs, which had bigger and better programs.

I learned a lot at Punxsutawney, including how to lose, which might be one of the most important lessons I've learned in my life. After I had been there about six or seven years, I suffered through a disastrous losing season. I discovered that you just can't win without good players. I was the same teacher, the same coach, doing the same things, but we lost game after game. It gave me a deeper understanding of what coaching is all about, of what is possible and what isn't. How much I knew was not all that mattered. I could know every way to throw a bounce pass, every man-to-man defense, and everything about attacking a zone, but if my players couldn't execute it, the team wasn't going to win.

I suffered through that year, and so did my players. Every night I had the same ritual. I walked down to the local newspaper at about eight o'clock and commiserated with Ben Jones, the local sports writer. I went into his office and looked at the wire stories to see what was going on in basketball and other sports. I read the local papers from around the state and visited a friend, Ted Swartz, who had a clothing store. He was a good golfer, a fine gentleman, and a sharp dresser, and we became very good friends. I went to see him when I got out of school and we'd just talk. The whole thing was really bothering me.

I had a player on my team whose father was a minister at one of the local churches. One night the father picked me up and we drove around a little bit. He talked to me about winning and losing and told me not to take it quite so seriously, which helped me regain my perspective.

On the nights we lost, I would go for a long walk, regardless of how cold it was. I had to be by myself. I thought long and hard about why I wasn't as successful as I wanted to be. I knew I was down, but I was determined it was not going to deter me from what I wanted to do. My theory about coaching and other professions is that those who are less determined or less motivated will weed themselves out. Some may have all the desire in the world, and technically they may be as good as or better than the next person, but if they don't want to pay the price, they're not going to make it. You've got to go to clinics. You have to work for short money. You have to have an understanding family. I had no lack of incentive or motivation, and my family was always supportive, so I remained totally committed to becoming a better basketball coach.

By the time I reached my eighth year at Punxsutawney I was getting frustrated. I wanted to move and had written to a lot of colleges and some top high schools. I had an interview at Bucknell University, where two players I had sent there became captains of the team. I was runner-up for the position, and nothing else seemed to be opening up. I started to think about leaving coaching, and said to myself, "I'm not going to spend the rest of my life in Punxsutawney even though it's a nice town and I've been happy here." I considered a job as a salesman for high school class rings, but didn't take it.

My former student David Long had gone to Duke University, not as a player but a student. His father traveled there frequently to visit him, and he asked Terry and me if we'd like to go along to see a game. We flew down in his twin-engine Piper and I got a chance to look at Duke, one of the top programs in the country. As a thirty-two-year-old backwoods high school coach, I definitely was impressed and thought the whole trip was sensational.

I was still playing a little basketball, and one afternoon we played a game in Reynoldsville, about fifteen miles away, against the "Redheads," a traveling group of redheads who played pickup teams of teachers to raise money for charity. When I got home, Jesse Long, an attorney friend, called and asked if I would be interested in going to Louisville to see the Final Four. I hadn't taken a day off in eight years, and I wasn't even sure what the Final Four was, but I knew it involved basketball and that was enough for me. I went to the administration and got a day off.

Jesse didn't have a ticket for me, but the plane ride was free. We got to Louisville, went to a hotel, and I had to do some fast talking to get the clerk to give me a room. I bought a ticket from some scalpers and found myself in the last seat of the last row of Freedom Hall, a huge, egg-shaped arena. I was behind the basket and up against the wall in the top row. But Duke was in the tournament and that made it doubly exciting for me. I walked around town and I didn't know any of the people, the players, or the coaches, but I felt as if I had "arrived."

I went back to my room after the game and read in the paper that Fred Shabel, an assistant coach, was leaving Duke University. When I had seen the campus on my earlier visit, I had met Bucky Waters, Head Coach Vic Bubas' top assistant.

When I returned from Louisville, I wrote to Bubas and told him I was interested in becoming his assistant. Talk about chutzpah! He was one of the most famous coaches in the country, just back from taking his team to the Final Four, and he gets a letter from an unknown high school coach in Punxsutawney, Pennsylvania, who wants to be his assistant.

Well I'm here to tell you that miracles do happen. Bucky Waters called me and said, "We want you to come down for a visit. We're having a recruit visiting from a very good high school in Pittsburgh, and you and Terry can come down with him for the weekend." I had to pinch myself to make sure I wasn't dreaming.

Chapter Three

So in late April or early May, 1963, I interviewed for the job. Bubas was light years ahead of everybody else and was the IBM of recruiting. He interviewed me personally for about three or four hours on a Saturday afternoon.

Bubas was a basketball coach, but he was also an executive. His interview was as thorough as the one I had had for the CIA. He went into all aspects of my background, my thinking about coaching, where I wanted to go, how I would handle traveling, and all the other demands of collegiate coaching.

It was an incredible experience, and I loved it. Terry and I went to a party that night so they could see how we handled ourselves socially. I think they were impressed with the way I talked to the recruit from Pittsburgh. We concluded the interview on Sunday. The starting salary was $6,000, plus a camp. This was after eight years of having a combined income (Terry taught also) of $9,000.

August, 1968, my first of many lectures at Five-Star, the nation's premier basketball camp.

Duke University basketball coaches and their wives, 1969. Left to right: Claire Brown, Hubie Brown, Terry Daly, Chuck Daly, Tootie Bubas, Vic Bubas.

Bubas asked if I would be interested in the job if it was available.

"No question," I said. I always trusted my gut feeling about jobs and had never debated about any job. But I couldn't believe they were really interested in me.

Around Memorial Day I got a call at Punxsutawney Area Joint High School. Vic Bubas was on the phone.

"How would you like to be a Blue Devil?" he asked.

I couldn't believe it.

We moved to Durham, where I became the freshman coach, and I was never happier. I traveled roughly sixty-five out of eighty-five days recruiting that year. I learned what IBM recruiting was all about. We'd have over 1,000 folders—one for each recruit—with a minimum of four letters in each folder. Duke was first and foremost an academic institution, but it was also one of the top three basketball programs in the country.

In recruiting, we first identified the prospect we were interested in, then sent a letter to garner information about that player, then sent a follow-up letter. We had to go all over the country because we had to find students as well as players. No one else was doing that at the time. I was completely immersed in the whole operation and was in absolute ecstasy. I went to New York, Philadelphia, and up and down the East Coast looking for players, finding players, and talking to their parents. I loved it.

Recruiting demanded a combination of personality and image. We were selling ourselves, our school, and our program. Relationships with kids' parents in their living room—that's what recruiting was all about. Going into homes, liking people, getting them to relate to you, and encouraging them to send their son to your school. I didn't know if I had all the right qualities, and I wasn't an aggressive recruiter, but I liked the job and knew it was what I wanted to do.

My first season in Durham we had to win the ACC tournament to get into the NCAA tournament, which we did. And not only that, but once again we advanced to the Final Four, where we lost to UCLA.

Talk about irony! The year before I had gotten into the Final Four games with a scalper's ticket that had me sitting in the last row of Freedom Hall. This year I was an assistant coach of one of the teams and was sitting on the bench. The contrast was so sweet that I have savored it ever since, and used it more than once as an illustration of what's possible in life if a person has perseverance and determination.

4 BLUE DEVILS, EAGLES, AND QUAKERS

"THE ROCK HUDSON OF COACHING" WAS THE NAME GIVEN TO ME BY ONE WRITER WHEN I WENT TO DUKE. I guess he called me that because I had all my hair, and I took it as a compliment then (I'm not sure I would now). Bucky Waters was very astute. He was clever, articulate, and very well organized. We worked in the same office and sat across from each other, but there was no competition between us. I was the freshman coach; he was the top assistant. We had a good relationship, and I tried to learn everything as quickly as I could.

Duke, known as the "Harvard of the South," was one of the leading academic universities in the country, so our first priority was always to recruit good students. We were capable of getting the best students in the country, but that didn't mean they were going to be good athletes.

We held study hall for the players and monitored the freshmen very carefully. We wanted them to come by our office at least once a week to talk. We met them in the mornings—Vic, Bucky, and I—to have breakfast with them and monitor how they were doing academically.

We had a big investment in our recruits—a four-year scholarship—so we didn't want them to get behind academically. Losing a player to academic ineligibility would make our entire program look bad, so we were always keenly aware

51

of our graduation rate. We kept after our players constantly. We knew what tests they had coming up and what papers were due and when. It was the best program in the United States and, for me, it was the best possible place to learn the business of collegiate coaching.

Durham was basically Duke University. It was a city of 90,000 to 100,000 people and part of the "Golden Triangle." There were three major universities within a short driving distance: Raleigh, with North Carolina State; Chapel Hill, with the University of North Carolina; and Durham, with Duke University. The whole atmosphere was very collegiate and very sports oriented. Our lives became synchronized with the community life at Duke University, which was cultivated and serene, a far cry from my rough-and-tumble Pennsylvania boyhood.

Terry and I leased an apartment for two years, then lived in a professor's house in Duke Forest for a couple of years. When our daughter, Cydney, came along we bought a house on the outskirts of town, but our life still revolved around Duke basketball. Vic's motto was, "You hire assistants and train them to become head coaches." I've tried to make that my motto throughout my career as well. The one prerequisite I have for hiring an assistant coach is that he be smarter than I am. The people Vic hired were all blue chip. When Bucky left, we brought in Tom Carmody, who went on to become head coach at Rhode Island, and Hubie Brown came in as freshman coach when I took over Bucky's job as assistant to Bubas.

UCLA was the powerhouse in those days, and I went to scout them several times. I started following John Wooden to his clinics. Whenever he went, I went. I wanted to pick up even one single idea that might help us beat him down the line. I became a great admirer of his. Watching his operation and listening to his philosophy told me that he too was what Pat Riley calls a "lifer" in basketball.

I had never seen a team practice the way UCLA practiced. They used the ninety-foot floor for almost every drill, which was part of Wooden's philosophy. There was a strange kind of quiet in Pauley Pavilion during those workouts. It was almost church-like. There was no conversation between the players, and the discipline was more intense than I had ever seen. They went through their practice as though they were in a time warp, and I sat there in utter amazement. I had been to a lot of other practices by other great coaches, and we used to think we ran a good practice ourselves, but none of them were like what I saw at John Wooden's practices.

I watched Lew Alcindor in a freshman game, before he became Kareem Abdul-Jabbar. He was a freshman playing against the varsity. I had seen him play in high school at Power Memorial in Manhattan. He allowed only a handful of schools to recruit him, and ours wasn't one of them, but I showed up anyway, hoping we could get our foot in the door at Power Memorial. There was no question about his game, his demeanor, his style, or his talent. When he stepped onto the court, I knew I was seeing a legend-in-the-making.

Assistant basketball coaches at Duke were in a high-profile position. Ours was one of the programs everyone watched. While there, I had interviews at Connecticut, Penn State, Memphis State, and Florida, and my name seemed to be frequently mentioned when there was a major job opening. I'm not sure if I was interviewed at Navy, but I was a candidate there. Some of these schools were very interested, but I decided I wasn't ready. I looked at their programs and I had a good reason for turning each one down. Florida didn't have a major arena; Memphis State was in the Missouri Valley Conference and didn't recruit blacks at that time; and I didn't think we could be happy living in Storrs, Connecticut.

I was interested in the Penn State job, but it went to Johnny Bach. I was still a high-profile assistant and was never unhappy that I didn't take the other jobs. After my sixth year at Duke, I said to myself, "I'm happy I stayed, even though I'm older, because I've learned so much, even in this past year."

Vic Bubas was a dominant personality in college basketball, and the thing he taught me the most about was organization. Total organization—mental, physical, emotional, and spiritual. He was totally organized in everything he did. He was always looking at the big picture and what the impact and consequences of each decision might be. He ran a strong program and didn't tolerate any nonsense. Once we were playing Penn State over the Christmas holidays and some of our kids were at a New Year's Eve party where there was some drinking going on. That was a major, major offense in the program at Duke, and Bubas wouldn't stand for it. He suspended six or seven players, but we won the game anyway.

During my sixth year at Duke, at an away game against Virginia, Vic called Hubie Brown and me into his motel room and told us he was leaving at the end of the school year. We weren't allowed to tell anyone, but he just felt it was time to move on in his career.

My name had been brought up for the head coaching job at Boston College by some friends in New York, and late in the season I was interviewed by Bill Flynn, one of the great athletic directors in the business. I decided that if I had a shot at the head coaching job at Duke, I wanted to stay there, but the situation was very unsettled. Bucky Waters had gone to West Virginia as the head coach and had done very well, and he had been with Vic since the outset of his program. We were in the finals of the ACC tournament and staying at a motel in Charlotte when I got a call from Bill Flynn offering me the job at BC. Duke was not yet ready to make a decision about Bubas' successor.

Fred Shabel, the man I replaced at Duke, was now at Connecticut and had just moved from coach to athletic director. I had great admiration for his administrative skills, so I discussed my situation with him. Then I went to Eddie Cameron, the athletic director at Duke, a gentleman if ever there was one, and talked it over with him.

Basically, Duke had a list of three people—Bucky, me, and Lefty Driesell, who was at Davidson before going to Maryland. I was the only assistant in the group. I said to Cameron, "I'd like to know where I stand," and he replied, "I'd like you to wait till tomorrow so I can talk to the president." I called the president and he said basically the same thing. I thought about it through the afternoon and skipped a meeting I was supposed to attend. Vic was a little perturbed, but there was a lot on the line and I wanted to do some thinking. I had to get this thing resolved.

The Converse shoe company had also come to me and wanted me to work for them, so I had a couple of options, and in my own mind I didn't think I was going to get the job at Duke. Bucky and Lefty were more visible than I, and visibility was important at Duke. Late in the afternoon, I accepted the Boston College job and told Vic before the game. I went into the arena with Duke that night, and the next day I flew out for my first press conference at Boston College. I don't think Vic was too happy about my decision. I wanted to be a candidate at Duke, but I could see it wasn't going to work out. I had made a decision that it was time for me to be a head coach, and this was the only opportunity I had. I knew it was going to be a difficult job, maybe more difficult than some of the jobs I turned down. But it was time for me to move on in my career.

The problem was, how could I fill Bob Cousy's shoes?

He had been at Boston College for about six years and was a basketball legend. He had taken his team to the NIT tournament and I knew I was going to lose a lot of key people. Bob Cousy was very honorable. He knew a year or two in advance that he was going to leave, and he didn't want to recruit players by telling them he was going to be around. That was the honest thing to do, but it left the cupboard a little bare for me.

Still, I went there knowing the kind of program they had. There was no money, and no offices. The room I was to use as an office had green linoleum on the floor with two desks and two chairs. That was it. I went to Bill Flynn and told him we would have to redecorate the place, because I couldn't bring kids in and let them see that kind of setup. He listened and let me bring in an interior decorator. Not only did we redo the basketball office, we redid his office, the athletic moderator's office, and even the football office. Everyone felt better.

"Are you satisfied?" Flynn asked.

"What about the gym?" I said.

We eventually got that fixed up, too. We were one of the first schools in the country to put down a tartan floor, trying

Moving day, 1969: Terry, Cydney, and I all packed and ready to move from Durham, North Carolina, to Boston and my first collegiate head coaching job at Boston College.

to jazz it up a bit. It was still a bandbox of a place, though, and the only way to solve that would have been to build a new fieldhouse. I never got that far.

The program at Boston had been successful because of Bob Cousy. People went there because of his name. It wasn't even really a program, as such. It was a personality cult based on the high profile of one man—one of the greatest players in the history of the game. Still, I liked Bill Flynn and I was treated well. But it was very difficult to recruit. Even college hockey was bigger on campus than basketball.

I scheduled my first team meeting at Boston College, and when the meeting started I locked the door and nobody else was allowed in. I made up my mind I wanted to establish who I was and what I wanted to do. One or two players were late and they missed the meeting.

We played our first game against Boston University, a big rival, and lost. I looked out the window of the gym and the Charlestown Bridge was there. I said to the sports writers, "Hey, guys, I ain't jumping."

It was a hard year. We didn't have a very good season, but it was a tremendous learning experience. It was my first head coaching job in college, and I had to find out who I was, how I wanted to coach, and how I could adapt to my personnel. Living in a major city was something I had never done before, but I learned to like it.

The next year I had a premier guard named Jimmy O'Brien, with whom I had a strong personality conflict. Finally I said, "Let's go to lunch." We went to a greasy spoon and sat down and talked it all out. We started out confrontational, but as we listened to each other, we started to understand and accept each other's point of view. That lunch completely transformed our relationship and laid the foundation for a close friendship. Later that season I had to go find him and tell him that his father had died, and that was one of the hardest things I ever had to do in my life. Jimmy was later drafted by the ABA and played for Pittsburgh. He was a terrific kid and has become a good collegiate coach.

Because the NCAA tournament took only conference winners at that time, getting into the NIT was a major goal for us. We were right on the border; we won sixteen games and needed seventeen to make it. We played an interesting game late in the season against Massachusetts, which had a player named Julius Erving. I devised a defense for him, and, if I'm not mistaken, he got only seven points.

We missed out on the NIT, which would have been a big thing for us, and now I had come full circle from Duke. I knew there were not that many kids interested in playing for BC, because we were not a basketball school like Duke. I used to drive from Boston to New York three or four nights a week, four and a half hours each way, to see high school games. I

Diagramming a play at Boston College, 1971. The player on the far right is Jim O'Brien, who later became head coach at the college.

drove to save money, but I also liked to drive because it gave me more time to think. I had a lot of fun at Boston College, and Bill Flynn was incredibly supportive.

There are different kinds of athletic directors in college. Some stay completely away and let you run your program, which is fine. Others show up when you win, but they're nowhere in sight when you lose. In the case of Bill Flynn, he was consistent. Win or lose, he always showed up in the locker room. He lived across the street and would say, "Stop by the house for a drink." I did, and I knew exactly where I stood all the time. There was no second guessing, no talking behind my back. He was up front and supportive of the program.

Living in Boston gave me a chance to see the Celtics play, and that was a treat. In 1970 they were at the end of their Golden Age, during which they won ten NBA Championships in eleven years, but they still had Bill Russell and were hard to beat. We were allowed into the games for twenty-five cents with our NCAA coaching card, and I'd arrange to get my players in for a quarter as well. The Celtics practiced around the corner in my neighborhood, and I'd go over to watch them but never got too close. I was strictly a fan, a viewer of the action. I'd sit wherever I could get a seat in Boston Garden. I wasn't a very visible person in Boston. High school coaches were more visible than I was.

Boston College wasn't an easy sell, and we sat by the hour stuffing envelopes and sending out recruiting letters. The initial letter had to be attractive enough to get the prospect interested. I recruited at a lot of Catholic schools because BC had a great reputation for its outstanding Catholic education. We sold the daylights out of the Boston environment. Not only would they be in a good school with high academic standards, but they would play against big teams in a metropolitan area. We were playing good teams in the New York and Philadelphia areas and had a pretty tough schedule.

Chapter Four

The gym was small, like a high school gym, and held only two or three thousand people. I decided we had to broaden our recruiting program. I couldn't be Bob Cousy and walk into a player's home and win him over on my reputation, so we went to Chicago and to other pockets of the country where we thought kids would be interested in us.

The toughest part of selling BC was that it wasn't well known. It was far down the priority list on sports pages. There was no TV coverage and only a student radio station. The kids knew all these things, and all the colleges in the area understood the problem. We had meetings with the media to try to sell them our program. The entire area was suffering in college basketball. Even Holy Cross would come in and try to sell its program. Providence had a high profile, more than the others, but that didn't help us. Ultimately, we came up with an idea of putting together all the local teams and going into the Boston Garden for a Bean Pot tournament. It was a takeoff on the hockey tournament; we had to try something to stimulate interest. The challenge at Boston College had me totally immersed in my job.

Dick Harter was the coach at Pennsylvania. They'd had a great season, something like 32–0, but got eliminated in the NCAA tournament and, bang, Harter went to the University of Oregon. The Penn job was open, and my assistant, Bob Zuffelato, said he was interested and wondered, since I knew Fred Shabel, if I would give him a call on his behalf. I called, but Fred wasn't available. He returned my call late that afternoon and I gave him my recommendation for Zuffelato.

At the conclusion of the conversation, Shabel said, "What about Chuck Daly?"

"Only through the proper channels," I answered.

They got permission to talk to me, and I went to Philadelphia for an interview. They had a great program at Penn, playing in the Big Five with coaches like Harry Litwack, Jack Ramsay, Jack McKenny, and Jack Kraft. It was incredible. The

60

Big Five was one of the few groups televising every game. They had a tremendous rivalry in Philadelphia between Penn, St. Joe's, Villanova, LaSalle, and Temple.

I knew what the job was all about, and when they offered it to me I accepted immediately.

The first order of business was to find an assistant. I had met a funny little guy named Rollie Massimino at a high school in Massachusetts and had helped him get a job at Stony Brook, a state university on Long Island. He was little, not more than five-feet, eleven-inches, earthy, had a great basketball mind, and was truly Italian. I called him and we met. "I'd like to have you as my assistant," I said.

He decided to come with me even though it meant a pay cut and he had five children to support.

That started a great, great friendship between us, which could be a whole book in itself.

One of the problems I had coaching at Penn was that it was a non-scholarship school. They also had the "freshman rule," which meant freshmen could not compete on the varsity, so essentially we were a three-year school playing against a lot of four-year schools. I looked at it as a good opportunity, though, because the program was in place and they played in the Big Five, with major television coverage, and I also received a salary increase. I was making $15,000–$16,000 at Boston College, and it went up to $22,000–$23,000 at Penn.

It seemed as if every career move I made was a struggle. First I replaced Bob Cousy, who walked on water in Boston. Then I took a job from Dick Harter, a guy who lost only three games in two years.

I knew there was potential for criticism at Penn, but it didn't bother me. My gut instinct was that it was a good job for me. It was a little difficult leaving Boston College because I had recruited some fairly decent players, but I didn't be-

61

lieve basketball was going to improve in Boston at the inter-collegiate level in the immediate future.

The first day on the job at Penn, I was interviewed by about thirty newspeople. In dealing with the media I decided to be as candid as I could, but careful not to say anything uncomplimentary about my players. I didn't want to say anything that could come back to haunt me. I wanted my players to play hard for me, but at the same time I wanted to be as honest as possible.

During the year, if someone wrote a negative story about me, I'd ask myself if it was true. If it was, I'd work at correcting the problem; there was nothing more I could do, and I moved on. I didn't believe in complications with writers. It was a no-win situation, because they always had the last say. If someone wrote a story that was untrue, I knew I had to say something about it, but I also knew I wasn't going to win; I was only going to make an enemy.

Generally I like newspeople, and I think part of the reason is that I enjoy trying to understand them. I read a lot of newspapers because I don't sleep very well. Most nights I'm up till one or two o'clock, and if I have four papers, I'll finish all of them. Because of this I have developed a love for newspapers, which has led to a kind of fascination with newspeople in general.

Coaching is a very visible profession that is subject to criticism at every level. Nevertheless, we're all human, we all have egos, and none of us likes criticism, even though we know it goes with the territory.

We bought a house in Cherry Hill, New Jersey, because property was a little less expensive there than in Philly. The big expressway into Philadelphia was the Schuykill Express-way, which everyone called "the Sure-Kill Expressway" be-cause of all the accidents. It was difficult getting into town,

Time out to talk strategy in the University of Pennsylvania huddle.

but I knew I would be going to northern New Jersey and New York a lot, and in Cherry Hill I was just ten minutes from Exit 4 on the Jersey Turnpike and ninety minutes from midtown Manhattan. Rollie and I rode up and down the turnpike three or four nights a week recruiting players. After practice, we would go up and back, stopping at his mother's place for a plate of spags, as he called spaghetti. I ate more spaghetti in two years with Rollie Massimino than I have the rest of my entire life.

When we went to Penn, Rollie and I were unknowns in Philadelphia, a very parochial basketball city, so we set out to meet as many people as possible. Rollie has a very special way with people. Although he can get under your skin and make you angry, it's impossible to dislike him. He's truly one of the good guys in our profession.

So we started preparing. Rollie was strictly a man-to-man coach and wouldn't even consider playing a zone. I said it wouldn't be a big problem and told him to come into the office the next morning and we'd talk about it. I've always had one rule with my assistants: they have to beat me to work in the morning. I never say they have to be there at a certain time, just that they have to be there before I am. Our first weeks together, Rollie always beat me to the office, and we would spend three hours a morning planning practice with constant fighting between us. He was stubborn and so was I. The battle never abated, but out of it came more knowledge about basketball than I have ever learned in such a brief period. Rollie is such a great basketball man.

We went into the season and things were shaping up pretty well. We had a good team and played Temple on opening night. The place was jam-packed, with the TV cameras all around. Coming out on the floor, Rollie and I walked together. You could feel the tension in the air, the electricity. Rollie turned to me and said, "It was worth the $5,000 pay cut for me to come with you to Penn."

In December, we went to Rochester to play in the Kodak Classic, and played USC in the finals of the tournament, a team ranked higher than we were. At halftime I decided we were switching from a man-to-man defense to a zone, which Rollie scornfully referred to as "Hands Up Harry." He said we couldn't play it, and he didn't want to be a part of any team that played "Hands Up Harry." The second half we played a 1-2-2 zone, won the game, and Rollie wouldn't speak to me for three days. He was that kind of guy. Whenever we lost, I had a tougher time getting him back up than I did the team because he took losing so personally. I've always thought it was ironic that when he won his national championship at Villanova, he played a zone defense and has been giving coaching clinics on it ever since!

Our first year at Penn was the best. We compiled a 25–3 record, were ranked third in both polls, and got beat by the University of North Carolina in the Eastern Regional finals. I don't think I, Rollie, or even Ray Carazo, my other assistant, were prepared to coach in that big of a game. I also think we let the media influence us. We played a great team and didn't know it. Not only did UNC have a solid starting team that included Bob McAdoo, but they had Bobby Jones coming off the bench. We just didn't know how good that team really was.

Hot Rod Hundley did the game on television, and after it was over he asked to interview me on national television. He started the interview by saying, "I'm standing here with . . . I'm sorry, I forgot your name." I jumped in and said, "Don't be embarrassed. Right now, neither my alumni nor my athletic director can remember my name, either."

Stuff like that didn't bother me. I spent my whole career being a pretty anonymous guy.

One of the great things about basketball in Philadelphia was playing at The Palestra. It was like going into Fenway Park or Maple Leaf Gardens or watching a golf tournament at the Augusta National. It was filled with history and tradition. The Palestra was located on our campus, and all the Big Five teams played there. Being inside it made you feel as if you had gone back in time. The arena was built around 1930 and held 9,000 to 10,000, which was unheard of in those days. It was the Mecca of basketball in the East.

Every team in the country came to Philadelphia to play. That was part of their recruiting strategy because everyone wanted to play in The Palestra. It was beat up and had small dressing rooms, but we made what improvements we could. We painted the seats, the hallways, and even the floor. We also got the coaches' rooms fixed up, all in an effort to make it a little better recruiting facility. I'm not sure it was necessary because it was such a magic place that you could feel the emotion in every part of the building. I loved just walking into it.

Chapter Four

I looked for every gimmick and every edge I could at Penn. We were one of the first teams to use a rebounding ring inside the rim so the ball couldn't go through, making every shot produce a rebound. We also used a smaller rim that allowed the ball to go through but taught the players to put a higher arc on their shot. We started using jumping machines and got a device that would return the ball for shooting free throws. My athletic director, Fred Shabel, was a basketball guy, and he wanted us to compete in the Big Five, so we had few budget problems. The fans were probably as good as any in the country. Their knowledge of the game is legendary. And, of course, the place was always filled with smoke. Mostly cigar smoke.

We recruited all over the country because we had to get students as well as players. We were part of the Ivy League, and the academics were much more demanding than at most other schools. Every year I tried to get at least one great player from the Delaware Valley area, which meant Delaware, Philadelphia, and New Jersey. We were usually able to do this because we worked hard at it. But even so, we had to go far afield to bring in players.

It got harder and harder for us because it was costing somewhere arounc $20,000 to go to Penn and we could not give our kids any financial help. Their only option was to work—in the cafeteria, in the bookstore, in the dorms overnight. I had players who would come to practice after going to classes all day, having been up all of the night before with dorm duty. It was very difficult for all of us. That's why the Ivy League cannot compete at the Division I level.

In July, 1978, I got word that my mother had to have an operation on her gall bladder. I knew it would be traumatic for her because she had never been in the hospital in her life.

We were in the waiting room when the doctor came out. He didn't have good news.

"We found cancer all through her system," he explained. "Things don't look very good."

I bolted from the hospital.

In every situation in my life, I had always been in complete control of myself. No matter what. I could handle anything. But this was different.

This was my mother.

I must have walked two or three miles. I kept asking myself all the questions, How? Why? Why my mother?

When my father died it was different. I can't explain it, but it's different when a man dies, even when it's your dad. When it's your mother, well, mothers are just special, that's all.

My mother was a beautiful woman. She never hurt anyone in her life, and she never said an unkind word about anyone. She loved everyone and it truly didn't matter about race, creed, or color.

I went back to work because we were getting ready to take our team on an exhibition tour of Italy, but before long I got another call saying my mother had been rushed back to the hospital.

I drove through the night, half dreading, half knowing what to expect. She had had chemotherapy treatment but couldn't take it. She didn't want to continue with the treatments.

For the first time I began to realize that basketball wasn't the most important thing in my life.

You can become so obsessive about what you're doing that sometimes you even put it over your wife and child, which I've often done. This isn't right, but that's what you do when you become the center of your own universe.

My mother was in a hospital in Kane, and I stayed at the home of Don Magnuson. I went to see her every day. She was coherent, but I could see she was failing.

When I went into her room, she'd say, "Did you pay all the bills?" It was very important to her. She wanted all her bills paid at that point in her life.

She got worse as the week went on and fell into a semi-coma. I started sleeping in the hallway overnight. I wanted to be there when she died. It was important to me.

I hadn't been running back and forth to see her after I left home. We went back once or twice a year, and occasionally Mom visited us. We hadn't been in close contact because of the distances involved, but now I wanted to be with her at the end. I was feeling guilty. I realized I hadn't done enough. I could have given her more money, taken her on a plane ride, visited her more often.

I'd sit in that hallway and say to myself, "Why didn't I see her more often? Why didn't I spend more time with her?"

This went on for eight or nine days. I read a lot of books because I had to do something to occupy my mind. Not being active is very hard for me.

One night I was out in the hallway, dozing. At two or three o'clock in the morning a nurse came out and said that my mother had passed away. I went into the room and was angry with her because she died without me being there. I wanted to be at her side at the moment of her death just to let her know how much I cared.

I didn't know it at the time, but I was learning about living through dying. For the first time I began to think of my own mortality. You grow up thinking you are invincible. Nothing can touch you. You're caught up in yourself and you think you're going to live forever. Then something like this happens and you realize how vulnerable you are.

It is a terrific loss when you lose your mother. It is something you never forget. You may not think about it on a day-to-day basis, but it's always there—the thought always returns. I still talk to my mother every Sunday I'm in church, and I don't talk about basketball, either.

5 TURNING TO THE PRO GAME

MY LIFE WAS ABOUT TO CHANGE. I had had six great years at Penn, but I had gotten to the point where I wanted to move again. As exciting as the job was, there was a certain sameness to it, and that worried me. At one point, Wayne Embrey of the Milwaukee Bucks had asked me if I was interested in a pro job, but at the time, I wasn't. I was still happy at Penn.

Pro basketball was big in Philadelphia, and I went to some of the games, though not as many as I did in Boston. But I did get to know the 76ers' trainer, Al Domenico, and Gene Shue, the coach. I was so busy in my own job that I didn't get a chance to get very close to them.

In 1977 I met Billy Cunningham, who had part interest in a Holiday Inn and was running a travel agency and a health club in Philadelphia. Cunningham was a bright guy and a smart businessman, and we played golf a few times. One of the local sports announcers, Al Meltzer, was leaving to take a job in Chicago and there was a party for him at Cavanaugh's near Penn Station. I went over and saw Jack McMahon, an assistant coach of the Sixers, in the crowd. Jack was another basketball "lifer." He played at St. John's in Brooklyn and had been around the NBA scene for a long time. He became a very, very close friend of mine.

Word was out that Gene Shue was in trouble as coach of the 76ers. "Aw, that's not true," Jack said.

69

Cunningham was at the table, but he didn't comment on the situation. Instead he said to me, "Where are you going later?"

"Nowhere," I told him.

"We're going up to Fran O'Brien's," he said. "Why don't you join us?"

I had nothing to do, so I went over. We were standing around having a few drinks when Cunningham said, out of the blue, "If things were right, would you be interested in going to the 76ers as an assistant coach?"

I was caught off guard by his question. I didn't know Cunningham that well and didn't know how much he knew about me or about the kind of coach I was.

"Well, yes, sure, I guess I'd be interested," was all I managed to say.

Three days later Shue was fired and Cunningham was named to take his place.

I went to see him coach a game against the New Jersey Nets that Friday night, but didn't talk to him. Nothing happened Saturday or Sunday, and I figured nothing was going to happen. On Monday morning, Pat Williams, the 76ers' general manager, called.

"Would you be interested in coming to the 76ers?" he asked.

I told him I would like to think about it. I'd had several college overtures, including Tulane and, indirectly, Cincinnati, but those jobs didn't appeal to me. They seemed like side moves. I went to my new athletic director, Andy Geiger, and told him what was going on.

I met with Cunningham and Williams in a room at the Hilton the next day and we must have talked for two or three hours. They offered me the same money I was making at Penn—$35,000. I wasn't very smart; I should have asked for more, but the idea of going to the pros appealed to me. I would be working with my friend Jack McMahon, whom I liked a lot, and that was very appealing. Billy Cunningham had been a great player with a great mind, and I felt I could keep learning from him. Penn gave me my release, and I went right to work with the 76ers.

My first game was against the Knicks in the Spectrum, where the "Zink," David Zinkoff, announced me as one of the assistant coaches of the Philadelphia 76ers. The next night we went to Washington. All of this was brand new. I'd never traveled with a pro team, or even been around one, and I wasn't sure how to act or what the relationships would be. We went into the locker room at halftime and George McGinnis, one of the stars of the team, pulled out a cigarette and started smoking it in the dressing room. I was stunned. I had never seen anything like that before in my life. I looked over at Billy. He wasn't reacting to it, so I didn't either. "Well, this must be how they do it," I said to myself. It was the start of a long learning process.

One thing I could do well was analyze the games. I knew enough basketball and had seen enough pro games to know when things were right and when things were wrong. As we were busing home after the game in Washington, I sat with Billy and Jack and we talked about the players. I made a couple of comments, and Jack sat up in his seat. "I can't believe you could recognize those things in such a short time," he said.

I knew then I could make the switch from college basketball to the pros.

We were successful at the start, but only to a point. Billy was trying to learn to coach, and I was trying to learn the league. We got along well, and I wasn't in a hurry to be a head coach, so our marriage was a good one. He was smarter than all of us. I could help him with the drills, and he let me do that because I could do it better than he could. He had a gut feeling about the players. He understood their mentality. He knew who was conning him and who wasn't. I knew I could learn all this from him. In turn, I wanted to help him as much as possible.

While coaching in college, I had gone to Hubie Brown's practices after he went to the Atlanta Hawks, so I was able to help with our offensive sets. We had some great personnel—Darryl Dawkins, Lloyd (World B.) Free, Bobby Jones, Doug Collins, George McGinnis, and a man known as Dr. J., Julius Erving. Maurice Cheeks came a little later. It was a phenomenally talented team, but we lacked a commitment to play defense and a sense of team unity. Sometimes too many individual stars can be a deterrent to success.

Jack McMahon had been around a long time and he knew the league, so we all brought something to the table. We knew we had to develop our talent until it became a team, and that meant playing defense as well as offense. We partied and we had fun. The chemistry was perfect, and our team slowly got better. And we recruited, or, rather, scouted. I was still at it.

If we were flying to Chicago, I would go to another city— perhaps South Bend or Ann Arbor—to look at some players. We were trying to keep on top of everything. Pat Williams was one of the smartest basketball executives in the game. He believed in collecting as much information as possible. I haven't known many people like him. All day long he was on the phone talking to people and taking in this mountain of information, sorting it all out and figuring out how it could help him. This is what you have to do to be a successful general manager in the NBA, and Williams did it well.

Once he sent me to Norfolk, Virginia, to check on a kid who played for Michigan State. He was only a freshman, but Pat wanted a full report on him. I saw Magic Johnson play one game and my report said: "He flew the airplane, he drove the bus, he cooked the dinner, he turned on the showers, he scored all the points, made all the assists, got all the rebounds, and smiled at all the girls." I was that impressed. The only other freshman I had ever seen who came close to Magic

Johnson as far as pure talent is concerned was Darryl Daw-kins. He got out of high school and went right to the pros. But the first time I saw Magic, I knew he would be one of the great players of all time.

Jack found another kid in Dayton, Dwight Anderson, and Jack loved him as a player. We could maneuver the draft in those days to take the kind of prospects we wanted, and Jack wanted us all to go to Dayton to see him perform. So the four of us—Jack, Billy, Pat Williams, and I—flew into Dayton and went into the kid's gym for a game. He didn't know we were there. Nobody knew. We went in with disguises. Billy wore a hat, I wore dark glasses, and we sat in different parts of the gym. We wanted to get different impressions of him and compare notes later.

The game began and I could see the kid was good. But right in the middle of the game, he turned around and slugged another kid. Billy got up and walked out of the building. When we saw him leave, we left. We met him outside and he said, "We're not interested in him." The kid never made it, and maybe this is the first time anyone ever told this story.

Nobody was keeping any charts on what we were doing. I had seen Hubie Brown do it in Atlanta, so I started doing it for our team. I was still trying to learn, still trying to teach myself everything I could about the game. The charts re-vealed that our fast break wasn't very effective. We were fifty percent or below in all our games. I went to Billy and said, "If we draft anyone at all, it has to be a point guard."

We were in Houston watching the East-West game from Las Vegas when the phone rang. It was Billy. He was watching the game from someplace else.

"Do you see this kid?" he asked.

"Yeah, who is he?"

"His name is Maurice Cheeks."

Chapter Five

Later that year, Pat Williams was holding tryouts in Cincinnati. He had ten or twelve college seniors together and was putting them through drills and scrimmages. The whole thing was done for one purpose—to get a look at Maurice Cheeks, but Maurice didn't know it. We really liked him, but we were trying to finesse our first- and second-round choices, hoping he'd still be available in the second round.

Pat had done his homework, as he always did, and felt Maurice would still be available in the second round. He was right, and we got Maurice Cheeks, who became one of the great point guards in the league.

I learned a lot from Billy Cunningham. He was a film addict, and he taught me the value of studying tapes. He couldn't get enough basketball. He'd go to Dean Smith at North Carolina and talk to him for hours, but he also listened to me because I had a little more background in the coaching aspect of the game than he did. He also taught me how to make decisions when everything seems equal. A lot of times a bench coach is faced with what seems to be a fifty-fifty proposition: for me, it's do I bring in Vinnie Johnson for Joe Dumars, or do I send Dumars out there for Isiah Thomas? When do I bring in Dennis Rodman? When do I go to Mark Aguirre? How long do I keep them out there? This is the essence of coaching. You have to make the right decisions, at least fifty percent of the time. You have to get it right or you're gone. I try to keep a certain routine about substitutions, but I also go by "feel."

In 1981 I was becoming a very visible assistant coach in Philadelphia, just like at Duke. I knew I would be getting some head coaching offers. One year at the All-Star game, Bob Bass from San Antonio asked if I'd be interested in coaching his team. Cunningham stepped in and said, "Not now—not at this time of the year." He didn't want to lose me halfway through the season. I understood how he felt, so I didn't feel bad about losing the San Antonio job.

Not long after that I became a very hot item. San Antonio was still interested and so were Dallas and Detroit. Jack McCloskey had been named general manager of the Pistons and he came to Philadelphia to talk to me about the head coaching job. He invited Terry and me to Detroit, where we met with Bill Davidson, the owner of the franchise, and talked for two or three hours. Oscar Feldman, who was Davidson's partner and close friend, was also there with his wife. They explained the entire situation.

The next day Terry and I flew to San Antonio for another interview. I had also been asked to stop in Dallas, but I called them and said, "I don't think you're that interested." The truth was, I couldn't handle three teams at one time.

I went to California for a league meeting. I was making pretty good money with the 76ers—around $90,000 with my playoff share and other incentives. That was good money for

I took my first course in "How to Handle Superstars" while coaching for the Philadelphia 76ers. The instructor was Dr. J, Julius Erving.

75

Chapter Five

an assistant, and they were even giving me a car. I had asked the Pistons for something like $360,000 over three years.

McCloskey called my room at the hotel. "You're the man I want," he said.

"OK, go back to Detroit and talk to Oscar Feldman about the contract," I responded.

I flew back to Detroit by myself for some more talks with the Pistons. Oscar met me at the gate and took me to a room at the Marriott. Before I even sat down, he said, "I'm offering you $90,000, $100,000, and $110,000 on a three-year deal." He tried to convince me how much potential there was in Detroit, how much money I could make. We talked for about three hours, went downstairs to get something to eat, and then I flew back to Philadelphia.

McCloskey called me on a Sunday night. "That's our offer," he said.

"Then I'm not coming," I answered.

My request was not out of line. It was a fair market price. I knew I was going to earn every penny of it because the Pistons were hardly a good team. Just a couple of years earlier, in 1980, they had won a grand total of sixteen games.

Cydney was in Cherry Hill High School, and that was another factor that was important in my decision. I'd moved around enough during her early school years and now I wanted her to remain settled for the rest of her high school years. The San Antonio job fell through, too, but I wasn't worried. I was sure something else would come along.

The next year only one job opened, in Atlanta, and they had already picked Kevin Loughery as their coach. I knew I wasn't getting any younger, and I said to myself, "Wait a minute—I'm over fifty years old and I'm still an assistant coach. If I'm going to move up, now is the time. I can't be choosy anymore. I've got to take the next job that comes to me."

Up to that point I hadn't made any mistakes in choosing my jobs, but now I had to make the big move. I was worried about Detroit. They had thirty years of nothing. Their attendance was poor because people didn't like the Silverdome for watching basketball. I knew Jack McCloskey wanted me because he had watched me in the Big Five at Penn and knew the kind of defense I coached. As a former coach, he knew exactly the kind of person he wanted to run his team. But I couldn't in good conscience take the job because of the money. I didn't think they were making enough of a commitment to me.

At any rate, we were going along pretty well in Philadelphia. Cunningham had become a very strong coach and didn't need my help much anymore. I realized that and it didn't bother me. That's how it went. During my last year there, we got a new owner—Harold Katz. Pat Williams stayed on as general manager, but I sensed that the Sixers were going in a different direction. I knew for sure it was time to move on.

During an exhibition game in Dallas, I ran into Bill Musselman, general manager of the Cleveland Cavaliers. He had a terrible team. The Cavaliers couldn't win anything and were always firing their coaches. We had lunch, and he asked me about my plans. He told me he thought the Cavaliers were going to make a coaching change and wondered if I was interested in the job. Cleveland would be a tough place to coach, but I felt I had to make a move. I told him I was interested. He got permission to talk to me and Hubie Brown, who was doing cable TV at the time.

I went to Cleveland for an interview and realized immediately what a chaotic situation it was. I reminded myself that I had always stepped carefully in changing jobs, but that didn't stop me; I was ready to do something major. We had our talk and they seemed interested.

Chapter Five

In December, 1981, we were practicing in the Boston Garden when I got a call out on the floor. It was my wife. She told me to call Hubie Brown. I called him and he said, "I've taken myself out of the running in Cleveland and I want you to know so you can be prepared because they're coming after you." When I was in Cleveland, I had asked for $125,000, $150,000, and $175,000—something along those lines.

When I got back to my room, Bill Musselman called. He said owner Ted Stepien would really like to have me as his coach, so I called him. I told him I wanted $125,000 for the rest of the year—from December 1 until the end of June. I wanted to make some money right away. I went to Katz and Cunningham and told them what I wanted to do, but they didn't think I would leave. Katz was a little stunned by it. The Sixers said they would have to get a draft choice in return for letting me go, which I don't think had ever been done before. I may have been the first coach "traded" for a draft choice. They wanted a number one pick, and the whole thing got a little sticky. They finally settled for a number two, and I was on my way to Cleveland for my first head coaching job.

Even if I coached only one game in Cleveland, it would make me a better coach, I told myself. I liked Stepien socially. He was a lot of fun. But I could see right away how shaky the whole situation was. When I got there, they didn't even have enough players to practice with. Some were hurt, some didn't want to practice, and some didn't want to play. One of their starters had gone to a funeral.

"Where is he?" I asked.

Nobody knew.

"When is he coming back?"

They didn't know that either. He didn't show up for several days and nobody knew what was going on. We had to send the assistant general manager to find him. I had only been there a week, and I knew I was in big trouble.

The Cavaliers had some pretty good personnel. I had Billy Laimbeer and James Edwards on that team, and Stepien had made some big investments by bringing in Edwards and Scott Wedman as free agents. Basically, he was on the right track. But he was antsy to win. I was starting Edwards because Laimbeer was twenty pounds overweight and not playing all that well. If I could ever get both of them on the court at the same time, I thought we might have something.

I got a room at the Holiday Inn and never moved out. Something told me not to set up housekeeping. Stepien wanted to talk to me after every game. Every single night we had to talk; he was that type. We would go up to his office and discuss personnel. This started happening after just two weeks. I remember one night we had a long, long discussion. The next morning I picked up the paper and everything we talked about was in there.

"Ted, we've got a problem," I told him. "We've got a leak in this office."

"Yeah, I know," he said. "It's me. I'm the one who told them."

That's the way he operated. He was an outstanding businessman, but owning a basketball franchise is not like running a regular business. Basketball is different. You have to have basketball minds running the basketball team. Otherwise, it won't work. I tried to tell him that, but I don't think he ever believed me.

I woke up every morning wondering whom he had traded or what changes he wanted to make. It was always something. I won my first game, against Atlanta, and Stepien gave me a dollar bill with his autograph on it. I think he was trying to make me feel good, and I appreciated that, but the whole operation was too loose to be successful.

Stepien wanted to be in on the team meetings and that was never a good idea. When I fined a player, he would reprimand me for fining him. He wanted to be close to the

79

players, very sociable. It was just the way he was. Right away
I told his attorney, whom I liked, to start drawing up some
separation papers because this thing wasn't going to work.

I had tremendous mood swings. One day I'd be optimistic
and think things might work out. The next day I'd be way
down, and the next I'd be ambivalent. I was only kidding
myself. The trainer used to sing the same song to me every
morning: "It's all happening at the zoo." He knew what was
going on. Everybody wanted out, especially the players.

"You're probably getting fired today," Stepien's attorney
would say to me on occasion. That isn't much fun to hear,
even if you do have a three-year contract. It was no way to
start a work day.

One night I got a call from the attorney. Stepien wanted
to meet me at his club in downtown Cleveland. It was sort of
like a nightclub, and one of the Cleveland writers was sitting
at the bar. I sat down and had a drink with him. Stepien was
in the middle of emceeing a show, which upset me, and I
talked at great length to the writer. Stepien finally sent word
over that he was ready for me. I sent word back that I wasn't
ready for him. I was still talking to the writer.

Stepien motioned me to a corner table. It was a Monday
night, not very busy.

"Why don't you quit?" he asked.

"Why don't you fire me?" I said.

He was playing games with me. He was a fun guy, but kind
of off the wall. Pretty soon I had my attorney talking to his
attorney because I could see trouble ahead.

One day I went to practice and none of my assistants were
there. Stepien had called them up to his office without telling
me. I fined them for not being on time for practice, but I knew
where that was leading.

We had a strange team. We'd be up by twenty or twenty-
four at halftime, fifteen at the end of the third quarter, and
could never hold on to win. It was very frustrating. We went

out West and Stepien showed up in Oakland. He told me I would not be in their plans the following season. I was getting threats every week, but this sounded like more than another threat. It sounded, in fact, like a final separation.

When we got back to Cleveland, my attorney flew in from Philadelphia and worked out a settlement. I received close to $270,000 in severance. It was very fair, but I didn't like losing my job. I'd rather have stayed, even if it was very difficult.

After ninety-three days, I was a failure as an NBA coach. I was feeling pretty low, and a lot of people were asking pointed questions about whether or not my career was over. It was March, 1982. I'd get up in the morning, read two newspapers with my tea, and go down to Billy Cunningham's health club for a little workout. I'd be back home at 9:30 with nothing to do and nowhere to go. I didn't have an office or anyplace to hang out. None of the people I used to know were calling anymore. As a "lifer" in basketball, I was having plenty of doubts about myself and where I was going.

One thing that's very important to me is consistency. I like it when everything is the same. People. Situations. Circumstances. I can't stand people who say they're my friend one moment and turn their back on me the next. When I came home to Cherry Hill after being fired by the Cleveland Cavaliers, it was a disaster. My phone never rang and nobody came around. It was as if I had died. As a head coach, I had had plenty of people around, but after I was fired, they forgot they had ever known me.

It wasn't like that with Koko, our French poodle. She didn't care whether my team had won or lost. It didn't matter to her whether I was an NBA coach or unemployed. She was just glad when I was home.

We got Koko when I was with the Philadelphia 76ers. I had never wanted a dog, and I was dead-set against getting this one. But with the job I had, traveling all the time and seldom

Koko, our French poodle, doesn't care whether the team wins or loses.

home, I knew my wife could use a companion. And Cydney, our daughter, was about six years old, and Terry and I decided it would be good for her to have a dog.

We had an Easter hunt for Cydney every year, and the year we got Koko, we left notes all around the house telling Cydney where to look for candy and gifts. I directed her, saying, "Go to the hall closet," "Look behind the umbrella stand." Finally I said, "Check the laundry room." In the laundry room was a beautiful cocoa-brown poodle. Cydney screamed with delight and started hugging the puppy immediately. I guess we've never stopped hugging her. She was feisty right from the start and very outgoing. She barked as if she were a German shepherd at anyone who came near the house. She loved to play ball. I'm convinced she always thought she was winning.

And she was. Because when you have people who love you, you can never lose. When I lost my job in Cleveland I started to learn how true that is, and I came to realize how

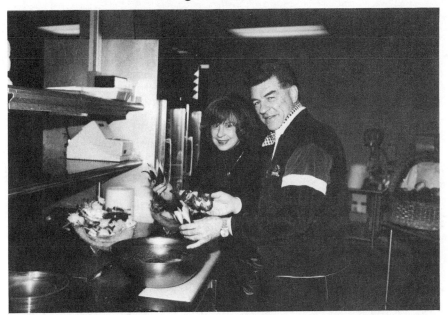

Relaxing with Terry at home.

important my family was to me. They were consistent when nothing else was. They understood the predicament I was in and how I felt, and they were completely supportive.

I started playing more golf, and it was my salvation. I'd hit a ton of practice balls and play all day. I began meeting some guys—an insurance man, a repairman from Sears, and a few others. They helped me get through the long days. My mind was troubled all the time. I was nearly fifty-two and didn't have a job and didn't know where I could go. Once you've been in the pros, you become a little tainted and there's no going back to the college ranks. Although Rick Pitino and a few others have done it, those were peculiar situations, and I didn't feel it was a viable option for me.

I could be an assistant again, but where? I didn't think I was too damaged by what happened with the Cavaliers because everyone knew how messed up they were. I thought I could rise above that situation, but when my phone never rang, it was hard to keep my spirits up.

Suddenly, a TV job opened in Philly. The Sixers needed a colorman. I was interested but wondered how they felt about taking back a guy who had left them. I knew Harold Katz wasn't particularly happy about my leaving, so I was surprised when Pat Williams called. He thought I could do the job, even though I hadn't had any experience on TV or radio except for occasional interviews. The job didn't pay much, maybe $30,000–$35,000, but I didn't have anything else and this would get me back on the scene.

I didn't know what I was in for; they just threw me to the wolves. I knew nothing about broadcasting, but I was supposed to work with Neil Funk on the broadcasts, Jim Barniak on the cablecasts, and Jim Gray in the studio. I had to do a pre-game show with the visiting coach, for which we paid him fifty bucks. It was unheard of to pay anyone for an interview, but I suggested it and the coaches loved it. Fifty bucks was fifty bucks.

I also had to do a halftime show in the back of the studio and a post-game show, live, on the floor or back in the studio. That wasn't all. We did some simulcasts, and I had to do a pre-game radio show with my little tape recorder, which I didn't even know how to run. At halftime, I had to do a tape show for the radio. So they had me doing five or six extra shows as well as working the game. But I loved it. I knew the league and had no trouble making comments. I knew the players and the coaches and could talk about them in an intimate way. I decided to have fun with the whole thing and it turned out to be a ball.

By now the Sixers had Moses Malone, and he helped them win sixty-seven games. That, of course, made our jobs much easier. Everybody was interested in the 76ers, so they were interested in what we had to say. I used to pray that Philadelphia would have a tough game so we could have a good broadcast. But they were killing a lot of teams and we had to do a lot of fill-in stuff.

Katz had agreed to my going on the air, but he didn't want me going to any of the practices.

"Fine, no problem," I said, and that whole season I went to only one shoot-around and no practices. I played golf every day I could, and even though I wasn't making much money, that was one of the happiest years of my life. I had the money from Cleveland in the bank and that eased my mind.

Late in the 1982–83 season, Jack McCloskey called again. The Pistons were making a move on Scotty Robertson, their coach, and there was a big uproar in Detroit. The media didn't think it was fair to fire him. He had won thirty-seven and thirty-nine games, and people like Joe Falls, a sports writer for the Detroit *News*, were really upset. Jack still wanted to upgrade the defensive end of his game and he knew that I stressed defense.

I came to Detroit for another talk with McCloskey. Terry came with me, and they took her on a trip through West Bloomfield and Birmingham to show her how nice the area was. We had dinner at the Novi Sheraton, a place away from the city, because they didn't want anyone to know we were meeting. I told him I wanted two years with an option, starting at $125,000 the first year. Oscar Feldman said, "I'm offering you $100,000 to start."

He was low again—this time by $25,000.

I couldn't understand it. I wasn't getting any other offers, but I didn't think they were being fair. We went back to the Northfield Hilton and I was mad.

Later we had dinner again at Charlie's Crab with McCloskey and his wife, Leslie. As soon as we sat down, Jack said, "You were disappointed with the salary, weren't you?"

"Yeah, I really was," I admitted.

"Let me see what I can do," he offered.

They came back and offered $125,000, $150,000, and an option year, and that's how I came to be the coach of the

Pistons. The date was May 17, 1983. I was fifty-two years old and pretty much of an unknown in Detroit. Jay Berry said on the air, "Who is this guy? Chuck who?" I smiled and thought of all the "Sparky who?" headlines when the Cincinnati Reds had hired their new manager a few years earlier.

I was excited about the job because the Pistons seemed to have a plan for what they wanted to do. Sitting in Scotty's office that first day, I said to myself, "I don't know how long I'm going to be here. They've had nine coaches in ten years or ten coaches in nine years, and I don't know if I can do a better job than Scotty Robertson. But Jack wants me to beef up the defense and I'll do that and we'll have some fun as we try to improve and see what happens."

I made a commitment to get to know the players, both on and off the floor. I began socializing with them. I wanted to know what was in their heads, whom I could depend on and whom I couldn't. We had a front line of Kent Benson, Bill Laimbeer, and Kelly Tripucka, and I didn't think that was a strong shot-blocking front line. I could see that we could be a strong offensive team, but were going to struggle on defense.

The Pistons were one of the few teams that had only one assistant coach and no real scouting system. I hired Dick Harter, who had gone from Penn to Oregon and happened to be out of a job. I knew about his great reputation in Philadelphia, but I barely knew him as a person. I knew he was a good defensive coach, and that's what I needed the most. I always had instincts about hiring people. I used the Vic Bubas rule of only hiring coaches who were better than I was. If I didn't, how could they make me better? I didn't know how much of a threat Harter would be, but I didn't care. I felt he was the right man for the job and he was the one I wanted. We became great friends over the next several years.

I could see it was going to be interesting working for McCloskey. He was a charming Irishman, and very personable, but I knew he could be tough. He is probably the toughest competitor I've ever known in basketball. He just wants to win, period.

I sensed he still had some of the coach in him, and I knew that might be troublesome. A lot of people warned me that I'd have to accept his input in coaching the team. That didn't turn out to be much of a problem because he had some good ideas. Still, I didn't think the general manager should be telling the coach how to coach, any more than the coach should be telling the general manager how to general manage.

I decided to let one of my assistants deal with Jack. He would hang out in his office, find out what was on Jack's mind, and relay the information to me. Some of it I accepted, some of it I rejected. It worked out well. He was getting his ideas out without treading on my territory, and I loved it when he'd come up with something I hadn't thought of. It was a good balance.

On the last day of the 1984 season, we played in Atlanta, and if we had won, we would have won the division. That's how much we had improved. We were up to forty-nine wins. We lost the game and ended up second, but it was a very promising start.

PART 2
INSIDE GAME

6 BOSSES, BONUSES, AND BODIES

WHEN YOU MAKE YOUR LIVING IN THE NBA, YOU SEE LIFE FROM A LOT OF DIFFERENT PERSPECTIVES. We play in all parts of the country— East, West, North, and South—and we have to rely on each other to survive. We're thrown together for eight straight months, and we have to get along or the whole thing isn't going to work. It's three coaches, twelve players, and a trainer against the world. We don't have time to take on any extra problems.

Such as racial problems.

I've never sensed any undercurrents of racial tension in our league. The NBA has overcome this more than most businesses because everyone is in it to win and racial problems are not conducive to winning. You've got to be careful about it, though, because the media is there to report everything you do and everything you say. What better example than the incident sparked by remarks from Dennis Rodman and Isiah Thomas after our playoff loss in Boston in the spring of 1987? I can still see the whole scene.

It was hot in Boston Garden, about 98 degrees in the shade with no air conditioning. I perspired so much I ruined a good suit. This was the seventh game of the Eastern Finals and it was close, back and forth the whole way, and I was thinking maybe we could steal it.

Adrian Dantley dove for a loose ball, something not at all characteristic of his play, and Vinnie dove for it also. They smashed heads on the floor, and both were stunned. Dantley was taken to the hospital, and Johnson was useless the rest of the game. We wound up losing.

The locker room in Boston was close and confining, and the press was everywhere. It seemed as if a thousand people were in there. I believe that even when you lose, you show some class and give the other team due credit. I always talk to my players first and then go across the hall to congratulate the other coach and his players. No big deal. It's just something I've always done.

I went into the locker room and said something like, "Hey, guys, we got beat. Let's handle it. Give them their due." Then I walked out of the room.

Actually, I was in a bit of a bind because I was addressing two issues at one time, and the questions were coming at me from all directions. First, a report was out that the New York Knicks were interested in me as their general manager, and now that we were eliminated, everyone felt I could talk about it. Second, I had to answer questions about the game.

All this was going on when somebody whispered to me that Dennis Rodman had made some remarks about Larry Bird. Right away I thought that maybe I hadn't said enough to my players. Maybe I should have done a better job of telling them how to conduct themselves. The questions kept coming at me from all directions.

The next thing I heard was that Isiah Thomas had come to Rodman's defense and agreed with what Rodman had said about Bird. The writers were saying that my captain was making racial remarks about the star of the Celtics. I could just about figure out what was going on. Dennis tends to get emotional and was probably speaking out of frustration. Isiah, never one to let a friend down, saw all the media around Dennis and stepped in and tried to help him out.

What Dennis had said was that if Larry Bird were black, he'd be just another player in the league, but because he was white, a big deal was always being made about him. Or words to that effect. The writers went to Isiah, and he agreed with Rodman. Now the whole place was jumping.

I wasn't concerned. These were my guys, and I knew them and I understood what they meant even if they hadn't chosen their words too carefully. But I also knew that if you give the press an opening like that they would exploit it, and there were going to be some repercussions over what Dennis and Isiah had said.

When we got back to Detroit, we were supposed to have a team dinner at the Pike Street Restaurant in downtown Pontiac. Management always treated the Piston players in a first-class manner at these social functions. When Isiah showed up he had already talked to Bill Davidson and Jack McCloskey about what happened in Boston. They decided that the best thing to do was for Isiah to meet with Larry Bird and try to diffuse the whole thing. Isiah was to fly to Los Angeles, where he would go on TV with Bird and get it all straightened out. I said to Isiah and his wife that it would be best to get the matter resolved as quickly as possible.

But, as I understand it, Larry Bird wanted nothing to do with a meeting on TV. He said the remarks didn't bother him, so why should they bother anyone else? He was being magnanimous about the whole thing. The truth is, I had nothing to do with getting things squared away, which the two players ultimately did in a private meeting. I just knew where Dennis and Isiah were coming from and wasn't all that upset about it.

As coaches, we're there to serve the players—to think of ways to help them improve so we can win more often. Our job is to prepare them to play well and, then, during the games, to make the right moves to help them win. I hear a lot of talk about a coach's "doghouse." I don't have a doghouse. I would never do anything to hurt our chances as a team because I'm too interested in winning.

If I get mad at a player, that doesn't mean I'm going to sit him down and not play him. I've done that perhaps twice in my years in Detroit, but I knew it was wrong, small on my part, and I've fought against it ever since. My ego has nothing to do with whom I play. I put the guys out there who I think can get the job done, because winning is where the real rewards are in basketball.

One thing I like to do with my coaches is take them up north, to an out-of-the way place in Michigan, and have a brainstorming session before the start of the season. It's just the three of us, and we do nothing but sit around and talk basketball. I get to know them, they get to know me, and we're all on the same page. I did this when Dick Versace and Ron Rothstein were my assistants, and I do it now with Brendan Suhr and Brendan Malone.

In my early years in Detroit Dick Versace had a friend, Ron Gibson, who owned some restaurants in Lansing. He had a place near Traverse City, right on Lake Michigan, and he offered it to us. It was ideal—lots of room yet very secluded. And no telephones. We did not want to see anybody or talk to anybody. It was going to be all basketball.

"I'll do the cooking, you guys do the thinking," Ron said.

We went to Lansing to pick him up, and did he bring along the food! Steaks, lamb chops, shrimp, lobster, and exotic dishes with names I couldn't even pronounce. We talked basketball all day long for about three days, morning until night. We'd be at it until three o'clock in the morning, stopping only to eat.

Ron made some fantastic meals. He spent all day in the kitchen while we were at the dining room table or out on the porch. We went over everything. Personnel. Plays. Offense. Defense. Everyone had his say.

I feel it's important for me to get to know my coaches as people, especially if they are new. I want to know how they think about things, what they believe in and value, what guides them in the decisions they make. And it's equally important for them to get to know me. The players go their own way when we travel, and it pretty much gets down to me, my coaches, and the trainer.

It's important that we work hard, but it's also important that we enjoy each other's company and have some fun. I'm at the point in life where I don't want any problems with my coaches. Who needs it? The only problem with going up north is that we all gain five pounds.

When Dick Versace was on my staff, he was a workaholic. He was new to the league, and I sent him out as our advance scout in the first year. He understood his role completely. An assistant's role is to help the head coach do his job, and to do anything to make it easier for him. Dick understood that better than anyone else. He would do all the film work, take all the notes, and get me ready for every team. Plus, he was an intellectual sort of guy. He was interested in a lot of things and was a great friend on the road. We would go out to lunch and dinner a lot and we'd sit together on the airplane. He was always upbeat and very enjoyable. And he liked to challenge me. He was always questioning my moves and I liked that. I don't want "yes" men around me. I want guys who can think for themselves and make suggestions. I have the final say, yea or nay. But they can have an input. In fact, I encourage it.

I got Ron Rothstein from Atlanta, and he proved to be a brilliant coach. He worked for Hubie Brown and Mike Fratello, and I respect both of those men. Ron was particularly good with the defensive part of the game. He brought a lot to our staff, especially to me personally. He had an under-standing of everything—how to play the screen and roll, how to play the baseline screen, how to play the vertical screen. He knew what to do on a back pick. He knew it all and he could teach it. With Ron Rothstein handling the defense, we became a tough team.

When we lost Versace in the middle of the 1988–89 season, I wanted Brendan Suhr from the Atlanta Hawks. He'd been an assistant coach there but was in the front office at the time, and I heard he wanted to get back on the bench. Jack McCloskey got permission to speak with him, and, coincidentally, we were going to Atlanta that week. I called him up and said, "Let's meet, I'd like to talk to you."

We went to a place called Houston's and had one of those three-hour dinners. I felt very comfortable with him. I didn't know him all that well—we'd met a couple of times, but that was it. I'd heard nothing but good things about his work. I didn't want someone coming in trying to change things. Dick Versace said to me on one occasion that we had to change our entire offense. We had just gone to the finals against the Lakers and he wanted to implement a whole new plan. I said to him, "Where did we finish this season? Who won in the East? Who came within one shot of winning it all in Los Angeles? We are not going to change anything." He got my message.

What I look for in an assistant coach is someone who wants to work with me. I want to have a good relationship, which to me is as important as good coaching. I said to Brendan Suhr at dinner that night, "Look, I've made every mistake you can make in coaching. You can't tell me one mistake I haven't made. What I want you to do is come to Detroit and have some fun. I want you to enjoy working in Detroit. That's very important." That's how we hired him.

Brendan Malone wasn't particularly happy about the move. He had been there before Brendan Suhr and he wanted to come off the road and become a bench coach. I didn't want him to do that, because I liked the job he was doing on the road. I knew it was a tough assignment, and maybe I was penalizing him by keeping him out there, but he was doing a great job for us.

I got Brendan Malone from the Knicks. He was an assistant with them before they moved him into the scouting department. He'd been around a long time and was a very likeable guy who knew what he was doing. He was a well-known high school coach in New York, including Power Memorial, the school Kareem Abdul-Jabbar went to, but Brendan didn't coach him. He relates very well to people, and maybe I'm selfish by keeping him on the road, but I don't want to lose his great contributions.

I have Brendan Malone sit on the bench during the playoff games. I try to have my two assistants work on everything together, and I'm fortunate they get along. They're both important to me. You can't have friction on your staff if you're going to get the job done. It can become too much of a problem. These guys have been tremendous, and they lift me up when I'm low. They are there when I need them. They are loyal, dedicated, and talented. How can I ask for more?

The one thing I keep telling them, as I do all my assistants, is to think about their next job—where they might like to work. Who will take my place when I leave the Pistons? I don't know. I know Brendan Suhr wants to be a head coach, and I'm sure Brendan Malone does, too. But that decision won't be up to me. Anyway, it may not happen for a while.

Training camp is vital to the success of a professional basketball team. Not many people pay attention to it because it doesn't get a lot of ink in the papers with football in full

swing and the World Series commanding most of the headlines.

But that's where it all starts—at camp, in the first few
weeks of October.

I put a lot of emphasis on our training camp. The truth is,
there are only two times I can really coach the team—in the
playoffs and in training camp. That's because I get the full
attention of all my players at those times, and they're very
coachable. They listen and they concentrate. My job is a joy
at the beginning and the end of the season.

The middle? Well, I'll give it to them as a Christmas
present, and just hope they don't fall off the ladder putting
up the lights.

I ask a lot of my players in training camp. That's the place
where they establish themselves. I tell them, "Don't come to
me in January and say you should be getting more minutes.
Do it now, today, in training camp. You show me you deserve
to be on the floor and you'll be on the floor."

I have to get their attention right away and remind them
of all the old disciplines they have to follow. The best way to
do that is to let them know training camp is serious business.

I didn't go up north with my coaches before the start of
our second championship season. I wanted to change things
a little, so we stayed in The Palace. We took over a suite,
closed the doors, and did our brainstorming right there. We
had food brought in and got our business done in two days.
(Truthfully, I need this session more than they do; I'm never
ready to go back to work. I haven't straightened out the slice
in my driver yet.)

We train at the University of Windsor, and I like going
there. I like the atmosphere. Any time you cross an inter-
national border, life becomes a little different, and that keeps
me from getting bored. Being in another country is stimulating.

We arrange the schedule for the players to be free at 7:30 each night so they can go out and have a meal for themselves. We have two workouts a day—one in the morning and again in late afternoon. There are a lot of nice restaurants in Windsor, and with their evenings free the players can have a relaxing meal before getting a good night's sleep.

We stay at the Hilton Hotel, where they treat us well. They serve afternoon tea and always save a table for me. I stop by before going back to practice for a cup of tea and some scones. It makes me think I'm in London. I usually don't get enough tea, so I stop at McDonald's and bring another cup to practice because I need the caffeine.

I've eliminated the players' per diem for lunch because I'd rather not have them going out and getting hamburgers or hot dogs or not eating at all. We set up a nice buffet for them because I like to keep them together.

The players are free to go out at night, but we don't want them going back to Detroit. We've got some heavy fines for that violation. We're in camp only seven days and we want their complete attention all the time. If they want to go home, all they have to do is ask and we let them go every time. But not without asking.

Our first day in camp is media day. We meet with the press from 5 to 6:30 P.M., and then we have a nice dinner for the team. We might show a short film, and Jack McCloskey will say a few words. I'll speak for a few minutes, going over our plans and our fines. I don't like to say too much because they've heard it all before.

The one message I try to get across is about playing time. I know every guy wants to play forty-eight minutes and get forty-eight shots, but that doesn't happen. I try to explain this to them and hope they understand. Some do, some don't.

Now, about the famous mile run.

Bernie Smitovitz (Channel 4, Detroit) and I in the training room ready to get our ankles taped (to cover up our socks).

On our first day of drills we work the mile run in between the morning and afternoon sessions. Everybody has to run a mile or he's not allowed to work out. I started doing this while coaching at Penn. Billy Cunningham picked up on it with the 76ers, but instead of a four-lap mile, we stretched it to a five-lap mile. We like to go six laps in Detroit.

After all, aren't we the champions?

Darryl Dawkins could never make it in Philadelphia. I'd go out there with him—just the two of us—and I'd pull him around the track.

The reason for the run is obvious. We want to find out who's in shape and who isn't. Bill Laimbeer hates it. It preys on his mind all through the summer. That's OK. He comes back in condition to play.

The players dread the run, but it can be fun. We keep their times, and no one is allowed to stop. Some of the smaller guys—the guards—will stand at the finish line cheering for the bigger guys who are still out there, laboring around the track. We've had Isiah go out there and lead some of them home. When they all finish, we go to the ninety-foot game.

We have our first four practices plotted out minute by minute. Short cuts are a necessity in an NBA training camp that lasts only six or seven days, but we make sure things get done quickly and properly. We don't want to lose our players by keeping them out there too long.

We put in our offense, our defense, and our out-of-bounds plays. It's a refresher course for them, but it's important. I like to play a lot during camp. We'll bring in NBA refs from the area and go at it on the third night because scrimmaging early is essential for a veteran club like ours.

Every year in training camp I'm reminded of the huge difference between college teams and the pros. When I was at Penn, we'd practice our half-court offense and it ran like clockwork. I'd just sit back and admire it. But when we started to scrimmage and played the full court, it was a disaster—poor execution, sloppy ball-handling, bad passes, and missed shots. I'd throw up my hands, wonder what the problem was, and just to make myself feel better, go back to the half-court offense. I wasn't kidding anyone, least of all myself. In the pros, I play full-court the first day, not only because NBA players can't be fooled, but also because they have to play all-out all the time to be at their best.

I like the rookies to get to practice ahead of everyone else. I want to get them taped by the time the veterans show up, and I also want them out there getting extra instruction from our coaches, learning our offensive sets.

One of the toughest things I have to do is cut the roster. I hate it; it's the hardest part of my job. I've got to go to a kid who has dreamed his whole life of becoming a professional basketball player, a kid who has worked hard and made many sacrifices, and tell him we don't need him. That hurts me as much as it hurts him. I try not to get too friendly with new players. I remove myself from them because I know that'll make it easier when I have to let them go. It's even more difficult when I've got to cut a veteran.

It's a lot easier for me if I can tell two or three players at once rather than each one individually. I used to launch into detailed explanations, but found out they didn't do any good. They just wouldn't accept, or even hear, my words. I've gotten to the point where I say, "Guys, we're gonna make a cut." Then I read the list of those remaining with the team and say, "Talk to Mike Abdenour and he'll make the arrangements for you." This may sound cruel, but it's the way I have to do it because those interviews were just tearing me up.

The toughest cut I ever had to make was when Spencer Haywood tried a comeback with us. I think Will Robinson, Jack McCloskey's assistant, set it up. Haywood played for Will when Will coached at Pershing High School, and they've been close through the years. It wasn't a bad idea, but I could see right away Spencer wasn't going to make it. I knew I had to tell him, so I asked him to come to my room at the Hilton Hotel.

There I was, a semi-rookie coach, telling one of the former great players in our game that we couldn't use him. He could have made it tough on me because his very presence in camp was a significant story. The media was going to play it up big no matter what happened to him. But he made it easy for me. He said he understood my position and we shook hands and parted as friends.

I like my guys to room together in camp. If they want single rooms during the season, that's OK; all they have to do is pay the difference. But in camp I want them living together. This has led to some interesting relationships over the years. Isiah Thomas and Bill Laimbeer used to room together, but they were like an old married couple, fussing and fighting all the time. They finally went to Mike Abdenour and told him they wanted separate rooms, which they got.

Then one morning I saw them making up. I think all teams have these "lovers' quarrels." It's a long season.

For players, the end of training camp is like getting out of jail.

I too am happy when the exhibition games start. By the time camp is over, every bone in my body is aching, and I need a chance to rest my feet. I don't mind soaking in a tub or a sauna even if it's Phoenix one night and Portland the next night.

I probably look at the exhibition season a little differently than most coaches. We play eight games, all in different parts of the country, and I enjoy traveling to the non-NBA cities. I don't care who wins the first game, but after that it's all business, and I want to win. I don't like getting into a losing habit, even when the games don't count. I don't want a losing mentality pervading my team. Ever.

Nothing is harder on a player's body, and therefore more jeopardizes his career in the NBA, than the grueling demands of the schedule. Travel takes its toll on every team, not only physically, but also mentally and emotionally. Players and coaches talk about it, but nobody does anything about it. Not even injuries are as much a threat to a player's health and sanity as the eighty-two-game schedule.

In the 1989–90 season we played something like twenty-seven back-to-back games. The NBA has a rule that if you play in a city one night, you have to catch the earliest plane out the next morning. That means a lot of 7:15 A.M. flights, and getting up at 6 A.M. How can that be good for anyone's health?

I often try to catch an afternoon nap, but that's hard to do. Something is always going on and I am always being disturbed. When we play two nights in a row, or four nights out of five, it is hard to practice, work on films, or even have meetings. We just play the games and are on our way. I don't know how many times I have said, "Thank God we don't have a game tonight."

This is why having our own airplane has helped us so much. It was a big investment on the part of our organization and Bill Davidson the owner, but it has been well worth it. It has made us a better team, and contributed significantly to our back-to-back championships. I may be wrong, but I think Isiah Thomas had something to do with it. I understand he went to Davidson and told him the value and benefits of having our own plane. More than anything else, the plane lengthens the careers of the players, and this is important when it comes to your superstars.

Take an Isiah Thomas or a Michael Jordan. If we're flying commercial, or even charter, and we have to go through the airport, they're easily recognized and badgered by fans for their autographs. In itself, this is OK, and it's part of the

Unwinding on the trip home with Brendan Malone aboard Roundball I.

business. But it also means more pressure for them, more energy expended. Then we have to wait for our bags.

We have a twin engine Bach one-eleven—Roundball I— and it has been renovated to accommodate our players, our coaches, and our trainer. The players are big guys and they all have special seats. We have three sofas on the plane if the guys want to stretch out. The coaches sit in the back. We'll have our broadcaster, George Blaha, along with us, as well as Harry Hutt, who oversees the broadcasts. Sometimes Jack McCloskey or Matt Dobek will come along, but no media personnel are allowed except Blaha, and that's because he works for the Pistons. I think the rule is that you have to earn more than half your income from the Pistons to get on the plane. That rules out everybody else. I'm told insurance has something to do with it, too.

Anyway, we've got a four-seat section with a table. That's for the card players. Bill Laimbeer, Vinnie Johnson, and Mark Aguirre are the regulars, plus Dennis Rodman, Gerald Henderson, Scott Hastings, or whoever else wants to get nailed that night. Billy is the leader of the card ring. He loves to play cards. Game films are always playing on the VCRs, and all of a sudden Billy will say, "Run that back." He's seen something out of the corner of his eye on one of the tapes we've got running on the TV monitors, and he wants to see it again. He's bright, and he hardly misses a trick.

Up in the front section sit Isiah Thomas and Joe Dumars. John Salley is usually up there with them. We have different groups that sit together. They read, they sleep, they talk. Once in a while, on a longer trip, they'll watch a movie, but not too often. Mostly we've got the games going on the monitors.

There are twenty-four seats on the plane. We have two flight attendants and two pilots, and the flight attendants make sure there is always food on board. Stuff that's quick and easy—chicken, pizza, chips, sandwiches. Dusty Graves is in charge, and she watches over everyone like a mother hen. She's terrific. She makes sure everyone has his favorite drink when we get on board. No hard stuff. That would make it seem too much like a bar or a restaurant, and the guys don't want that. They voted against it. They don't want to get in at one o'clock in the morning and take the chance of getting into an accident while driving home.

Nobody is forced to look at the films while we fly. We put them on as a convenience, and it helps cut down on some of our film time. I am very sensitive to how much film we look at. You can drive players crazy with films, and over the years we have cut way back on our film sessions.

When we first got the plane, we had to learn how to use it. We could be back home in bed between one and two in the morning from any place in the eastern part of the country. Should we have an early practice, a later practice, or just a team meeting? Flying commercially, we wouldn't have had the luxury of a choice, and normally would not practice at all, but now we had extra time and wanted to use it wisely.

When we're out West, sometimes we don't leave until the next morning. It's better for the players to get a full night's rest before we leave. I always have the condition of my players' bodies on my mind, and I don't like to wear them out. I like them to be as fresh as possible. That's one secret to coaching in this league. That's why we very seldom have hard practice sessions. I want them to save their strength for the game.

Since we've had the plane, the quality of our play has improved. Other teams have noticed this and many of them are investigating or have already bought their own planes, or at least are flying charters almost exclusively. It just makes sense. In fact, the league office is looking into the possibility of having everyone fly charter.

Life in the NBA can get tough at times, but our bosses have tried to make it as easy as possible for us.

7 LIFE IN THE NBA

I'VE HAD MY SHARE OF CONTRACT PROBLEMS IN DETROIT. When I came here in 1983–84, my first contract called for $125,000, $150,000 and $175,000—two years and an option. The option year meant they hired me for two years, guaranteed, and it was their option whether or not to retain me for the third year. The salary was determined in advance and was not renegotiated.

We won forty-nine and forty-six games in those first two years, which was a good mark in Detroit, but management was in no hurry to sign me for the third year. That bothered me because I felt I had done a good job for them. They finally picked up the third year, and then we started some very difficult negotiations for a new contract.

The Pistons have always been tough with me. I'm represented by Albert Linder, an attorney from Philadelphia, who is more of a personal friend to me than strictly an agent. At one point during the summer of 1986, Jack McCloskey said if I didn't agree to their offer in forty-eight hours, he was going in another direction. I was a semi-free agent and wasn't satisfied with the new contract, which would have paid me $200,000 and $250,000 for the first two years, plus $275,000 for the option year.

My salary didn't seem fair compared to that of other coaches in the league who were making more money, but I

finally agreed to their terms. The first year of the new contract was the 1986–87 season. My contract expired on June
1 of the following year, about the time we went to the finals
for the first time against the Lakers. So technically I coached
in that series without a contract. That was upsetting.

We started all over again with new negotiations in the
summer of 1988, with nothing getting settled. CBS contacted
me and asked me to come to New York to interview for a
position as color analyst on the NBA telecasts, and I agreed
to meet with them in late September. I decided I had nothing
to lose by keeping all my options open. I took my attorney
with me and we met secretly in a hotel. They didn't make a
specific offer because they didn't want to get anyone in the
Detroit organization upset.

Three years earlier, in 1985, the Philadelphia 76ers had
wanted to hire me as their coach when the guaranteed years
of my first contract in Detroit ran out, but the Pistons refused
to let me go unless they were given a number one draft pick
for me. That's how things always seemed to go for me.

After talking to CBS, I went back to Detroit and told
McCloskey that since I didn't have a contract for the coming
season, I was interested in leaving and going to CBS. He was
stunned.

"What am I going to do?" he said. "Camp opens in another
week."

Jack was a coach himself, and I suggested that he take the
job or give it to one of my assistants—Brendan Malone or
Dick Versace.

"Let me get back to you," he said.

I wasn't using the CBS possibility as leverage to get more
money; I really wanted to go to the network and get into
broadcasting. CBS didn't mention a specific salary, but I had
a pretty good idea that it would be in the $350,000 range. It
would be a two-year deal and I liked that part of it. But unless
I got a clean bill of health from the Pistons—a release with

their blessings—CBS would not take me on. They just didn't want any contract disputes after the fact.

My problem with the Pistons was very basic—it was about money. Jack McCloskey was surprised when he heard about the contracts of some of the other coaches in the league—like Larry Brown making $700,000 in San Antonio. But understanding the problem wasn't helping me solve it, and I was getting anxious to move on. "I've got to talk to Bill Davidson," McCloskey said.

Davidson indicated to Jack that he wouldn't let me go, so I asked for an appointment. I went to his business office and he was brief, but adamant. He said he couldn't let me go at that late date, with training camp about to open. I didn't tell him everything that CBS had told me, but I think he knew from his sources in the league office. I understood his reaction, just as I understood McCloskey's reaction. I had put them in a very difficult position.

I explained that I didn't want to walk out on them, but I had to take care of myself. I eventually decided not to make a big issue of the whole thing. I felt I owed that much to them. But still, I had no contract.

We went to a league meeting in Orlando, Florida, and were at a social function when Jack came to me and started talking contract again. The sticking point was over a bonus for getting through the first round of the playoffs. They had been giving $10,000, but he wanted to eliminate that entirely because he said we should win our first-round games.

I got very upset. I got stubborn and he got stubborn, and when you have two stubborn Irishmen going head to head there's always the possibility things will never be resolved. They had offered me $400,000 a year for three years and that was fine, but I felt they were trying to nickel-and-dime me with the bonus money. On the other hand, I no longer wanted to move. Jack and I went around and around at the Orlando party arguing about the money.

"Why don't you at least give me something?" I asked.

"OK, how about $2,000?"

I went to my attorney laughing. The whole thing was becoming ridiculous. We had a chance to win the NBA Championship and we were haggling over a few thousand dollars.

I could see we were at a stalemate, so I finally said to my attorney, "OK, I'm not happy with what they're trying to do, but I can make enough extra money on the outside to make up for it. Let's go ahead and do it."

It turned out that we were so good I made about $70,000 with the other extra bonus clauses. I tried not to think of Larry Brown and his $700,000.

I don't know our owner, Bill Davidson, well, at least not socially. I've been to his house a couple of times for dinner, but that was when the Pistons were thinking about firing me, so the occasions weren't exactly conducive to building a strong personal relationship.

Bill struggled a lot in his early years with the Pistons, but he's reached a point where he has chosen to put a little distance between himself and the franchise. He looks after his other interests and has good people to run the day-to-day operations of the team so he can relax and enjoy it. Obviously, he's a very successful man, and I happen to like him. He has let me do my job, under the supervision of Jack McCloskey. He hired me to coach and never once has he interfered. He has never come to me and told me what I ought to do, and I respect him a lot for that.

He can be tough, and he has no qualms about firing people if he doesn't think they're doing the job. I don't know how many coaches he's had in Detroit, and I don't think he liked firing any of them—that's not his nature—but he did it because he felt it had to be done.

He hired Jack McCloskey, who has proven to be an outstanding general manager, as evidenced by his record. He's the one who put this team together. Davidson lets McCloskey run the basketball operations, and Tom Wilson the administrative and management end of it. Davidson keeps his distance but stays on top of it through these two men.

Bill enjoys life. He has simple tastes—a good meal and a drink or two. He often has dinner at The Palace before the games. He's well respected around the league and likes to mix with people, but he's also a hard-nosed businessman who has great vision. That's why he built The Palace and why he let us have an airplane. He's innovative and always looking ahead.

However, he nearly fired me a couple of times.

In December, 1985, we were on a western road trip and were having a terrible time of it. We weren't a good team yet, but we were decent. But everything fell apart and the road trip turned into a nightmare.

Bill Davidson, me, and Oscar Feldman.

Chapter Seven

We were bouncing around the West Coast, losing games in Portland, San Francisco, and Seattle, reeling like we were punch drunk. It was the week before Christmas, and the weather, which had been threatening all week, was turning worse. We had taken eleven straight unscheduled flights and didn't know if we were coming or going. We even had to travel by car on three of the trips because the fog was so bad. Nerves were frayed and tempers on edge. The whole situation was really wearing us down, and we faced the prospect of flying all the way across country to play in New York before returning home for Christmas.

We played in Seattle on a Thursday night and got to the airport on Friday morning to fly to New York for our game with the Knicks in Madison Square Garden on Saturday night. The fog was so heavy we just sat at the airport and looked at it. Nothing was taking off or landing.

We had about fifty pieces of luggage with us, which Mike Abdenour retrieved from the commercial flight we were scheduled to take. We headed over to the Boeing hangar because someone said visibility was better a little further out and we might have a chance to take off from there. But nothing was happening there either, so we sat around some more.

By late afternoon I knew that even if we took off immediately, with the three-hour time difference, there was little chance of getting to New York before midnight. One possibility was flying prop airplanes to San Francisco and leaving from there, but the guys vetoed that idea. Apparently there was something in their contracts that said they didn't have to fly props.

Finally, I got on the phone with Scotty Sterling at the NBA office in New York and told him he had to decide whether or not to cancel the game because it looked like we were going to be stuck in Seattle.

"It looks like we're not even going to get home for Christmas," I said, and at the time I really thought we wouldn't.

But then we found out that Jack Ramsay's Portland team had traveled from Phoenix to Seattle on two rented Lear jets. They held ten or eleven passengers each, and it cost something like $50,000, but that was the only way they could get to Seattle for their game with the Sonics. Those two planes were at an airport just outside Seattle. Mike Abdenour collected all the luggage again, and we piled into some rental cars and headed for the other airport.

We got there about ten o'clock at night, and I divided up the team. I took the coaches, the trainer, and rookies with me and put the players on the other plane. I went into a coffee shop and bought about a hundred bucks worth of sandwiches, juice, pop, and pie for the trip.

We had to stop in Minneapolis to gas up and got to Teterborough Airport in New Jersey at about five in the morning. We took taxis into Manhattan and finally reached our hotel at 7:30 A.M. We played the Knicks that night and lost by one point.

The next morning we flew back to Detroit. As we dragged ourselves through Metro Airport, I watched Isiah Thomas walk to the luggage claim area. I have never seen any person in my entire life look so tired. I think he was at the point of crying.

I felt everything was unraveling and I was losing my team. The losing, the fatigue, the travel problems, and everything else were weighing down so heavily on me that I wasn't sure how I could go on myself, much less motivate my team. Night after night we got constant pressure from the media asking what was wrong with the team and what I was doing about it. It was all over TV, on the radio, and in the papers that I was on the way out.

Jack McCloskey was sturdy through the whole thing, and that meant a lot to me. But I noticed that Bill Davidson called him off the road, where Jack was scouting, and that wasn't a good sign.

Then Davidson asked me to his house for dinner, not once, but twice, which was highly unusual. His cook made us marvelous meals and we sat around and talked, but we never discussed any of our problems. I was thinking this might be it—this might be Bill's way of letting me down easily, and I was very apprehensive. But it never got to that. He just wanted to chat about the team. He was a perfect gentleman about it all.

One evening shortly after that meeting, on a particularly snowy and icy night, my wife was entertaining the Piston wives, and I had gone to a movie.

When I got home, my wife had a message for me.

"Isiah Thomas called—he wants to talk to you," she said.

I called Isiah back.

"We need to talk. Meet me at the McDonald's on Orchard Lake Road. Wear a hat."

That sounded a little melodramatic, like cloak-and-dagger stuff, but he didn't want either of us to be recognized. We both showed up wearing hats and dark glasses.

It was just the two of us. He told me how much he liked playing for me and that he felt like he had been set free.

"When I'm with someone, I'm with them one hundred percent," Isiah assured me.

"But Zeke, I don't know if I can solve this problem the way it's going. I just don't know."

"Don't worry," he said. "We're going to be all right."

That was it, a very short meeting between us. As I drove home, I figured he must have gone to the owner on my behalf. I knew they were close and talked about things like that.

We played the Boston Celtics two or three nights later, and Isiah had the game of his life. He scored something like

35 or 37 points and beat them single-handedly. We went on to win 23 of our next 27—including a ten-game winning streak—and the heat was off.

I learned two things from this ordeal. First, there are certain things beyond my control. We had the same players and the same coaches, and we were doing the same things the same way during both the losing streaks and the winning streaks. Second, you've got to be patient and persistent because you never know when things are going to turn around.

We've had losing streaks since then, but we've proved that we know how to win when it counts. And the "book" on our team, repeated constantly by everyone from TV commentators to the guy on the last bar stool, is that we win because we play good defense.

It's true.

But every team, from high school to the pros, tries to play good defense. Defense wins championships. But how do you do it? How do you get guys to play defense when all the glory is on offense?

If you study the game by reading, listening, watching, and learning from others, you realize that defense is the only common denominator to winning. I've read a lot by and about successful basketball coaches, and I've learned that if a team's defense is consistent, the team will win more than it loses, even if it has only average players.

I believe that 90 percent of the coaches in our profession want to be known as defensive-minded coaches. The problem is convincing the players. Even though they know the best way to become known as a macho player is to play tough defense, it's still a hard sell.

A player's mentality is always geared toward scoring. That's what the game is all about. Scoring produces victories and makes the crowd cheer. When the ball goes through the hoop the player is the hero. Every eye is on him and every cheer is for him. He likes it. Who wouldn't? He wants to do it again, so he takes another shot, and then another, and another.

When you score a basket, you are a success, and kids who want to be basketball players develop an appreciation for offense long before they know anything else about the game. They want to score. That's where the glory is, that's where the headlines are, that's where the money is. As these young players develop, their coaches have to battle them constantly to work on the more difficult parts of the game. They have to teach them to chase their man around a screen, be in position to rebound, and dive for loose balls.

When you go into coaching, you must decide what philosophy to follow. There are successful coaches who are defensive-minded, some who are offensive-minded, and some who balance both. In my own case, I believed from the start that defense was the answer to winning. My conclusion seemed logical because defense was the one thing that could be consistent every night.

When you coach high school players whose talent is limited, you have no choice but to teach and play defense. I realized in my first high-school coaching position that I would never have a great offensive team because I had only one or two kids who could shoot the ball. I had to teach them the other parts of the game and what we could do to compensate for our lack of offensive firepower.

I was always seeking information and trying to learn as much as I could about the game and how to coach it. I loved to travel, so I went to every basketball clinic within the constraints of my schedule and budget. In the 1950s we had little television and virtually no audio-visual aids. There were no instructional films, and only a few entertainment films on basketball. I watched all the other high school teams, all the playoff games, and I was never so proud that I wouldn't steal ideas from them.

I listened to all the great coaches—Adolph Rupp, Clair Bee, Bobby Knight, Hubie Brown, Pete Newell. I heard every one of them and many others over the years. After a while, a lot of it was repetitious, but if I came out of a clinic with just one idea that I could adapt to improve myself or my team I considered the clinic worthwhile.

I was always open to what other coaches were saying. I'd scribble notes as fast as I could write. Sometimes I even took my wife along to take notes because she knew shorthand. I was determined to see the other side of every issue.

As I listened to all these great coaches, I became more and more defensive-minded. I soon learned I couldn't play man-to-man defense with my high school team because I would lose too many players through fouls. Our team didn't have enough talent to win with even one or two starters out of the game, so man-to-man defense wasn't an option. We started playing some zone defenses instead. I tried to mix things up, getting all I could out of playing man-to-man while no one was in foul trouble and switching to the zone when someone was. It was a constant juggling act, but it forced me to make a deep study of both styles of defense, and I learned a lot about both.

I also read coaching articles in *Scholastic Coach* magazine. This may seem simplistic by today's standards, but it was all we had then and I made good use of it.

Coaching was a never-ending learning process. I had to keep working at it as the years went by, through my time at Duke, Boston College, Penn, the Philadelphia 76ers, and the Cleveland Cavaliers.

When Jack McCloskey hired me to coach the Pistons in 1983, he wanted me to improve the defense. He thought I could do it the way we had in Philadelphia under Billy Cunningham. I knew right away, however, that I couldn't do it unless we traded for some people who already *knew* how to play defense. In the pros you don't have enough time to teach players how to do it.

I accepted the position because I needed the job and I felt we could work around the issue. Detroit had good offensive personnel, and I never told McCloskey we couldn't build a successful defensive team with what we had.

I had a two-year contract and a one-year option, and I knew I had to win games to keep my job. Detroit was notorious for changing coaches. Since I felt the Pistons could be a good offensive team right away, I planned around that. We had Kent Benson, Kelly Tripucka, Bill Laimbeer, Isiah Thomas, and Vinnie Johnson.

However, they had deficiencies on defense that they couldn't possibly overcome. They lacked size, leaping ability, and could not block shots. And even from an offensive standpoint, they had nobody who could post up, so we couldn't get to the foul line to slow down the other team's transitional game.

I've always felt that my first year in Detroit was the best coaching job I ever did. We won forty-nine games, after the team had won thirty-seven and thirty-nine games the previous two seasons, and we got into the playoffs for the first time in seven years.

In professional sports, the management signs the checks, chooses the players, and pays them, so they always have a higher opinion of the athletes and their abilities than do the men who have to coach them. Consequently, management has a tendency to expect more than is possible.

After we started making the playoffs, I went to McCloskey and told him we had to do something about Tripucka. He was outsized at his forward position and he was never going to be an outstanding defensive player. Except for Isiah Thomas, we didn't have the quickness in the backcourt to get back on defense. In fact, before I got to Detroit, the Pistons were getting killed on defense because of the play of their guards.

Isiah would go to the basket, Vinnie Johnson would follow him in looking for a rebound, and nobody was back to defend.

We got Adrian Dantley for Tripucka, and this helped our defense tremendously. Not because Dantley was an outstanding defensive player, but because he was able to get to the foul line, which slowed the other teams down and allowed us to set up properly on defense.

Then we started to add personnel. We picked up Joe Dumars, Dennis Rodman, and John Salley in the draft and Rick Mahorn from Washington. All were defense-oriented players. We picked up more speed, became more physical, and we developed some shot-blocking ability.

Then we turned our attention back to the offense. We established a playoff-like tempo that allowed us to score 90 to 100 points a game. I realized immediately that playoff basketball was different from regular-season basketball. You don't get as many points in the playoffs because everyone plays more intensely. So why play one way during the season and another way in the playoffs? If we could develop a playoff style throughout the season, surely it would help us when we got to the biggest games of all.

It was hard to slow down the tempo because of the players we had. It went against their grain. Slowing things down restricts a player like Isiah Thomas, who is a flat-out, push-the-ball-up, into-the-lane, dish-it-off player. He kept playing his way, and I didn't know what to do about it so I left him alone. He would push the ball up the floor as only he can do and we'd have Laimbeer, Mahorn, and some of our best players still down at the other end of the court.

I knew it wasn't going to work. It was a conflict between my style and Isiah's talent. We finally got around it by going to what we called an "early offense." We took the ball under the opponent's basket, gave it to Isiah, and let him go up the court with it and work with our number three man, usually

Adrian Dantley, in the post. This went against our philosophy, but it allowed us to change tempo, which is a very important element in basketball. It also kept Isiah happy.

By slowing things down, we frustrated the rest of the league. They wanted to run up and down the floor and score a lot of points. But check the records. No matter how many points a team averages during the regular season, it will fall ten, fifteen, or twenty points in the playoffs. So why not get accustomed to playoff basketball before the playoffs begin? But to do this, your players cannot be selfish. They have to give up their personal statistics for victories.

What helped a great deal were my outstanding defensive coaches: Dick Harter, Ron Rothstein, and Dick Versace. In our meetings and all our planning sessions, we worked on the things I always wanted to work on, the fundamentals of defense: how to double down, chase off the screens, and play the low post.

When Rothstein showed up, we put in all these things. I was very excited, but I have to say that things didn't go well at the beginning. It was tough getting it all across, but we stayed with it and the players began to understand what we were trying to do and they accepted it to a degree. Not all the way, because they still loved those points.

At this point, we had developed a team with a taste for winning. We got to the quarterfinals, then the semifinals, and they could begin to see the Holy Grail. They started to feel as if they could become NBA Champions.

All this is a credit to the players because it wasn't an easy philosophy for them to accept.

All of them came around at different stages, in different ways, and began giving us their full cooperation. It was a constant selling job on our part, every day in every way, with never a letup. There was some complaining, but not during the games. We had to keep after the players because they're not robots, and they are not perfect. But the more we won, the more they accepted our ideas.

That's when we tried to incorporate another key ingredient in my coaching philosophy, which is to involve players in strategy and decision making whenever possible. We tried to share everything with them and asked them what they thought about it. You can say all you want as a coach about how things ought to be done, but if you've never been an NBA player—which none of us ever were—you can't always be sure you're right.

We could tell them what we thought was the right way to play in a certain situation, but if they were at all intelligent (and most of them are), they'd come back and say, "I can't play it that way, but I can do a good job of it if I do it this way."

It just makes sense that if you let them do it their way, they'll work harder at it to prove they're right.

Sometimes you have to go along with your players, even if you don't like what they're doing. With a player like Isiah Thomas, you have to say, "OK, we'll do it your way until you show me you are wrong."

Maybe the most important factor in playing defense is defensive rebounding. There's a basic philosophy that goes back to the invention of the game that all coaches spout but don't necessarily believe. I probably say it a thousand times a year: "If you don't give them a second shot, you'll never lose a game." You can't possibly lose if you hold them to one shot on every possession. They can't shoot well enough to score enough points to win.

Boxing out and not letting your man get a second shot is the single most difficult thing to sell to your players. It drives you insane as a coach. I never stop saying it, even though I know they hate to hear it. I hate to say it, but in the biggest games of the year, I say it even more . . . and a lot louder than during the season.

121

Defense isn't very entertaining, but if you want to succeed it is the only way to go. If I have any phrase that sums it all up it is "Defense wins championships." It's not very colorful, but it works for us.

Coaching is a never-ending learning process.

8 Trials And Tribulations Of A.D.

THE ADRIAN DANTLEY TRADE WAS A PIVOTAL POINT IN OUR PROCESS OF BECOMING A CHAMPIONSHIP TEAM. A lot of people didn't like the deal, but those who didn't weren't paying close attention to our team.

I go back a long way with Adrian. We were at an All-Star game banquet years ago and he was sitting at our table. I said to my wife, "Terry, that's Adrian Dantley," and she knew immediately who he was.

I said to her later that night, "I have a feeling that some day I'll be coaching Adrian Dantley in Detroit."

He was quite a player. I had recruited him at Penn. In fact, I recruited him pretty hard. He lived in Washington, and I went there often to talk with him and his mother. He was playing at DeMatha High School, one of the top programs in the country, and I was really impressed with his talent.

When I came to Detroit, I thought there were three players in the league who were virtually interchangeable in terms of their overall talent and style of play: Dantley, Kelly Tripucka, and Mark Aguirre. Kelly, of course, was on our roster, but even then I would have traded him for either of the other two because they were so much alike in size, salary, background, and ability.

After about three seasons in Detroit it became evident that we had to make a change in personnel, particularly at the "three" position, if we were going to improve. I went to Jack McCloskey and said, "I think we've gone as far as we can with this group. We've got to make a change at one position."

I was talking about Kelly Tripucka's forward position. He was an outstanding offensive player, but we had been giving up thirty-five points a game in the playoffs at his position. It wasn't all his fault because other guys were playing there as well, and maybe we didn't double down enough. But it was his spot, and it wasn't working out for us. Jack said he'd think about it.

More than two years later I was at social function at Penn State University, where my daughter was attending school, when someone came up and said, "Hey, ESPN just reported that you got Adrian Dantley from Utah for Kelly Tripucka."

Adrian had a tough reputation in the league. He had his problems with Frank Layden, the Utah coach, but there were other reasons for the friction on that team as well. I knew it wouldn't be easy dealing with him because he had the reputation of being a difficult player.

I didn't know the specifics of the problems he had in Utah, but I was willing to start out fresh with him. I was happy to get him because he was thoroughly professional in terms of his body, his attitude, and his mental toughness. He was a little small for his position, but we developed a system of isolating him and letting him go one-on-one with his man. He was almost unstoppable and he elevated our entire team.

Billy Cunningham came to me before an exhibition game in Phoenix in 1986 and said, "You've moved your game to a new level."

I wasn't so sure of that myself, but if Billy said it, it had some validity. I still considered him one of the most astute observers in the game, but I wanted to see it translated into the W and L columns.

We started the 1986–87 season and Dantley gave us the post-up player we never had before. He could put his back to the basket, drive, and get to the foul line from eight to twelve times a game, which was very significant. When you have someone who can get to the line that often, you don't have to stop the other team in transition as often, and this enabled us to cut down dramatically the number of easy baskets scored against us. It makes it harder for the opposing team to score when you're getting to the line often and stopping the other team's fast breaks.

We also had drafted John Salley and Dennis Rodman in the spring of 1986 and had obtained Rick Mahorn from Washington a year earlier. All three were excellent shot blockers, so our entire defense was getting better. We went along like this for a couple of seasons and then I started getting uneasy with my team. We were having too many isolation plays for Dantley. Too often the four other players on the team were just standing around watching him play.

I talked this over with Jack McCloskey, who has an excellent basketball mind and is never satisfied with his roster. He thinks he can always make things better. I know he's always talking to people on the phone, and I believe he would trade anyone on our team if it would make us better. He doesn't regard anyone as an untouchable. I told him what I felt and got the impression he agreed with me.

I was watching Dantley very closely, and I could sense some signs of age starting to creep into his play. Not in his overall effectiveness, but in the way he ran the court. Nothing was ever mentioned to me about this, not by my assistants or anyone else. It was just sixth-sense stuff on my part.

All through my first four or five seasons with the Pistons, I had Mark Aguirre in the back of my mind, although I knew he was having his problems in Dallas, and Jack started having some serious talks with Dallas about Aguirre.

I liked the fact that Aguirre was much younger and a terrific offensive player. Dantley, meanwhile, was in the twi-

I can get angry easily, but I get over it quickly.

light of his career. He was a very tough-minded player, but his best days were behind him. He'd been in the league a long time. I also started to notice that he was becoming more and more withdrawn from his teammates. Joe Dumars was his best friend, and they got along fine, but I didn't see much chemistry between Dantley and the rest of the guys.

I didn't think Dantley was happy with the way the team was being run because we were guard-oriented. He said this to me a couple of times, then became less conversational. I tried to talk to him about this on a few occasions because I knew a gap was developing between us, but it didn't do much good. He could be a pretty silent person.

In the middle of the 1987–88 season, we had a couple of road games against the Los Angeles Clippers and San Antonio Spurs, two of the worst teams in the league. We lost them both. Dantley had become very possessive of the ball and wasn't at all happy with the way things were going. He was getting resentful and everything seemed to be coming to a boil.

We were taking the "red eye" home from Texas when Isiah Thomas came to the back of the plane.

"I need to talk to you," he said. "We're in trouble and I think our season is finished." He wasn't happy with the chemistry of the team. He felt too many guys were watching and weren't involved in what was going on. Dantley had been getting the ball and taking it to the basket more than he had ever done before.

I knew what Isiah was trying to say.

I went to the front of the plane and said to Dantley, "I need to speak to you."

"I can't see you tomorrow," he said, "I've got an appearance."

"OK, I'll see you at eleven the day after tomorrow." We had a shoot-around scheduled and I planned to talk with him before we went onto the floor.

127

Chapter Eight

I've never been good at holding onto my anger. During our all-night sessions in Philadelphia, Jack McMahon used to tell me that by morning Irishmen would always forget what they were mad about the night before. That was me. I'd get hot about something one day and the next I'd have forgotten it. I was getting some of these feelings about meeting with Dantley, but I knew I had to have it out with him, and I knew it was going to be a tough session.

He came in at eleven, and I told him what was on my mind. He told me how he felt. We both aired our differences in a healthy way. His attitude improved tremendously, and he had a great second half of the season. We went to the seventh game of the finals in Los Angeles before losing in the last minute, and I felt we ended up on a high note.

When we started the next season, the old friction was back again. Isiah Thomas is the leader of this team and maybe he felt he was being challenged by Dantley. I couldn't see anything on the surface, but I could feel it. Our whole staff was talking about Aguirre again. We knew he might present a new series of problems, but if we didn't move on him soon, we were afraid we might not be able to get him.

During a game in Boston, we really messed up out on the floor. I hollered something to Dantley and he hollered back at me. That had never happened before, and I wasn't very happy about it. I knew we were nearing the end.

At our next practice, I went over to where he was sitting at sidecourt.

"Adrian," I said. "We need to talk."

"I have nothing to say. It's all been said and it wouldn't matter anyway."

"But we've got to get this out in the open and talk about it."

"No," he insisted. "I have nothing to say."

The final outcome after that brief exchange was never in doubt.

Fortunately, Dallas seemed to be more and more interested in making a deal. We got very close at one point, but it didn't happen. Then in February, 1989, when we were in Los Angeles to play the Lakers, I decided to ride to the Forum with Jack McCloskey and our two assistant coaches. Usually I ride the team bus with the players because I think it's important for me to be with them, but for some reason I changed my mind that day. We were riding along when, right out of the blue, McCloskey said, "It's all done."

That's all he said, but we all knew exactly what he meant. I didn't say anything when I got to the dressing room because the deal wouldn't be finalized until the next day. We played the Lakers and it was a helluva game. Dantley was outstanding, playing both ends of the court and scoring something like nineteen points in our victory. I think he sensed something was up.

The trade was completed the following morning, and I had to find Dantley to tell him about it. The two things I hate most about this job are cutting players in camp, youngsters whose whole goal in life is to play in the NBA, and telling veterans they have been cut or traded. You're smashing people's dreams, and sometimes their careers, and it's not easy to do. I'm not built for it emotionally, but it has to be done.

I have learned over the years to do it by saying as little as possible, because the more you talk, the worse it gets.

I went to Dantley's room and knocked on the door. He didn't say much when he let me in. Finally I said, "There are a lot of circumstances involved and there's not much point in discussing them anymore, but you've been traded to Dallas for Mark Aquirre."

He still didn't say much. He was the strong type.

My eyes teared up when I left his room. He had done a lot for our franchise, and I was sorry it had to end this way. He had helped me in my career, and I appreciated that, but sometimes things don't work out the way we all hope they will.

Isiah Thomas was a close friend of Mark Aguirre. They both grew up in Chicago, were drafted the same year, had the same agent, and talked all the time. Those two plus Magic Johnson were a tight group. They hung out together all the time and were almost like blood brothers.

Some say Isiah has a strong influence on Bill Davidson. He does have his ear, there's no question about it. Isiah was in favor of the trade, but I don't know how much he had to do with making it happen. He was looking at it from a selfish standpoint. He knew he had another six or seven good years in Detroit, and he wondered how long Dantley would be around. He wanted somebody younger on his side.

Aguirre reported to us in Sacramento, but I couldn't play him because Dantley had refused to report to Dallas. From what everyone was saying, Aguirre was going to give me more problems than any player I had ever coached.

I'd heard about his problems with Dick Motta but didn't want to go into any of that with him. I didn't make any calls to find out what went on in Dallas. I wanted to form my own relationship with Mark, and I wanted him to know me as much as I wanted to know him. This is something I believe in. I like to start fresh with everyone, and that's the way I decided it was going to be.

Mark showed up at the game in a gorgeous suit. I know enough about clothing to know it was expensive; it probably cost in the neighborhood of $700. I usually have one of my assistants sit next to me on the bench, but I told Mark I wanted him at my side during the game. I wanted to start educating him about our system.

We played a sensational game. The best player on the floor that night happened to be Dennis Rodman, who started in place of Dantley. He was incredible—rebounding, running, defending—just fantastic.

I leaned over and tapped Aguirre on the knee. "Mark," I said, "I have the best back-up number three guy in the whole NBA." I was giving him a not-too-subtle hint that if he wanted a job on our team, he'd have to earn it.

We moved on to Golden State. Normally it would have been a day off for us, but I called a practice because I wanted to see what Aguirre could do. We had our "Bad Boys" image at that time and our guys even played it tough in practice. I put Mark on the second club to see how he posted up. I have a strong belief that a coach really doesn't know a player until he coaches him every day.

We got ready to play, and Rick Mahorn said, "I have Aguirre." It sounded ominous, and I loved it.

Mahorn kicked the hell out of Aguirre every time he went down low. I watched him closely. He was getting pushed around pretty badly, but he was taking it. Rodman switched to him and Aguirre had to struggle just to get off a shot. He was finding out what we were all about.

I let them stay out there a long time, longer than usual. As we walked off, Aguirre was sweating and all but dragging his feet on the floor. He walked past me with a chagrined look, holding both hands above his head, and said, "I have no rights here—none at all."

I knew then that somehow everything would work out.

Some days it seems like this is the only rest I get.

9 THE GOOD BOYS

I'M NOT SURE WHO STARTED CALLING US "THE BAD BOYS," BUT THE NAME STUCK. Fair enough. Our team adopted this persona during our first championship season when they needed something to bring them together. The nickname became their rallying point. I wasn't in love with it because I thought it could create some negative publicity, and sports teams from Detroit do not need negative publicity. But I knew it was just a gimmick. I knew these players as well as anyone, and if they got a little rough on the floor, they were not that way in my dealings with them. They are tough, talented, and strong-minded, but they are also very coachable.

Isiah Thomas

To be a successful coach in the NBA, it's essential to have a good relationship with the superstars on the team. Paul Westhead learned this lesson the hard way. He coached the Los Angeles Lakers to a championship, and a year later he was fired. He had an alleged disagreement with Magic Johnson about how the game should be played and Magic won. This should not detract from Westhead's ability as a coach. He's been successful throughout his career, and went from the Lakers to little-known Loyola Marymount, which he turned into a national power.

133

If you don't get along with your best player, you don't survive. You have to give up some self-esteem, and maybe some ego, to pacify him, but it must be done or your chances for success are zero. I knew immediately I could never win in Detroit unless Isiah Thomas was in my camp. It has nothing to do with him or me—just the way things are in the NBA. It happens on all teams. Coaches handle it in different ways.

Take a look at all the polls. Isiah Thomas is a very popular player, a true superstar, and he deserves some special consideration. Not favoritism, just some strong, solid understanding.

I went through a little of this when I was with the Philadelphia 76ers. I saw how Billy Cunningham had to handle Dr. J. It required a special touch. Players at this level have the celebrity status of rock stars. They're recognized and idolized wherever they go. They can't walk through an airport,

To be a successful coach in the NBA, you've got to have a good relationship with the superstars on the team.

a hotel lobby, or go to a restaurant or shopping mall without being recognized and besieged with autograph requests. They're very special people who get very special treatment. Who could handle it all? You think of the other people who work with them and you wonder what's left for them in terms of their own egos. They have to make adjustments, too.

I didn't really know who I was as a person until I was at least thirty-five years old, so how can I expect a kid who comes from a tough background in Chicago—where some of his brothers did time in prison, where his whole neighborhood was involved in drugs and various kinds of crime—to handle with perfect poise and equanimity the money, status, and everything else that he suddenly finds coming his way?

Basically, Isiah is a very nice person. He is sensitive to other people, and everyone knows how gifted he is on the basketball floor. He has a superior intellect, and an ability to perceive his profession beyond the reach of others. He has been on the streets, and he knows all the games people try to play with him, so coaching him can be difficult just because he is so much different than the others.

When I first came to Detroit, I just let him play his game. That became a problem because I couldn't always understand what he was doing. Some nights he'd be a scorer, but other nights he'd be the assist man. I thought about it a great deal and finally decided I couldn't worry about it because I couldn't change it. Isiah was our emotional and physical leader, and it was my job to develop a team around him. It was the only way we were going to get better. We weren't going anywhere unless he took us there.

I've had my run-ins with him, some hot ones, too. These things are unavoidable when people work so closely together for such a long period of time. But I always knew I had to have him on my side if we were going to be successful.

Bill Laimbeer started to come to the fore and became a leader in his own way, and so did Rick Mahorn. But the bottom line was that we would rise or fall with Isiah Thomas. If he had a good practice, the team had a good practice. If he had a good game, the team had a good game. What was hard to accept was that he couldn't always be good. We expected perfection from him every night, and it was impossible for him to give it to us. His body, for one thing, wouldn't allow it. He's only six-feet, one-inch, which makes him among the smallest superstars in the game. Some nights he just couldn't do it physically, and other nights he wasn't there mentally. The truth is, some of the games bored him.

Still, we wanted him to be Isiah Superstar every time he went on the floor.

It's easy to go along with him because he was so dedicated to the game. I've never known him to be out of shape. He takes good care of his body so he can get the maximum out of it. Probably not a day in his life goes by that he doesn't practice. He's always trying to improve himself. He has the advantage of having a gym in his home, and some nights he works as long as three hours on his game. When he came to some practices, he would play at only 50 or 60 percent. Finally I realized he had done much of his work at home.

Some of our players had a problem with him, until they came to understand what he was all about. Isiah can do anything he wants to in a basketball game, and he has proved that over and over. He can score sixteen points in ninety-four seconds, which he did against the Knicks in a playoff game in 1984, and he can go against the Lakers in Los Angeles and pull his team from seventeen points behind to beat the World Champions before their own fans. He couldn't make any of the three NBA All-Star teams and got only one point in the balloting for the MVP award, but consider his performance in the finals against Portland. When the biggest games of all were on the line, he was the premier performer in the series. He knows how to win. He is our leader, and anyone who doesn't admit that doesn't understand our team.

136

The Good Boys

★ ★ ★

One night we were out of sync. Nothing was working for us, and I was mad. I said to Isiah during a timeout, "What's your greatest asset?"

"Leadership," he replied.

"Dammit, then lead," I yelled.

We won the game.

Do the players like him? I suppose it's like all groups. Some do and some don't. I think he understands how his teammates feel about him, and I know he's not afraid to voice his opinion. He'll call team meetings and lay down the law. If he doesn't like the way things are going, he'll tell them about it.

"Go ahead, have your meetings," I told him. "I don't care." What else could I do? He was going to call them anyway. He's that kind of leader.

There's no beer or alcohol in our dressing room. That's Isiah. He and Bill Laimbeer put in rules like that to keep everyone straight. They set their own curfews and enforce them. They understand the financial rewards for winning and the price they have to pay to win.

We have a group of very intelligent guys. They know what they have to do to win, and we talk about it all the time. During the season, we're on an island all our own. We have twelve players, three coaches, and a trainer. That's it. It's us against the world. We are scrutinized every night. Every move we make is recorded, dissected, analyzed, and evaluated. We have to be careful what we do and say. That's why we need leadership, and that's why a player like Isiah can be so valuable to a coach. That's why I go along with a lot of the things he wants to do.

Vic Bubas at Duke taught me to bite my tongue. There are a lot of things I'd love to say at times, but it's better to be quiet. I want to tell my players a thing or two on the bench, but instead I put my hands in my mouth or lower my head or simply turn away and look at something else. This form of self-discipline is very hard to acquire, but it's necessary if you're going to win in the NBA.

Basically, it's not that difficult to go along with Isiah because he cares so much. He knows how good he is, so his performance on any given night is not what's important to him. Winning is what's important to him. He's a kid. He's fun. He's got a lot of life, and he enjoys the game. He studies the game, and watches everything he can on TV. He knows what's going on all over the league. He knows he operates in two spheres: basketball, which is a children's game, and the business world, which can be very serious. He knows he's going to be a very wealthy man, but he also knows he can get burned. He's become cautious about a lot of things and a lot of people. When you get a player like him, you learn to appreciate him.

Isiah is very bright, which makes him a challenge to coach, but it's much better to have a superstar who is involved than to have one who doesn't care. If your best player doesn't care, you'll have problems that will never end.

Joe Dumars

The draft is very important to any team, but coaches don't get to see many of the players in person. I can watch them on TV or tapes, but it's tough evaluating them from a screen. If I'm going to draft a player and pay the kind of money that's invested these days, I want to watch him practice as well as play, preferably without him knowing I'm there. I want to see what happens when he goes to the bench, I want to see his actions toward his coach, his interplay with his teammates, his relationships with all those around him.

The Good Boys

I want to go to his home town and listen to what people have to say about him. I did this when I was a scout with the 76ers, but I haven't had this luxury in Detroit. I know talent is paramount, but I'll take a little less talent if a guy has a great work ethic, a great attitude, and is a good person. He'll need all these things as a professional.

I had heard good things about Joe Dumars from McNeese State, but I had never seen him perform in person. I saw tapes of him playing in some All-Star games in Hawaii, and I was impressed.

When I'm reviewing prospects, I get a legal pad and write notes about each one. When I watched Joe's tapes, I wrote only three words: "He's a player." What I had heard about him was confirmed by the tapes, and I knew he was going to be an excellent player—good both on and off the floor.

I didn't know if he'd still be around when our turn in the draft came. Houston needed a guard, and Dallas was very interested in him, and both teams picked before we did. On draft day, Houston passed on him. We breathed a sigh of relief but were still worried about Dallas. The Mavericks had two picks ahead of us, but they took Ueve Blaab and Bill Weddington—two big guys from Indiana and St. John's. They left Joe sitting there, naked. We took him immediately. He reminded me of two players that we had in Philadelphia— Maurice Cheeks and Bobby Jones, both great ones.

I'd been using a three-guard rotation with Isiah Thomas, Vinnie Johnson, and John Long, all veterans and good players. John Long was tough-minded defensively and physical, but now I had four guards and had to work out a solution. I used Dumars a little, but I couldn't find many minutes for him. I kept waiting for him to make mistakes, but he didn't make any. He got better and better with each game, and I knew I had a real problem on my hands.

I knew Isiah didn't want to be the point guard all the time. He liked to shoot and wanted to be more of an all-purpose

139

guard. I thought maybe I could work Dumars in with him, which would give us some flexibility. But you just can't have four guards and try to play them all. I knew I had to make a decision, and it would be a hard one. My problem—one of my faults as a coach—is that I have trouble demoting players, maybe because I care too much about hurting people's feelings.

I was getting some pressure from Dick Harter, my assistant, and also hints from Jack McCloskey, to give Dumars more time. Nothing major, just hints here and there. I knew Joe was a very special person and that I couldn't keep him out of the lineup. But that meant I had to move John Long down the line.

John was a dedicated worker, a veteran who gave it his all. I was going to take his time away and that's never easy. He was unhappy when I told him but didn't make a big fuss about it. I think he understood what I had to do and why I had to do it and we're still friends. But it's never easy telling a player he is being moved aside for someone else.

Joe is open and honest about everything. You know where he stands all the time. He can distance himself from some of the problems and come up with some very sound solutions.

One day Isiah Thomas came into my office with Joe. The team was struggling, and Isiah looked worn out. I could tell he had been up all night looking at tapes, trying to figure out what was going wrong. Isiah had some things written down that he wanted to go over with me. "I'll listen," I said, "as long as I have my say."

Isiah went to the board and started to list the things that were wrong. We went back and forth, Isiah and me. Joe just listened. Isiah said he was so worried about everything he couldn't even sleep. He was talking and I was listening, then I was talking and he was listening.

"At least he cares," I said to myself. On some of the technical things he brought up I conceded he was right, and on others I told him he was wrong. We went through everything: offense, defense, traps, screens, the works. I could see what he was getting at. A lot of it revolved around the problem we were having with Adrian Dantley, but the whole thing got pretty abstract and hard to follow.

After we finished, I said to Joe, "What do you think?" He hadn't said much the whole time.

"I say we leave it the way it is," he answered.

That was tough because he was standing up to Isiah. But Isiah knew Joe was an intelligent person, and also honest and fair.

We talked a little more and I adopted some of Isiah's suggestions and rejected others. But I was happy to see that Joe was not afraid to speak his mind. That's why he has so much respect on our team, and why he and Isiah get along so well. They have a mutual respect for each other.

What Dumars did that day, I call "Crisis Management." He was asked for his opinion and he gave it, openly and honestly. That's the way he is. He has his off days, but he knows how to handle them.

When we were in New York for our second-round series in the spring of 1989, Joe wasn't doing too well and I pulled him for Vinnie Johnson. He didn't like it, and I knew he was unhappy. But he made a great statement the next day. I called it the "line of the week." He said, "On this team, you wait until you are chosen."

Joe has come a long way on our team. For the Lakers, there's no question who their most valuable player is: Magic Johnson, with James Worthy second. At Phoenix, it's Kevin Johnson, with Tom Chambers second. Here, it's tough. Isiah Thomas is a great player and a great leader, but Joe Dumars is outstanding, too, and so is Dennis Rodman. You take these three and Bill Laimbeer and you have the heart of our team.

Joe really came through for us in the Portland series after getting word of his father's death. No one knows how difficult it was for him because he cared so much for his father. His love was genuine, but so was his sense of responsibility. He knew what he had to do, and he knew what his father would have wanted him to do, so he stayed with the team.

We have stretching drills before practice, and the guys always get down on the floor in the same groups. Joe and Isiah are always at the far right corner, side by side, with Laimbeer facing them. Vinnie Johnson is out there facing the other way. Positioning is very important. Rodman is here, Aguirre is there, and there are always a bunch of guys around the basket, including William Bedford. I can get a lot done during these drills. I mingle among the different groups and listen to what they're saying. I might needle them and they'll needle me back. I'm always looking for information, always trying to find out what's on their minds.

I've learned that Dumars is very secure within himself, and because of this he has no trouble deferring to others. He doesn't have to be the center of attention. He had an interesting relationship with Adrian Dantley. I never saw two guys who were closer. They were together all the time, around the hotel, on the planes, on the buses, going to dinner, everywhere. I think Joe found Adrian amusing and really enjoyed his company. He found it stimulating and educational. Dantley was a pro's pro. He understood the mentality of the league—every aspect of it, from management to coaching to playing. I think he was a good influence on Joe. He taught him a lot. They made quite a pair when they were together.

Bill Laimbeer

Bill Laimbeer is a man who loves all kinds of competition. Cards. Darts. Golf. Basketball. You name it, he'll take you on.

I find this interesting because of his background. He came from a well-to-do family and could have taken it easy his entire life. Instead, he constantly set different challenges to prove himself. His father is a top executive for a major corporation, and Billy never had to go without anything in his life. But he's always had a fierce determination to make his own way and has gone after everything as if his life depended on it.

Basketball has never been easy for him. For one thing, he can't jump. Two inches is max for him. But he gets rebounds because he's taught himself how to do it. He's a big guy who can't play under the basket, so he has developed one of the most devastating long shots of any big man in the history of the game.

He tried out for the U.S. Olympic team and was the worst-looking player at the camp. He went to Europe and came back. Nobody gave him much of a chance. But through sheer determination and hard work, he turned himself into a pro player.

I know all about his reputation of being a cheap-shot artist. He throws elbows and pushes people around. If there's a scuffle under the basket, there's a good chance he'll be part of it. But he's only doing what he feels he has to do to survive. He can take a lot of physical punishment. I've watched him closely over the years, and he used to have a Gandhi-like approach to pain. I've seen some guys really put it to him—namely, Bob Lanier when he was with the Milwaukee Bucks and Robert Parish of the Boston Celtics. They gave him some mean shots, one even decked him from behind, and I had a hard time trying to understand why he didn't go after them. That bothered me a lot. It didn't help Billy, either. People questioned his courage.

As he developed and matured, he began to strike back more often. Again, I look at it as a case of survival.

Chapter Nine

Billy likes to challenge himself. One year he'll try to be the best free-throw shooter in the league. Another time he'll try to lead our team in rebounds. It's a game he's playing with himself, a game within a game to keep himself motivated.

He's very intelligent when it comes to basketball. He'll make some great suggestions, but he can also be difficult to manage. Once he decides something should be done a certain way, he's going to do it that way, no matter what anyone else may think. I can't get into too many confrontations with him because he's too valuable to us. If I start disciplining him, I'll lose him, and then we'll start losing.

This is a tough thing to handle because you have to be careful about not playing favorites. The guys know how Billy is, so they understand why I treat him the way I do. When our minds are together on something, it's terrific. But our minds are not always together.

He showed me more in our series against Portland than I ever expected of him. He worked as hard as anyone on either team, and I know he pulled some of the other guys along with him. I still see him going up and getting rebound after rebound, just when we needed the ball to stay alive.

Billy has a phrase he's fond of repeating. He always says, "Play forty-eight minutes."

So we play forty-eight minutes.

That sounds easy enough, but check out the teams who do it. I mean, all the time, night after night, season after season. Some teams play forty-seven minutes, some play forty-six. Some play twenty-four and go home.

Billy will harp on this in our huddle. I'll be trying to talk and he'll be shouting, "Forty-eight minutes—we gotta play forty-eight minutes!" He gets mad at his teammates and he gets mad at me, but it's OK because he also gets mad at himself. You can't get down on someone who wants to win as much as he does.

No matter what happens—no matter what's been said—he can always come back. He can put things in the past.

He is the most booed player in the league. I don't know how he takes it when we go into certain arenas and the fans get on him like they do. I'd be crawling under the bench, but I think he relishes it. It is another challenge for him. You can yell at him, but he is going to beat you. Most guys couldn't handle all the abuse, but he walks out there in that arrogant way of his and that gets them ever madder. He doesn't care. Watch how many times he smiles at them.

"I hate Bill Laimbeer," people say to me.

"You wouldn't hate him if he played for your team," I answer.

I like Billy because he plays the total game. There is much more to basketball than scoring. Some people only watch the ball and never see all of the by-play going on. That's the most interesting part of our sport, and nobody handles it better than this man. Rebounding, boxing out, covering a screen, working without the ball. If you watched only him for an entire game, and understood the intricacies of the sport, you would enjoy yourself in ways you never thought possible.

Nobody knows this, but Billy nearly retired before the start of our second championship season. I saw him at a golf tournament just prior to training camp and sensed that something was wrong.

I said to myself, "He doesn't want to come back—he's had enough basketball."

I was very concerned. I called Isiah Thomas, and I even called Billy's wife, Chris. I was right. He had had it.

When you're a professional basketball player, you're together with your teammates for a long time. We'd been together for eighteen of the previous twenty-one months, and that was a lot of togetherness. It can wear at you. The season is long and the summer goes by quickly. You barely have a chance to unwind before it's time to go back to camp.

It is normal to yearn for a more normal existence, even a nine-to-five job, with weekends off with the family. We make a lot of money in this business, but sometimes money isn't everything.

Isiah told me he was sensing the same things about Billy. "I'll handle it," he assured me.

I called Jack McCloskey and told him what was going on. He said he'd talk to Billy. I didn't want to get into any long conversations with Billy because I didn't know how much good it would do. I felt better going through Isiah, Jack, and Billy's wife.

Billy finally said he'd come to camp, and I knew he would be in good physical condition because that's how he is. But I wondered about his mental state.

We always report at five o'clock in the afternoon on the first day of camp. That's media day. We do our stuff with the press, then I like to have a nice meal with the players and look at a few films. I didn't have a lot to say because what are you going to say to a bunch of guys who just played 200 games for you? But I kept Billy in the corner of my eye.

The next day, we started out with a layup drill and right away I could see we were into it. I watched Billy very closely, and he went right along with them. He was banging right in there. I knew then that he was going to be all right and so were we.

Vinnie Johnson

Vinnie Johnson is one of the guys who has been with me all the way in Detroit. Only three are left: Vinnie, Isiah Thomas, and Bill Laimbeer. Vinnie is a classic one-on-one player, straight from the Brooklyn schoolyards. He understands that that is his contribution to our team. He could be described as selfish, except that's what we pay him to do—come in and score—and the team understands it.

I wonder how many times his last-second shot against Portland will be replayed on VCRs throughout Michigan and around the country.

There aren't many guys you can pull off the bench, cold, and tell them to go in and score. I usually run a play for Vinnie right away to see what he's got, and some nights he is simply unbelievable. He's not young anymore, and has never been a great defender, but he's a player. He knows when he plays defense, he gets more minutes.

Vinnie gives us instant points whenever he comes off the bench, and that's invaluable. I'll put him in when our offense is sputtering and say, "Score, Vinnie!" and he scores. It's incredible. I call it a high-wire act: he goes in there in dangerous situations and gets us out of them. He is loyal and loves to play. He's a purist when it comes to basketball. He'll shoot the ball, but he'll also dish it off, depending on what's best in a given situation.

He's a bit of a pouter. When he isn't on the floor enough, he gets upset with me. I can see it in his mannerisms: the way he comes off the floor, the look on his face. I can tell it by the way he responds on the bench. A lot of times I'll have one of my assistants talk to him and try to get him out of it. Sometimes I'll talk to him.

The good thing about Vinnie is that I know I can talk to him and he'll always come out it. By the next day, he'll say, "OK, it's over—let's play."

The thing I like best about him is that he loves to play. Every day he comes to play, even in practice. He'll take guys on in a scrimmage, holler at them, and tell them he is going to whip them. Everybody likes Vinnie because they know he's real.

In the final seconds of our last game with the Lakers for the 1988 title, Vinnie was coming down the floor with the ball and he had Rodman on his right wing on a three-on-two and one-half break. I had some timeouts left and I had to make a split-second decision. Do I call time and try to set something up? Or do I let the play go on?

I knew what Vinnie was going to do—pass it off to Rodman. I decided to let it go. Magic Johnson was back defending. All year long Rodman had taken the ball to the basket in similar situations and looked for a layup or someone close in to pass to. Magic had five fouls, so he wasn't going to defend too close. He didn't want to go out of the game on fouls.

But instead of driving or passing the ball, Rodman pulled up and shot. I stared in disbelief. Then I jumped to my feet and screamed, "What the f— is he doing!" I was immediately ashamed of my reaction, but it was too late. The TV cameras caught me in the act and broadcast my outburst to twenty million viewers.

I can't fault Dennis for taking the shot; he was wide open. But that's not what he does best, and it's not his play. The ball clanged off the rim from about fifteen feet away and we lost. I should have called time and set up a play for Vinnie. But that's nothing more than hindsight. When I had to make my decision, I decided to let them play. And I couldn't really get mad at any of them after they had played so hard. I made my choice and I had to live with it.

Vinnie Johnson is one of the good guys in our business. A fun guy. Basketball is very important to him. I don't know how he has done financially, so I worry about him down the road. He's had some good contracts and I hope he has been taking care of himself. He's one of the most sophisticated players in the game, and he also happens to be one of the best dressers on the team. He has great taste in shoes, clothing, and jewelry. He doesn't buy a lot, but what he does buy is very classy.

I think he is a contented person. He likes to drink a little and enjoy life. But he does stay in shape. One time "Stairmaster" asked him to work out with one of their new machines. He went to a gym in Farmington and absolutely destroyed the machine. He did things to it they didn't think possible.

He and Billy Laimbeer are pretty close and I see them going to dinner a lot. Vinnie's personality had a lot to do with our decision to protect his spot on the team over Rick Mahorn when it came to the expansion draft.

Vinnie is important to us, especially in the playoffs, because that's when the other team takes so much away from you—your fast breaks and your set plays. You have to go one-on-one to get baskets, and this is what Vinnie does best. There's been a lot of talk over the years about getting rid of him, and every year the subject of his age comes up. But then he comes back and has another good year. If he played for some other teams in our league, I'm convinced he could average twenty points a game. With us, in our three-guard rotation, he doesn't get enough minutes to get that many points. He has been a rock for me. An absolute rock.

Excuse me while I put on the tape of his shot with 0:07 left on the clock.

Dennis Rodman

The NBA scouts a variety of different All-Star games in its never-ending search for talent, including one for lesser players in Portsmouth, Virginia, and that's where we found Dennis Rodman in the spring of 1986.

When Jack McCloskey came home from that game, he could hardly contain his enthusiasm. He had seen a kid, he said, who was just unbelievable. He was an unknown, from Southeast Oklahoma State, and something of a hot dog, but

Chapter Nine

Jack loved the way he played. A lot of people didn't appreciate his on-the-court-antics, like raising his hand to the crowd and challenging the other team, definite no-no's in the NBA, but Jack was intrigued by him and liked his enthusiasm. Jack has a little of the riverboat gambler in him, and thought he might be taking a chance, but was inclined to do it anyway. He is secure in his job, so he can be a little gutsy, and this turned out to be a big plus for us.

Rodman went to a bigger All-Star game in Hawaii but didn't play well, so despite Jack's initial enthusiasm we pretty much wrote him off because of his poor performance. There was another series of games coming up in Chicago near the end of the season, and fortune intervened on our behalf. Mike Abdenour, our trainer, is an enthusiastic student of the game himself, and although he was supposed to be on vacation, he decided to go to Chicago to check out Rodman for himself. Dennis played, but again he didn't do much. In Chicago, they had NBA coaches running the teams for the first time so they could see how the players would react in a pro atmosphere. Most of management definitely cooled off on Rodman after Chicago.

While in Chicago Mike discovered that Rodman had some asthma problems that affected his performance. He didn't feel well for any of the games there, but only Mike knew it.

With this new information, we decided we wanted Rodman after all, but when we got to the draft, we also knew we needed height, so we took John Salley on the first round. It was a no-brainer. We needed a big man and he was the last one left.

In the second round, we took Rodman. It didn't cause much of a stir because everybody remembered how he played in Hawaii and Chicago. We took Rodman and Salley to a rookie camp in Windsor, but they didn't play all that well. They were ordinary at best, and a lot of people were saying we had made a mistake with these two players. But we liked

150

them anyway. We thought they were two young kids who could run and jump and they could fill out our roster nicely.

From a coaching standpoint, I was impressed that they weren't overly interested in scoring but could pass the ball. You need players like that if you're going to develop a team concept, because most players just want to score. I didn't have a long-term contract for myself, but I wanted the Pistons to develop into a real team no matter how long it took. I decided to go with these two and make them a part of that team. To do this we needed a bench, and to have a bench you have to give non-starters the chance to play. These were two players I wanted coming off my bench.

I used them that way right from the beginning, and immediately the whole league took Rodman the wrong way. They didn't like his hot-dogging, and he was driving the other teams nuts with his style of play. They really grew to dislike him. I watched him closely, and what I liked was that he always came to play, even in practice. He was doing things that even had our veterans saying, "What's this guy up to?" He'd go in for a layup and soar through the air. He'd go up for a rebound and pull it down with a vengeance. He never let up. I knew we had a very special player.

I said to myself, "What kind of guy is this who doesn't want to shoot the ball?" All he wanted to do was run the floor and play defense. I could see his style of running and it excited me. He looked like a three-year-old thoroughbred, and I could see him running in the Kentucky Derby. I thought he could be a world-class runner if he ever put his mind to it. He was going to be an outstanding player, but I also knew he could be very sensitive.

We checked up on his family background and found out that life hadn't been all that kind to him. *Sports Illustrated* had reported that he had stolen some watches from the Dallas airport. Dennis had been working as a janitor at the airport. One night he was cleaning up and saw watches behind the bars of an airport store window. He hooked several of them that were within reach to give to his friends. He was caught but not prosecuted and gave all the watches back.

I saw in him a mustang out on the range—a wild colt who wanted to run loose, to be free. He didn't want any restraints on him, so I knew handling him would be a touch-and-go matter. But he loved to play and he loved to win.

As he became better and better, I heard guys around the league saying, "My God, what a mistake we made!"

Jack McCloskey had scored a coup. The guy was a fabulous player.

Last season on a trip out West we were struggling. In a game against Golden State Isiah Thomas took an elbow to the head, suffering a concussion, and couldn't play. Bill Laimbeer was ejected early in the game, and we had to fight through all forty-eight minutes. We lost, and when we got back to the dressing room, Rodman started screaming at everyone. He got on the guys who were not playing defense. He said he didn't want to be a part of any team that didn't want to put out.

I loved it. I listened but never got involved.

There was no stopping him. He went on and on. I let him go for two or three minutes, maybe four. He was yelling and throwing things all over the place. Nobody said a word. Not the players. Not the coaches. No one.

When he finished, I waited a few seconds, then said, "That's it—Dennis said it all." And I walked out.

I like him. He's a coach's dream. You can take him out of a game or put him back in and he accepts it all. He's easy to deal with because all he wants to do is win. Scoring doesn't mean anything to him. Where can you find a player like that in this day and age?

Last Christmas Day I was home with my family when Dennis pulled up in the driveway. He walked in and gave Terry a gift of Waterford crystal. It was his way of saying thank you. He and my wife have this little thing going about cinnamon-nut cake. He loves her cinnamon-nut cake. Every once in a while, she'll bake him one and I'll take it to him at the arena.

I worry about Dennis. He likes to drive too fast. I hope he's taking care of his money because I want him to get everything he can out of life. If anyone deserves it for the effort he expends, he does. Each season he gets better and better. He's still too emotional, and gets frustrated too easily, which is something he has to work on. I've seen him miss a shot and then be completely out of the game the next two plays. He gets so frustrated his mind goes blank. Even in practice, I've seen him get so angry with himself he'll kick a basketball up into the second tier.

"With a foot like that, Dennis, you can always get a job in the National Football League," I tell him.

He looks at me and smiles. How can you get mad at a guy like that?

James Edwards

James Edwards is one of the nice people in our league, a true gentleman. I have followed his entire career in the NBA. I had him in my ninety-three-day stint with the Cleveland Cavaliers, and he was a good player for me. Bill Laimbeer thought he should be playing in Edwards' place, but Laimbeer was twenty pounds overweight at the time, so I played Edwards instead.

Edwards doesn't have much to say. He minds his own business. Even though in our system we play him in the middle, he's really a forward. He's not a mean guy, so consequently he's not a great rebounder. But he is a flat-out competitor.

He came out of the drug scene in Phoenix, where a lot of accusations were made but nothing was ever proved against him. I look for certain signs in my players that reveal drug problems. Their eyes, for one thing. Their speech. Are they on time? Or are they late with a lot of excuses?

Ever since we've had Edwards, he has been as clean as a new shirt, clear-eyed and well-spoken, and hasn't been late one time for anything. I consider him a model citizen. He has a great attraction to women, or they have a great attraction for him. It doesn't matter, there's nothing wrong with it. He's a single guy and loves his life.

I may not have given him enough playing time in our first championship season—he only played about 1,200 minutes. I knew he needed more than that to work into the groove, but I couldn't work it out. The number nearly doubled in our second championship season, but at his age, I have to watch him and take care not to wear him out.

I wanted him from Phoenix because I felt he could make our bench stronger. That's how you win in this league. The teams with the most depth usually wind up on top.

We started John Salley last season but got off to a horrendous start. We had an extremely difficult schedule early in the year, so I knew it would be rough, but I certainly didn't expect to be only 13-11 after twenty-four games. When you're the defending champions and barely staying above a .500 percentage, you know you'd better make some major adjustments, and quickly.

Everyone was talking about our demise, how we were going down the tubes and didn't have a chance in the world of repeating as champions. I wasn't too alarmed because I figured we would get going once the schedule evened out for us.

We went to Sacramento and I thought about making a change in the starting lineup, Edwards for Salley. I knew James could play the low post, and he would give us some scoring strength. Even though he fades on a shot, he has a terrific eye.

I was out late one night, then went to the hotel bar for a nightcap. Brendan Suhr was there, and so was Isiah Thomas and some of the players. I told them what I was thinking about. I wanted their input. They were unanimous about the change. I let them talk, and I listened. I finished my drink and walked out of the room, telling them I would make coaches out of them yet and pay to see them work.

John Salley

When we drafted John Salley, he had the reputation of being an in-and-out player. He came into our rookie camp without a contract, and that was a good sign. It meant he was serious about his job. Right away we could see he had a great personality and that he was a good kid. He was hard to get mad at.

In training camp, it was hard to define the kind of player he was. He wasn't a shooter, but he could run and block shots. When I first came to Detroit, we had no low post players and nobody who could block shots. You can't win consistently in the NBA without those two elements. These two kids gave us running ability, and they could block shots, so I figured they would fit nicely into our team. I was determined to work them into our plans.

They started slowly but at a nice pace. John, though, can be an enigma. He has become very media conscious and is popular with everyone in the press. That's because he's always accommodating, upbeat, and says a lot of funny things. Everybody likes him. He does all the talk shows and a lot of commercials. He looks and acts like Arsenio Hall. He seems to know everybody in show business, which is fine, but I have to bring him into my office from time to time to remind him of his priorities—that everything he has, everything he gets, stems from one thing and one thing only: the fact that he is a professional athlete.

"Hey, John, don't forget what got you here," I keep saying to him. "Let's concentrate on basketball. The way salaries are escalating, you stand to make a lot of money if you keep your priorities straight."

He had a very mediocre eighty-two games in our championship season of 1988–89, but he, along with Dennis Rodman, Vinnie Johnson, and James Edwards, gave us the best bench in the league. Vinnie and Edwards are primarily offensive threats, while Rodman and Salley are defensive players, so I had a lot of flexibility in the way I used the four of them.

Salley and Rodman gave us the deepest bench in the league and were very important to our success. But I always had to stay on John. He had the needle out for everyone, and he's not afraid to say what he thinks. The surprising thing is that he is a bit of a loner in terms of the rest of the team.

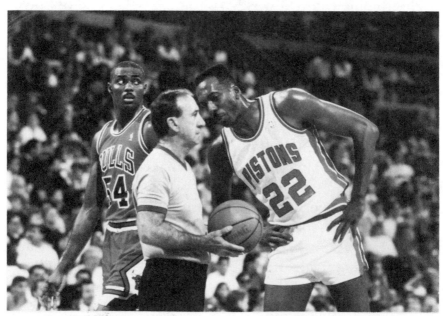

John Sally confiding one of his innermost secrets during the Chicago series.

When we got into the playoffs in 1989, we saw more of the real John Salley and what he is capable of. He raised the level of his game and went out there to win. This past season he kept his level at a higher rate throughout the year, yet his name kept popping up in the papers in connection with trade rumors. It had to be unsettling to him.

I finally had to sit him down and tell him not to worry about it. I told him he wasn't going anyplace. He had bought a big home in Detroit, a mansion with sixty-four rooms that once belonged to Cardinal Dearden, and was becoming quite the man about town. He was involved in a lot of different things—promoting his own line of shoes and clothes, making all kinds of appearances, and even doing stand-up routines in comedy clubs. Again, I told him, "Hey, John, that's great, but don't forget basketball."

More than once I found myself screaming at him on the floor. Then later we'd be walking through the tunnel back to the dressing room and somebody would come up and pat me on the rump. It would be John. It was his way of saying, "It's all right. I understand why you're yelling at me."

John is very likeable. He can always break you up.

"How come Daly doesn't yell at James Edwards the same way he yells at you?" a writer asked him one day.

"That's because they went to school together. They're the same age," John said.

This man likes to kid around a lot, but when we get to the end of the season and everything is on the line, he is as serious as anyone.

Mark Aguirre

No player on our team has had to make more adjustments to our style of play than Mark Aguirre. Not only has he done it, but he's also done everything else we've asked of him, and that's why I like him so much. I'm a Mark Aguirre fan and not ashamed to admit it.

He has done a very difficult thing. He has put our team ahead of himself, and he's earned my respect in the process.

When we got him for Adrian Dantley, Dennis Rodman was in the process of becoming a star in our league. Dennis got so good that I was holding out Adrian Dantley through the entire fourth quarter of some games because of Dennis' defensive ability. When I did this, we almost never lost. It wasn't easy on Dantley, and when we got Mark, I knew I was going to have to do the same thing with him.

He was going to have to sit and watch—and at crucial times during the game—more than he had ever done in his life. I knew he had his own ideas of how to play the game. He was an incredibly talented offensive player, but he had his problems on defense. And we were a defense-minded team.

I knew Isiah Thomas could help him out, but only to a point. If Mark was going to become a part of our team, he would have to do it himself. He would have to change his thinking as well as his style of play. He found out almost immediately that our guys cared about winning and little else. He found out about the concept of team play. He looked and he learned. He tried to work in the best way he could.

It's hard not to like Mark because he is such a likeable guy.

"You're too sensitive," I told him one day.

"Yeah, you're right," he said. "I'm too sensitive."

How can you get mad at a guy like that? He is moody and can be tough to coach, but I'm glad he's on my side.

Just stay in shape, eh?

William Bedford

One of the reasons we're such a good team is our attitude. Our guys know it takes sacrifices to win. For instance, our players police themselves. They have a "no alcohol" agreement among themselves, and they won't even allow beer in the dressing room. We don't have any big drinkers anyway.

Vinnie Johnson will have a few and so will Scott Hastings, but that's about it. I don't have a curfew because I don't need one. The players take care of it themselves. They set their own times when they should be in bed. They even call bed checks on themselves. Why should I have a curfew? If the players want to sneak out, they can. I know. I used to do it myself.

It's a changed world. These guys realize the money that's available and what they're flushing down the toilet if they get into trouble with drugs and alcohol. Their careers are short enough as it is, and they know they'd better make it while they can. To my knowledge, we don't have a drug problem on our team. I had some problems in Cleveland but never in Detroit.

William Bedford was on drugs but got caught. In fact, he has two strikes against him. Once more and he's out. But Bedford was tested three times a week this past season and he was clean all the way.

Bedford is an interesting case. He's a good-looking man but has a frustration level that hurts him. He's got the size, seven-feet, four-inches, and he can catch the ball and shoot it. He has the potential to be a good offensive player, but his work ethic is limited. Some days he can be an unbelievably good player in practice, but he's not consistent.

We struggled to get him through this past season. With James Edwards and Bill Laimbeer getting older, Bedford can be an important piece of the puzzle in the near future if he wants to be, and that's why Isiah Thomas said all those promising things about him at our celebration in The Palace. He was letting him know how valuable he could be to our team. He was giving him a challenge.

So far it's been hard to trust Bedford on the floor, and in coaching you go with the guys you can trust—the ones who know all parts of their job and play both ends of the court, the ones who know how to rotate, how to box out, how to get to the free-throw line. That's how you're going to win, and that's whom you trust. But you can also get too comfortable trusting the same players, so you have to keep reevaluating yourself and everyone on the roster. I don't know if we can improve Bedford's work habits. We've tried. We've kept after him summer, winter, autumn, and spring. It's the old business of parents expecting more of their children than their children expect of themselves. We see a lot in him and are trying to go down the line with him.

We can push him only so far, and beyond that the motivation has to come from within himself. In our system of defensive basketball, we play as a unit. We have a support system in which everyone helps everyone else. We can't have anyone out there on their own. This is one thing Bedford has to learn. I watch him in practice. He'll go out and work on three-point shots. We don't need him to practice that part of his game. We need him to get involved in all phases of the game. But that's the way he is, and it's hard to get him to change. Our players watch Bedford as much as I do. He has a lot to prove to them, as well as to me.

The Bench

We're always talking about our bench in Detroit. Some of our players don't get much of a chance to play, but when you're the coach, you want them to be ready when you need them. This isn't easy for them, and what I appreciate about my reserves is that they never complain about lack of playing time. They don't ask for any special consideration. Even when they don't play during practice, they stay ready. All are experienced, and that's very important. I've found out you can't play championship caliber basketball with all young guys at the end of your bench.

We were looking for a fourth guard when we came up with Gerald Henderson. We had fooled around with some young kids at our 1989 training camp, but it wasn't working out. The other players just weren't comfortable with them. If we were going to repeat, we knew we had to have somebody back there we could rely on.

It's not easy to sit there game after game and suddenly be called on to play. That's what we needed, though. We needed someone who could understand this situation and always be ready. Henderson had been there before. He had played with the Celtics when they won, and he was also with Philadelphia and Milwaukee. He had played for something like eleven NBA coaches, so he knew what was going on. He was down the line in his career, but he was still a good, solid player. He was good in practice, and the players had confidence in him. He turned out to be a great addition to our team.

I didn't talk to him too much at the start because I wasn't sure how much he was going to play and I didn't want to give him any false hopes. But he knew how we operated with our three-guard rotation, and he accepted it.

He is always very alert and is there when I need him.

We picked up Scott Hastings after he left Miami as a free agent. He had a reputation for being a pretty tough guy, and since we lost Rick Mahorn in the expansion draft, we thought he might make a good addition to our team. He was physical and could play the low post. He could also hit some outside shots. We looked at him as a possible back-up to Bill Laimbeer.

Scott is a jokester and has turned out to be a delight because of his incredible sense of humor. He keeps the guys loose, and that's important over a long season. I think he wants to be a coach. Like Henderson, he has accepted his role. One night in New York I used him when we got into foul trouble, and he made two steals, did a great job on Patrick

Ewing, and we won the game. He has been a plus at the end of the bench.

David Greenwood is another player who is getting toward the end of his career, but he gives us a dimension that we need to win. He was also a free agent, and Los Angeles looked at him but decided not to sign him. Since we couldn't be sure of William Bedford and his background in drugs, we added Greenwood as insurance. David is physical and can play in the low post. He is very dedicated to staying in shape, and that's important in coming off the bench. He made a major contribution in the Portland series.

I watch them down at the end of the bench. They have fun and sometimes devise little pacts among themselves. If you've got guys down there who are complaining, you're in trouble. They can create a cancer on your club. I don't think the guys on our club would allow it, but you always have to guard against it. These three players have understood from day one what their role is, and they have more than upheld their end of the bargain. They know there is some big money involved, and they're willing to work for it.

Rick Mahorn

It wouldn't be fair to talk about "The Good Boys" without talking about one of "The Bad Boys." Rick Mahorn.

One of the toughest days of my life was right after we won the championship in 1989, the day we lost Rick in the expansion draft. It killed everything for me.

We knew the expansion draft was coming up and we were going to lose one of our players. We had a nine-man team and could only protect eight. Thomas, Dumars, Laimbeer, Aguirre, Rodman, and Salley were sure to be protected, and the other two would come from the group of James Edwards, Vinnie Johnson, and Rick Mahorn. It wouldn't be easy to part with any of them because they were all important to us, all a part of the team. So we did what a lot of people do in their personal lives: we procrastinated. That may not have been wise, but we put off our decision until the very end, as if some magical solution would present itself at the eleventh hour.

Most of the talk centered on Vinnie Johnson, at least in the administrative offices, because of his age and because he had a new contract coming up. They figured he was the most expendable. I wanted to keep him, but I don't always get what I want.

The coaching staff met off and on with Jack McCloskey to talk about who we might lose, but we didn't do it frequently. It was never fully determined, even though Vinnie's name was in the forefront of these conversations. If you don't make the playoffs or if you get knocked out in the early rounds, your season ends in late April or May, and you've got some time to think about and prepare for the expansion draft. In our case, we played our final game on June 13, two days before the draft was held.

We didn't have any time to make our final decision. Even as we beat the Los Angeles Lakers, we hadn't made up our minds. At least I hadn't.

After game three in L.A.—a Sunday afternoon—we went back to the hotel and started reviewing the tape. I said to Brendan Malone, "Why don't you call Jack and ask him to come to our room so we can talk about our expansion problem." Jack came in and we went through the whole thing all over again. I could sense the feelings were changing.

Mahorn had a bad back, and we weren't getting much playing time out of him. We had a reputation as a very tough and physical team, and Mahorn contributed to that and helped us win a lot of games. But we were also getting into a lot of trouble and accumulating a lot of fines, and I wondered how this would affect us when we came back to try to make it two in a row. Would everyone be looking for us, including the league officials? Our reputation wasn't the best.

We thought we could make up for some of the things Mahorn did through the draft or possibly through a trade. What I didn't realize is that McCloskey had been in Chicago the previous weekend for an NBA tryout of college players. Brendan Malone was with him and so were two of our other scouts, Stan Novak and Will Robinson. They had gone into the Mahorn situation rather deeply and semi-agreed that he would be the one to go.

If that turned out to be the decision, I knew we'd be losing a good player and one who did a lot to help us win. He played low-post defense, was nasty, and he took us to another level with his attitude on and off the court. I liked him personally and the whole thing bothered me.

I tried to rationalize it all. We couldn't give up Edwards because we needed his low-post scoring. We couldn't give up Vinnie because of the way he could bring us back to life.

I knew we had to make some kind of decision, but before we ever discussed it, McCloskey said, "I've already made up my mind. The papers are done. It's going to be Mahorn."

We flew home after the finals, and McCloskey came back to me on the airplane and said maybe he could salvage it with a trade. If a team wanted to take Mahorn, we would offer them our draft pick instead. The only problem with that was that we picked last. Jack's idea sounded good to me because I desperately wanted to keep Mahorn and was willing to try anything. I thought we needed him to win again, sore back or no sore back.

We had a parade through downtown Detroit, and Jack was riding on his float with a telephone at his side. He was still trying to work out a deal. It was wild. The people along the parade route were screaming and yelling, and Mahorn was smiling back at them, and all the while we were trying to save his career in Detroit but not getting anywhere.

After the parade we went back to The Palace, where another celebration was under way. We were ushered to the stage, where all the players were to be introduced individually. They all got a great hand, but I wasn't enjoying any of it. The whole thing was working at me, and I could feel myself choking.

Orlando backed off because of Mahorn's physical problems, so that left only Minnesota. I heard later that Bill Musselman, the Minnesota coach, called Adrian Dantley to get a reading on our three players. Smart. He went to the right man. I understand that Dantley told him any one of the three—Johnson, Mahorn, or Edwards—would be a good choice.

It ended up that Minnesota took Mahorn. I went back to the locker room with Jack and my two assistant coaches. We had to think of a way to tell Mahorn. He had just gotten a tremendous reception from the great Detroit fans, and we had to tell him he was not with the Pistons anymore.

I asked Mike Abdenour to call Rick into my office. I wanted to be the one to tell him, alone. When he came into the room I think he sensed what was going to happen.

"All right," he said, "tell me where I'm going."

I blurted it out, and it was just like the day I had to let Dantley go. I had tears in my eyes. I knew we were ruining the whole celebration, but I didn't know what else to do about it.

The guys in the locker room found out about it right away. They had sensed it would be Vinnie, and they had prepared themselves for that news. Mahorn came as a shock to them.

The team "officially" renounced the Bad Boys image after they lost Rick Mahorn.

Every step a struggle.

PART 3

PLAYOFF DIARY

10

LET
THE
GAMES
BEGIN

SUNDAY, APRIL 22, 1990

We played the Chicago Bulls today at The Palace, our last game of the 1989–90 season. It was a meaningless game in that it didn't affect the standings or the playoff picture, but I didn't want to finish up on a losing note. At the same time, I wanted to minimize the risk of injuries going into the playoffs.

I had to bring Isiah Thomas and James Edwards back in to wrap it up. I didn't want to do it, but we needed the win to keep the proper momentum going into the playoffs.

We won the game but it drained us.

After the game, Jack McCloskey wanted to speak to the team, which he does only on rare occasions. He gave them a kind of pep talk—what had been expected of them during the season and what they had accomplished.

The mood in the locker room was jubilant, even though we all know the toughest part of the season is still ahead of us. We've had a good season, with the best record in the Eastern Division, and tied for the second best overall. Only the Los Angeles Lakers won more games than we did, and we're guaranteed home-court advantage throughout the playoffs until we face them in the finals. Even that doesn't upset me too much because I believe my team can beat anybody, even on their home court.

✮ ✮ ✮

After the game, Terry, Cydney, and I went out to eat. It is a tradition with us to always enjoy a special meal after the final game with just the family. We went to the Oceania Restaurant in Rochester for Chinese food, and the chef made us a marvelous meal.

"Are we going to have our family conference at the end of the season?" Cydney asked during dinner. That's another tradition in our family. When it's all over, we sit down and have a free-for-all discussion. We talk about anything on our minds, including individual plans and goals for the immediate future.

"Of course we'll have our post-season conference," I told her. She seemed satisfied but also a little worried.

Cydney is twenty-four and a graduate of Penn State University with a major in journalism and television. She's on her own now, working in sales for a large corporation, but

With Detroit restaurateur John Ginopolis, my daughter, Cydney, and wife, Terry.

she still likes to have input into what her father is going to do with his life. Over the past year she has become concerned about my behavior on the sidelines and would like me to calm down a little more. I couldn't ask for a better daughter—she's the greatest.

On the last night of the season, Vinnie Johnson likes to throw a party for the guys. I had told him earlier I'd be there, but after dinner I said, "I'm bagging it." We went home and I read the New York *Times*, the Detroit papers, and worked on my book a little. Then the phone rang. I've never changed my number in Detroit, so a lot of people have it. I don't mind when they call because I remember all too well what it was like when I got fired by the Cavaliers and my phone never rang.

Don Casey, coach of the L.A. Clippers and a good friend of mine, was on the phone. He told me they were meeting at that very moment regarding his fate. I know exactly how he felt. He needed to talk with someone, and I was glad to be there. A few hours later Matt Dobek, our director of public relations, called to say that Casey had been fired by the Clippers.

An hour later Mike Fratello, coach of the Atlanta Hawks, called and was in pretty much the same situation. He too wanted to talk. I spent some time on the phone with him, going over his options.

I was happy to be available for these two friends because others have been there for me when I needed them. Talking with a friend in a difficult time helps crystalize a person's own thinking. These are people I'm comfortable with and who are comfortable with me. On the court, I try harder to beat them than some others, and they do the same to me. It's part of the game and we all understand it. But when they're in trouble, or I'm in trouble, we help each other out.

We are playing the Indiana Pacers in the first round, a team coached by Dick Versace, my former assistant. I never had a better man work for me. He did everything I wanted, and I did all I could to get him the Indiana job. Now, the hell with him. All I want to do is beat him. We can be friends again when it's over, but the playoffs are no time for friendships.

MONDAY, APRIL 23

At 8:05 this morning Mark Champion called from WWJ to make sure I was ready for our 8:15 radio show that we do every Monday, Wednesday, and Friday. I was awake until 2:30 this morning, so I tried to go back to sleep for ten minutes, but I couldn't. I went down to the basement, where I have a microphone set up, and Mark called again at 8:15. He asks unrehearsed questions, and I do my best to answer them in a two-to-three-minute program. It's loose but informative, and I enjoy doing it.

After the radio show I had my morning tea, raspberry—not from a bag but loose tea from a can. I'm a tea connoisseur, which I guess I inherited from my mother. She made tea all the time and then read the leaves. I used to believe every word that came out of the bottom of my cup.

Our house has an instant hot water tap, so I can make tea or soup in a matter of moments. It gets a lot of use because I drink four, five, six, seven cups a day. I like tea for dietary reasons, but I also like it because it gets me wired. When I want to be careful, I drink decaf, but when I need a lift before a big game, I'll knock down two or three cups of the straight stuff.

With my tea I read the morning newspapers. I noticed that the league has fined Pat Riley $25,000 for holding out three of his regulars in the Lakers' final game in Portland. I understand why he did it, but I don't necessarily agree with his decision. In our business people pay a lot of money for tickets; it's very similar to the entertainment business. Every night you have new people in the building. For some of them, it might be the only game they see all year, so a coach has a responsibility to put his best team on the floor for every game.

I also think the integrity of the league might be called into question if a coach doesn't field his best team. You have to consider your opponent's standing in the division as well as your own. When we played Indiana at the end of the season, they were fighting for a playoff berth. When we played Philadelphia, they were trying to win their division. We owed it to everyone to play the best we could play. We all fear injury and we worry about fatigue, but those are things we have to live with. We can't control everything.

I have great respect for Pat Riley, who has had to go through a lot to get to the top of this business. The man is an outstanding coach. He's organized and very demanding. We see each other from time to time, and I think he knows how much I admire him, even though I sometimes question his taste in clothes (just kidding, Pat).

After my tea I headed for The Palace. I live in West Bloomfield Township, on Maple Road just east of Haggerty. I go the same way every day. East on Maple, north on Drake, east on Walnut Lake. I pass my church every morning, and every time I go by I say a Hail Mary. I just want to say thanks for a great day, for my health, for a job that I love.

I'm charged up every morning I go to work. I've been doing this for over thirty years, and it still excites me.

I really appreciate my assistants. I always kid them that all I have to say is "Brendan" and everything gets done. They're always two steps ahead of me, and this morning was no exception. They had all our reports ready, including a detailed account of every player on the Pacers. The reports are put into folders and distributed to all our players. These reports show not only statistics, but also the tendencies of each player: whether he likes to go right or left, whether or not he likes to put the ball on the floor and drive, how often he goes into the lane, how he likes to box out, and much

I'd be lost, on and off the bench, without the two Brendans.

more. We also give our players TV tapes of every opponent. We analyze all their moves so our guys know what to expect.

A lot of people think our coaches just sit on the bench and doodle during the games. Anything but. Brendan Suhr keeps every play run by both teams—what succeeds, what fails, and against what type of defenses. How he does it, I don't know. He stays in the game but also keeps up with his notes. When Brendan Malone goes out to scout another team, he keeps track of the frequency with which they run all their plays, and this goes into our reports also.

When we sat down for our private meetings before the workout, I said to Brendan Suhr, "I want to know the success of our plays against them for the entire year."

He didn't even blink. He went through our books and pulled them out.

We played Indiana five times this season but counted only four of the games because in our first meeting, the second game of the season, we were so terrible that the game

174

showed us nothing. We made something like twenty-five points in the first half, which may have been the lowest total in the history of the league.

Our players are very good about paying attention in meetings and studying at home, and I trust them to make good use of the material they're given. Whether or not this trust is deserved becomes evident at practice the next day; it doesn't take long to tell how hard they've studied when we walk through the opponent's plays.

I usually call practice for eleven o'clock every day, because we're here, there, and everywhere and get in at all hours of the night, which makes it hard to keep track of changing schedules. If I make all the practices at eleven o'clock, it's easy to remember. But today I scheduled it for half past one because I wanted my coaches to have more time to get their material together. I also wanted to give my players a little extra rest after their final game of the long season—and after Vinnie's party last night.

As the players came into the locker room before practice, I observed their reactions to determine what mood they might be in. I've got a pretty good feel for when a guy is out of sync with the team or out of sync with me. I don't like to get into a lot of confrontations because they can be too damaging, so I ask my assistants to handle them. If they can't, I step in and do it myself.

Billy was one of the first to arrive. He has never been late since I've been here because he doesn't want to get fined. I don't think he wants to part with a dime. Isiah Thomas came in early and that was a good sign. Everyone seemed to be in a good mood. I decided not to tape up, to just walk through the plays instead. We brought out the scouting reports and sensed a healthy, positive enthusiasm in the locker room. We passed out pens and pencils so they could take notes. I looked around the room and liked what I felt.

I could see they were focused, so I went to the blackboard and gave them a brand new play. They hung on my every word, absorbing it immediately. I talked about zones and the alignment of players and they absorbed that, too.

When we went out to work, the building was completely empty.

During the year, I allow the media into practice, but it's a lot better if we practice in private during the playoffs. If just eight or ten of the regular sports writers showed up, I wouldn't mind, but the number can get pretty large during the playoffs. When thirty or forty people are walking around and talking, I can't get the concentration I need from the players. I try to be sensitive to the needs of the media, especially since I'm part of the media myself, in a way, but the bottom line is that I've got to do what is best for the team, the owners, and the fans. Plus, I think some reporters might go back to their own teams and drop little hints about what we are doing in practice. I try to convince myself this doesn't happen, but I don't want to take any chances.

I didn't have any dinner because of an appearance at Kosin's clothing store from 6:30 to 9. I agreed to do it three weeks earlier and I didn't want to break my promise. I have a contract with them, and beyond that, I was a close personal friend of Harry Kosin before he died. So for nearly four hours I signed autographs and talked basketball.

One of the things I don't especially like about my job is the lack of privacy. When I first came to town, I was invited to a lot of charity golf outings, and I went to most of them. But as we became more popular, the appearances became more and more of a chore. No matter where I went—to the movies, a restaurant, or to a golf outing—all people wanted to talk about was the Pistons. I understood it and enjoyed it, but it still became very wearing. The last thing I want to do is hurt someone's feelings, so I usually decide it's best not to go at all. The truth is, I'm more interested in what other people do. I have a natural curiosity about other people, but I can never get them to talk about themselves.

When I finished at the clothing store, Ben Kosin gave me a Scotch, a nice tall one. I took a leisurely ride home and stopped for a Coney Island hot dog with everything and a glass of milk. I had a hat on so nobody recognized me. It was pretty late when I got home, and the house was shut down for the night.

I took Koko out for her nightly airing. She's about seventeen years old now and is blind and deaf, but we still wouldn't give her up for anything.

When I come home at night, even if I've flown the "red eye" and get in at 5 A.M., Koko is waiting for me. She's always glad to see me. The moment I touch her, she perks up and so do I. Wins and losses don't seem all that important anymore.

We watch TV together on the sofa in the den and she stays there as long as I do. Of course I'm the sucker. I always give in to her. I make sure she has her treats, as well as her food. This past Easter, we had some people over to the house and I gave Koko a full plate—a little liver, a little stuffing, a little turkey with gravy. I can never do for Koko what she does for me.

I savor moments with Koko because they are so precious. I know I won't have her forever, so I try to enjoy every possible moment with her. When you get to a certain age, there are lots of things to remind you of your own mortality. Koko helps me understand mortality and vulnerability.

Each night when I come back to the house, I take her out on our deck that overlooks a small pond. There's usually a breeze, and I hold her up and put her head into the wind because I know how wonderful that must feel to her. I want her to enjoy the fresh air because you never know what's coming in life.

After I brought Koko inside I noticed that some interesting magazines had arrived, so I looked forward to a little reading. But there on the kitchen table was the most obscene piece of cake I've ever seen—a peanut butter cake with peanut butter frosting. I'm usually careful about sweets, but what's the point of being a championship basketball coach if you can't break your own rules once in a while?

★ ★ ★

Last night after our final game with Chicago, my mind raced until early this morning. Once I start thinking about basketball at night, I have a difficult time getting to sleep. But once your mind starts, how do you turn it off?

The playoffs mean extra pressure on everybody, but it's absolutely the best time of the year to coach. Everybody gets with it. I don't have to ask for their attention. They know what it means and they are ready.

I decided early in the season not to talk much about repeating as champions until playoff time. John Madden taught me that. He admits that when he was coaching the Oakland Raiders, he made the mistake of trying to defend his championship in training camp and then after every game. "The only time you can defend it," John says now, "is when the time comes to defend it."

Well, now is the time to defend it, so I'll put it to them squarely. I've laid off my players all season, but now's the time to get serious if they want to repeat as champions.

I start thinking about our personnel and the things I want them to do against Indiana. Fortunately, I have an excellent staff. They work at their jobs. I feel OK because we have only one team to think about. During the season, we might have to get ready for four teams in a week's time.

I guess I'm not going to get much sleep tonight either.

The fact that Dick Versace has been my assistant worries me. He knows our habits and our tendencies, our strengths and our weaknesses. I have to figure out a way to counter his thinking. He knows that Billy is a great outside shooter, so he'll have somebody in his chest all night long. We know Billy isn't going to score, so we have to figure out ways to make him a decoy, ways for him to set up plays.

No, not much sleep at all tonight.

I am concerned about our team because of that ugly fighting incident with Philadelphia in our next-to-last home game. Our league hadn't seen anything like that in a long time. Everybody got into it, and Bill Laimbeer and Scott Hastings were suspended for our final road game in Indiana. They flew to Indianapolis with us, got word they were out, and flew back home.

Part of a coach's job is to know his players, and for me that's one of the great rewards and side benefits of the career I've chosen. I know a lot about our players, particularly Billy. He can dish it out with the best of them, but he's an extremely sensitive person. After his suspension, I was particularly concerned he might feel some distance between himself and his teammates. I wanted him to feel like he was still one of us.

I normally wouldn't have called a practice the next day on such a tight schedule, but we held one at Oakland University before our final game against Chicago. I wanted to have a shoot-around, but more important, I wanted the team back as a group.

We went through a light drill. Billy usually commandeers a basket on the main court as his own territory, but on that day he went to a far corner of the gym. He and Scott Hastings were shooting there by themselves. My coaches noticed it too. "We've got a little problem going here," I said.

I started asking questions and discovered that Billy felt left out of things, like he wasn't part of the action. But there was more to it than that. ESPN had run a story that said, among other things, that Vinnie Johnson apologized for Laimbeer's actions in the Philadelphia game. I asked Matt Dobek if he could verify that report.

179

Billy's wife, Chris, has a tremendous influence on him, and in many ways he's lost without her. When she isn't around he becomes even more sensitive, and she was out of town. I was getting worried. Billy is very important to us, and we couldn't afford to lose him at a critical time like this.

Vinnie Johnson was scheduled to be on my TV show that night, so I took him into the control room and asked him about the ESPN story. He said he never said any such thing about Billy.

"Then I think you need to tell him that," I said.

Vinnie got hold of Billy the next day and worked out the whole thing.

Billy was a great contributor in the Chicago game, very serious about it all, and it turned out he threw in the winning basket at the end. I felt a lot better.

TUESDAY, APRIL 24

Every year during Lent I cut out all sweets and hard liquor. I don't drink much at any time, so liquor isn't as difficult for me to give up as sweets. But I love desserts. If I had my way, I'd start all my meals with chocolate ice cream or chocolate cake.

Giving up sweets is especially challenging when we're on the road. I'm always given a nice suite of rooms when we travel, and often when I get back to the hotel at night the bed is turned down and there are two chocolate candies on the pillow. There I am, the head coach of a professional basketball team, in a nicely appointed suite, with two chocolate sweets sitting on the pillows just waiting to be eaten. Nobody would know, except me and God.

I'd stare at those little candies and even think about them when I went into the bathroom. One time, I couldn't resist the temptation any longer. I shoved the two chocolates in my mouth and started chewing, but before I swallowed I said to myself, "Hey, if you do this, all the things you stand for in life don't mean anything." I went into the bathroom and spit them out.

When I told this story to Dick Versace, he didn't understand what I was talking about. He said, "What's wrong with eating two little chocolates?"

I said, "Nothing, as long as it's not during Lent."

I spent about an hour in Dr. Berris' office getting a tooth fixed that fell out on our last trip to Indianapolis and finally arrived at The Palace about 10:30. I called the Ford Dealers about doing some commercials and then went into the dressing room to talk to my assistants about our practice plans. Today we had our first serious practice before the beginning of the playoffs.

Rod Thorn, who enforces the law in the NBA, has sent a directive about violence in the league and I had to read it to all our players, sign it, and fax it back to him, saying we had read it.

We had our best practice in three months. I divided the guys into two teams. A White Jersey team executed all the Pacers' plays, and a Blue Jersey team played our game. The Blues wiped them out. We worked on boxing out, transitional defense, executing a screen, and getting the ball under control when taking it up the court. I didn't tell the players this, but we could have beaten any team in the league that day.

I noticed Jack McCloskey watching the workout. He frequently comes down to see what's going on and we usually meet at the end of the workout. When he came onto the floor, I could see the look in his eye that said he knew the players were ready. I felt the same way, and it is a terrific feeling.

The player I always watch closely is Isiah Thomas, our emotional leader. He is responsible for our performance. He knows he can't do it every night, not when we play eighty-two games and eight exhibitions. But now it's playoff time and there are no nights off for him. When he's on his game, he gives the whole team a lift. When he isn't, that's when I earn my money.

On the flight to Indiana for our last regular season game there, Isiah came to us on the airplane with some suggestions he'd written down. We listened to him, as we always do, and what he said was very solid. He has an excellent mind for basketball. He loves the game and he lives it.

I gave Isiah my best motivational speech at practice today. I told him how important his performance is in practice as well as in the games, how he has to set the pace for everyone else. His greatest asset may be his leadership qualities even more than his abilities. But I don't minimize his abilities. He does all the little things and does them correctly, like handling the ball on a break, not turning it over. The guys know they can depend on him and his performance elevates their performance.

I asked him a question that had been on my mind.

"Zeke, what goes through your mind when you come down on a break and you suddenly see daylight through six guys and try to pass the ball through there and it gets batted away? I know it's an instinctive thing, but why do you do it?"

Isiah smiled.

"You know, every coach I've ever played for has asked me that same question. The truth is, I don't know why I do it. I just do it."

I figure it is a challenge to him, and he needs challenges in his life. Some of the games bore him. They aren't big games and he has a hard time working himself up for them. A big game is with the Lakers or the seventh game of a series. When Isiah has a challenge, that's when he's at his best. That's why he is such a clutch player.

Sometimes my assistant coaches don't understand why I do certain things. I hold a pretty light rein on this team, and I don't overwork them. I guess I'm a so-called "player's coach." That doesn't mean I'm easy on them—just that I try to understand them. I try to understand their mentality, and I try to understand them on and off the floor. They are, for all practical purposes, private corporations. They're all going to be rich men if they take care of their money. I try to understand that, too, while keeping them focused on the job at hand. It helps that I am interested. I've been to nine million practices and coached nine thousand games and yet I get excited about every one of them. That's why it would be hard for me to give up coaching.

THURSDAY, APRIL 26

Today was our first playoff game. I woke up at 5:30—too early. I went back to sleep until 6:30—still too early. I woke up again at 7:00, and at 7:30. Finally I gave up and went outside to get the paper. I always start my day with the papers, but this morning I couldn't concentrate. I was thinking about our game with Indiana, particularly the things that might be successful against them. And I worried a lot. Will Isiah show up? What will our attitude be? Will we be focused?

We'd had two great days of practice, but I was worried it wouldn't continue. I started going over the last-minute details, making mental notes to myself—so many I couldn't remember them all. I've got two assistants who wear me out sometimes. They're great, but they can drive me nuts with the details. I tell them, "Hey, guys, if we talk about this stuff too much, we'll miss the game."

A coach doesn't want to lose his players by burdening them with too much information. Only so many plays, only so many films. The most important thing is to keep them mentally and physically fresh. You can't wear them out on the floor or in the film room. If you can make it so they have a little fun, fine. But you can't always get it to that point.

We had a shoot-around from eleven to twelve, watched a little tape, and then I went to my office to catch up on some

correspondence. It was a long afternoon. A long, long afternoon. It's always that way before the first game because I
don't know what to expect. At about three o'clock in the
afternoon, I went for a walk around the building, and that
helped. I came back and went into the coaches' office, turned
off all the lights, and lay down.

I had to do a lot of television tonight because the opening
of the playoffs is a big television night. I had to do Bill Bonds
at 5:10, then all three local channels, then some national
stuff.

At five o'clock I walked into the press room and had a
piece of lemon pie. I can resist a lot of things but not lemon
pie, especially when I haven't eaten all day. I had fun on the
Bill Bonds show and then went back to shower.

I did all the things I had to do to get ready, but my mind
was going nine million miles an hour. I just had to hide it,
that's all. I went back into the press room, one of the three
greatest press rooms in the league. They were serving steak.
I don't eat a lot of steak, but I had one today. I resisted having
another piece of lemon pie, though.

Time is dragging.

"Geez, it's an awful lot of time until we play," I said to
Brendan Malone.

My two coaches went somewhere, and I was left by myself
to think, think, think.

Jack McCloskey came into our office and I could see he
was a little tight. We all get that way. It's like starting out a
whole new season or waiting for a baby to be born: you know
it's going to happen but you can't control your nervousness.
You're on edge all the time.

How can a guy who has been in the business his entire
life, a guy who has just coached the world champions for a
full eighty-two-game season, be so afraid?

It's the fear of losing, that's what it is. I've had to live with
it my entire life. I am a competitive person, and the fear of

failure, the fear of losing, overwhelms me at times. I've had to learn to live with it because it's unavoidable. It's always in my mind, although I try to fight it as much as possible.

Isiah Thomas came in early, which was a good sign. He looked very stern, which was another good sign. Normally, our guys have a lot of fun before the games—they're laughing and joking with each other. Not tonight. They were quiet and very sober. That too was a good sign for me. Maybe we wouldn't play well, but we'd be focused and would play hard.

The game began and we dominated the first quarter. Isiah was really sharp, and when he's like that, we all feed off him. He was playing well within himself. He was going to the basket, pulling up, and taking his shot. When I see that, I relax a little, but not much. Indiana looked a little nervous and somewhat tentative. It's the first playoff game for most of them and they were careless with the ball. That's what happens to an inexperienced team.

I started seeing fatigue in some of our guys, and I realized we've had too many days off. We weren't sharp. We substituted in the second quarter, but the guys who came off the bench didn't do a good job. I was pleased with our starters, but our bench has to come through for us.

Indiana gained some confidence in the second half, and I got so excited I split the back of my pants in the third quarter. My fanny was hanging out, big time. Thank God I had a pair of gray shorts on to go with the gray slacks.

Vinnie Johnson wasn't being aggressive enough in going to the basket, and I thought the same about Joe Dumars. We were settling for our shots rather than going after them. I said a few things, but mostly I turned away, which is one of the hardest things to do in coaching. I try not to say anything to them when I take them out of the game. They can be screwing up, but I don't think it's going to help matters if I get all over them. They're pros and they know why they're coming out.

We got into some foul trouble. I have a rule about personal fouls: I try to get a guy out of there before he gets his third in the first half. They give you six fouls in this league, but you really get only five because with the sixth you're gone. Indiana kept making shots, which tells me they are a good, young shooting team that won't go away in this series.

Terry usually goes to the games and is a good sounding board for me because she's objective. When she thinks I'm right, she tells me, and when she thinks I'm wrong, she tells me. She sits directly across the floor from our bench, right behind Jack McCloskey.

I could see Jack stand up, which he often does when he's mad. I always look at him and wonder what he's thinking. It's like having your newspaper editor look over your shoulder when you're trying to write.

We held on to win, 104–98, but it wasn't as easy as it looked.

After the game I went in for the press conference. The writers didn't ask any good questions, so the whole thing was over in a matter of minutes. Then I went out with Jimmy Gray, a reporter for CBS, and John McLeod, the former Phoenix and Dallas coach who is doing the color on our telecasts. My wife brought along a friend and we went to the Fox and Hound on Woodward in Birmingham. We had a couple of drinks and something to eat and started talking basketball. McLeod is looking for a job, and Gray was talking about doing a game on the network. I got caught up in the conversation in spite of myself. Basketball, basketball, basketball. Oh well, I guess it goes with the territory. We left about 1:30.

I got home and settled down with a book I've been reading—Scott Turow's *Burden of Proof*. It's a wonderful book that I enjoyed immensely, especially for its character development and portrayal of male psychology.

FRIDAY, APRIL 27

I put on the tape of last night's game and watched the second quarter to get a feel for what was going on and to formulate some plans for what we should try to do in the second game. I asked the two Brendans how we should play it, and they said we have to do a better job of playing the pick-and-roll. We have five or six ways of playing, but we have to improve or somebody like Reggie Miller might kill us. We'll ask for the players' input before making any decisions because they're the ones who have to make it work.

The game was on national television again, and I thought that might affect Indiana in the second game but I wasn't sure. My concern was not TV, even though I knew they'd be zooming in on me since coaches are high-profile in the NBA. My concern was the five-game series. I didn't want to lose in our building because when we go to Indiana, they could close us out on their home court.

With Jim Gray, of CBS-TV, a close friend and late-night caller.

We try to keep up with the other games, especially the teams we think we might play. We always watch Los Angeles. We can get overnight copies of any game in the league through a subscription service in New Jersey run by a man named Mitch Kauffman. He has satellite dishes and records every NBA game. If we need Chicago-Cleveland or Boston-New York, he'll have it to us the next morning. I love watching all the games on TV and don't miss many of them. I love all the comments. Some of the guys doing the games are terrific.

SATURDAY, APRIL 28

I don't like afternoon games, which is what we had today. For one thing, we can't have a shoot-around, which allows me to see my guys on the morning of a game. I like to make personal contact with them—see if they're clear-eyed and ready to go. Bill Sharman started shoot-arounds. He believed it was important to get the team together earlier in the day, and I agree with him. Now everybody does it, even though they're boring for the players. I especially like to have them when we are on the road because it gets the guys out of bed. For a 7:30 game, an 11:00 shoot-around is no problem. But when you're playing at 3:30, you can't expect them to be there at 9:00 or 10:00 and then be back at 2:00.

I try to keep the shoot-arounds simple. We do a little stretching, a layup drill, and something else to get them running up and down the court. No contact. Just something to loosen them up and get them thinking basketball. Sometimes we have a walk-through drill for some plays we're going to run that night. Sometimes we'll work on out-of-bounds plays, which in our league frequently mean the difference between victory and defeat in the last seconds. Or sometimes we'll just have a refresher course on things we've gone over before, and then a short meeting with particular emphasis on what the other team does offensively.

188

Early in my career I was replaced by a groundhog; later on I was upstaged by a Quayle—vice-president style!

The important thing is that I can see how they're feeling. Is anyone sick, hurting, or trying to cover up an injury? Is anybody depressed or preoccupied? If they are, I want to know about it. I don't want to find out fifteen minutes before game time.

I wondered if we'd come back with the same intensity we had in the first game. When the players aren't intense, I can't do much coaching. They're going to do what they want to do, and I can't do much about it. That's why I love this time of year. I can really get into coaching because the players are so coachable. They know it's going to be tough, and I know it's going to be tough, and that draws us together.

I knew Indiana would cut back our fast breaks by one-third because that always happens in the playoffs. They know everything we're going to run, and no one will get an easy shot. Their intensity will also be high, so they're going to play better defense. We have to bring our game up to match theirs. We have to know where to box out, where to rebound, and when and where to be physical.

I got to The Palace about one o'clock after making a few stops along the way—the bank, the cleaners, and a couple other places where people with more normal schedules routinely go.

I took a shower and prepared for my pre-game radio show. My mind was racing again, trying to think of everything we have to do. We have been off a whole day and I don't want to lose my train of thought. I have a card that I carry around during the playoffs with some of our offensive plays on it. Out of habit, I pull it out and begin to study it, absent-mindedly, even though I have it memorized.

I liked our intensity at the beginning of the game, but I was concerned because I saw a new Indiana team on the floor—a team that was neither nervous nor tentative. The newspapers have been on them because they were outrebounded so badly the first game, and now they were really going after the ball. It wasn't a free-wheeling team anymore, it was a much more physical team. They were ready to play our game.

"This may be good for us," I said to myself, knowing we could do it better than they could because we were more experienced. I liked the idea that they were coming at us. It's what we need. The score was 41–41 at the half, and I felt good. We were playing adequately, but I credited their aggressiveness for keeping it so close. I was happy about it. Happy for them and happy for the league, because I know a close game is good for national TV.

Most of all, I was happy for us because they were testing our work ethic and that will do nothing but help us. I was sure we'd be all right because all of our guys were working. I saw Isiah Thomas defend his man, and his feet were really moving. When he does that, even Michael Jordan has a tough time scoring off him.

At halftime we talked about the fact that they were executing better than we were. I told them we had to raise the
level of intensity on defense, particularly in rebounding. We
started well in the third quarter and began opening up a lead.
We were ahead 67–50, but it was obvious the Pacers were not
going to go away. They kept fighting back and stayed within
range the rest of the game. I saw what a great player Chuck
Person can be: Dennis Rodman was all over him, but Person
kept going up and nailing his shots, and he also got some
balls off the board.

Edwards got into some foul trouble, and that worried me
a lot. I figure we'll play Boston next, and they have just
annihilated the Knicks in Boston Garden, 157–128. Boston
will give us trouble in the low post because of their big front
line, and who can I get to help out Edwards? If he is in foul
trouble against the Pacers, what will the Celtics do to him?

I played Laimbeer twenty-four minutes in the second half,
which I don't like doing. Edwards had three fouls, and as I
tried to get Salley in to replace him he hooked a guy and
picked up his fourth. I didn't like taking Edwards out because
he hadn't played enough minutes, and he needs time to get
into his rhythm. The game was going on, but all I could think
about was Boston and the foul trouble Edwards will be in
there. Bird. McHale. Parish. Tough. Very tough.

Maybe I can look to William Bedford for some help. Maybe
David Greenwood, maybe Scott Hastings, but I haven't used
them that much during the regular season. They might be
able to come in and help out, but I'm not sure. Greenwood
might be best in the low post, but I don't know where he'll
fit into our offense.

Hey, Daly! Get your mind back on this game!

Our guys tightened up on defense, and we won by thirteen, 100–87.

I was happy when I got back to the dressing room, but I
was exhausted. Absolutely drained.

"This is the hardest game I've coached in two years," I told the two Brendans. And I meant it. I was totally whipped.

Jimmy Gray and I got caught in traffic leaving The Palace. I decided my best shot was to go north on I-75 rather than south, but I got all turned around and wound up swinging back right in front of The Palace. I was dead tired and we still had a forty-five-minute ride to John Ginopolis' restaurant in Farmington.

My wife and daughter met us there and we had a fabulous meal. I love lamb chops, especially in John's place. He cooks them Greek-style and I'm in heaven. The only places I order them are John's place and the Palm I in New York, where they also have $100 lobsters on the menu. I tell John he'll never be big league until he has $100 lobsters on his menu.

Sitting at dinner, I thought about the game. I was especially satisfied by today's win, because we beat Dick Versace, my former assistant, who knows our system and our defense so well.

While I mused about these things, who should pop into my mind but my old friends the Boston Celtics. Everyone says the way to beat Boston is to run the ball up and down the court. The Celtics are old and tired and this will wear them out. Sure. They're so old and tired they just put 157 points on the board and never slowed down from start to finish. Still, I figure we can slow them down because we're a better defensive team than New York and can do a better job of rebounding.

I was staring off into space when I became vaguely aware of someone nudging me in the side. It was Terry, telling me to eat. I'd completely forgotten my lamb chops.

MONDAY, APRIL 30

I get kidded all the time about being a pessimist, to which I always say, "A pessimist is an optimist with experience."

But as we flew to Indianapolis for game three, I felt strangely optimistic. I believed we would win the series.

I needed to keep the team focused, so I said to them, let's finish the series in three so we don't have to come back to Indianapolis. I told them we wanted no extra flights, no extra nights in the hotel, no extra practices. We don't want to work overtime because we are starting a long, long siege of games.

We went out to eat at a place called St. Elmo's, a popular steak house in Indianapolis, and I committed a cardinal sin: I ordered pork chops in a steak house. They brought a small cup of bean soup and a big salad with Roquefort dressing, plus two large pork chops and a baked potato. I ate the first pork chop even though it tasted a little funny. I cut the other one open and the odor was so strong I called for the waiter to send it back. They apologized and offered to bring me a steak; they didn't have any more pork chops. I told them I was full and couldn't eat any more.

The check came to about forty dollars apiece, and I thought of my mother. She would turn over in her grave if she knew what her son had just done. Forty bucks for a small cup of soup, a salad, and one spoiled pork chop. She could feed her whole family for a week with that kind of money and have some left over. I could see her shaking her head.

TUESDAY, MAY 1

We had a shoot-around and I felt we were going to play well. We had a little meeting and Billy Laimbeer said, "Hey, they're gonna play with great emotion early in the game. We gotta fight our way through it."

I didn't think the Pacers could play with emotion for forty-eight minutes, but they did. They started out playing a very hard, very physical game and went up 17–10. But the next time I looked we were ahead. Isiah had a superb game. He got his fourth foul and I had to sit him down, but when he went back in he just took over. He's at his best when he's distributing the ball and finding the open man in our offense. He capitalized on every Pacer mistake. I'd rather have him play this way than get twenty-six points a game. His problems start when he tries to take over a game when we're behind. He tries to go one-on-five, and that can never work. I'm lucky he understands himself so well.

Indiana had five or six thousand empty seats in the arena. The fans who showed up got into the game, but I'm sure the Pacers feel bad about all the empty seats. I've tried to explain to Dick Versace that it takes time. I tell him how it used to be when we played at the Silverdome in Pontiac. We'd get twelve or thirteen thousand a game and that was it. Not until we started winning big did the people come out. I tell him it will take time in Indianapolis. What I have trouble understanding, though, is why the college game is so well received in Indianapolis but not the pro game. Not yet, anyway.

We got into some foul trouble—Edwards, Salley, and Rodman—but we held on to win, 108–96.

The flight home took only thirty or forty minutes, but it's always special when you return after winning a series. There's a warm glow and serenity about everything, and you feel pride in your accomplishment and a sense of relief that you've made it past the hurdle.

But it didn't take long for the conversation to switch to Boston. The Celtics are two up in their series with the Knicks and we have to start getting ready for them. We've had some big series with them over the years and we are facing another one that will not be easy. They have an enormous front line and we have to figure out the right way to play them. In fact, I've been thinking about this since January. I know we have to get some defensive help to hold down their front line. We need a third guy in there—either Scott Hastings, William Bedford, or David Greenwood.

Trying to defense Kevin McHale, Robert Parish, and Larry Bird is certainly going to get us into foul trouble, so I know we have to get some help off the bench. You can't defense them straight up. You've got to double up on them, which leaves them with an open man, usually Dennis Johnson, who is hitting fifty-three percent of his shots. It isn't going to be easy at all. And I haven't even mentioned Reggie Lewis, their most athletic player. He concerns me. The whole Boston team concerns me. They always seem to be there, intimidating, threatening, ominous.

WEDNESDAY, MAY 2

I gave everyone the day off and decided to play nine holes at Western Country Club. I played by myself, just grabbing a cart and hitting two or three balls on any open hole I could find. I practiced a little, then went in to take a sauna. It's one of those pleasures in life I like to savor.

I have a busy schedule and often feel a lot of pressure. For me to be at my best, I have to set apart some time for myself and my family to relax and enjoy the simple pleasures that life affords. I like to talk with friends on the phone, have leisurely dinners with my coaches, and sometimes just get away from everything and be by myself for a while.

Golf is a good outlet for me, but I wish the season weren't so short in Michigan.

A perfect vacation day for me is to get up early, drive over to Western Country Club, and hit golf balls for several hours. This is great relaxation, and I love trying to make the ball go where I want it to go.

I get there at about 10 A.M. and go to the driving range, then the sand area, and finally the chipping area. I hit every club in my bag. I play by myself, and I'm never more content. When I play with others, I have to fend off too many questions and talk about basketball the whole time.

Chapter Ten

I practice until about 12:30, go inside for a lemonade and a sandwich, and then hit more balls until two or three o'clock. I'd rather do that than anything else. My mind is clear, I am relaxed, and I just have a ball by myself.

My love for golf started when I was a caddie at the Kane Country Club, a little nine-hole course. We couldn't afford to join, and my dad had no interest in golf anyway, but by caddying on weekends and sometimes on Thursday afternoons, we got to play on Mondays, when the course was closed.

We'd scrounge for balls in the woods and creeks, find half a dozen, and then four of us would play, sharing the only three clubs we had between us. It was no problem. We just passed them back and forth. You haven't played golf until you've tried to putt with a seven-iron.

When I got a little older and started keeping score, I had a twenty-three or twenty-four handicap. I bought myself a set of clubs when I got out of the service and became obsessed with the game. I actually started filming my swing. I'd wake up in the middle of the night and go to a mirror to check on my swing, and I started seeing a white ball against a black background in my sleep.

I never took a lesson. I just started working on my game. I would catch a tip here and a tip there and I'd read everything I could get my hands on. I went from a twenty-three to twenty-four handicap to winning the club championship. I got my handicap down to a two or three, and the day I took the title, I shot a sixty-nine.

I hold great admiration for golfers because they have to earn their own way. In basketball, enormous contracts are guaranteed for long periods of time. But golfers have to go out and earn everything they get. They've got to work at their game, whether they want to or not, or they're not going to make it. If they don't work hard, their game is going to slip and they'll pay for it. They have no one to help them but themselves. That's what I call a real challenge.

I had the privilege this past season of playing a round of golf with Raymond Floyd. I have a self-imposed rule that I put my clubs away on the first day of training camp and don't touch them again until our final game is over. But every rule has its exceptions.

We were in Miami and had an off day before our game against the Heat. Scott Hastings, one of my players, asked if I was interested in playing with Floyd. Was I interested! I had met Floyd at one of the Miami games and knew he was a friend of Billy Cunningham, so I broke my rule and went out to Indian Creek to play with him. Scott came along and so did Harry Stevens, whose commissary company services many of the ball parks and arenas around the country.

I don't remember what I shot and didn't even care. Floyd shot a sixty-five, and it was a joy just to watch him play because he's such a professional.

I really cheered for him when he tried to win the Masters last spring. We were flying from Cleveland to New York, watching the tournament on some hand-held TVs, and the guys were needling me when it started slipping away from Floyd. Bill Laimbeer especially was letting me have it.

When we got to the airport in New York, I went straight to the bar to watch the end of it. They had to hold the bus for me so I could see how it came out. I felt terrible when Floyd lost on the second extra hole to Nick Faldo. I was very quiet on the ride into Manhattan because I knew how Floyd must be feeling.

I've also gone to some golf clinics and had the chance to play with a few celebrities. I am privileged to have played with Jay Haas, Ben Crenshaw, Mark O'Meara, Governor James Blanchard, Glen Campbell, and Bruce Devlin. But the highlight was right after we won our first championship in 1988–89. At one of the few charity events I appeared at that year, I played in a foursome with Arnold Palmer. Try that sometime! If five thousand people show up, five thousand people follow Arnold Palmer. That meant everything he did, they watched. It also meant everything I did, they watched.

I said a little prayer to Gerald Ford's God before stepping up to the first tee, "Please, let me hit it straight." I didn't want to embarrass myself, but even more, I didn't want to hurt anyone. That scared me half to death. People were everywhere.

When we got to the seventeenth tee, we were held up for a moment. As we stood there waiting to hit the ball, Sam Snead joined us from the group behind. The man with perhaps the greatest swing of all time. A natural. A man who has been on the golf scene for more than fifty years, and one of the most celebrated players of all time.

He appeared in front of a mass of people gathered around the tee and nobody even noticed him. It was like he was invisible. That told me then and there how fleeting fame is, and just how much being a celebrity really counts for in the world. I didn't tell him who I was. I just went over and talked to him again for a moment, since no one else did. I felt very sad. It helped me put fame and popularity into perspective.

I got home about 7:30. Two games were on TV: Boston versus New York and Phoenix versus Utah. I was in my glory. I got my board out, a magnetic diagrammed court I keep in my den, and started working out some plays as I watched the Boston-New York game. I reversed some action to see how it would work out and tried to develop some things the Celtics haven't seen before. You do what you do best, but you try to come up with a few surprises.

In the last seconds of the game Boston was trailing and Larry Bird took a three-point shot to tie the game. He missed, and New York won.

It's funny in our business. When the Knicks lost two straight in Boston, all the papers had everyone fired in New York—general manager Al Bianchi and coach Stu Jackson. Now the Knicks are back in it and everyone is ready to enshrine them. But I still feel Boston is going to take the series. Anyway, it's a great night. I watched both games.

I took Koko out several times and she loved the cool night air. Sometimes the smallest, simplest pleasures in life are the most rewarding.

FRIDAY, MAY 4

We've had so much time off that the guys can't get focused, and we've had a couple of terrible practices. I'm having trouble focusing myself. We don't even have an opponent yet for the next round.

Here come the Knicks. They played sensationally in game four, scoring 137 points. I'm starting to get a little nervous because we haven't prepared at all for them. I think the Celtics will beat them back in Boston, but I'm not so sure anymore. I tried to watch the second game, but I got sleepy and was struggling to stay awake at the end. Once in bed, though, I started reading an Elmore Leonard thriller, and with the Celtics and the Knicks on my mind, I ended up staying awake until 5:30. Not a smart thing to do when you've got to get up for practice.

SUNDAY, MAY 6

When I arrived at The Palace for our three o'clock practice, there was one quarter to play in the deciding game of the Knicks-Celtics series. The guys arrived at 2:30, and we watched the end of the game in the dressing room. No matter how hard I tried, I couldn't sit down to watch the game. I was in and out of the coaches' room, wandering around nervously. I didn't know what was going to happen and that always bothers me.

199

Chapter Ten

All of a sudden, we realized the Knicks had a shot at winning. What had seemed almost impossible was becoming more certain by the minute.

The Knicks won, and we were stunned. I realized that parity in our league is not just a cliché. I've been saying all along that a lot of teams are becoming equal, and this proves it.

Fortunately for me, I've got some kind of coaching staff. The game in Boston wasn't over two minutes when Brendan Suhr handed me a manual of the Knicks. He had them all ready to go for our players, plus seven TV tapes. He was working on the other seven tapes and had them an hour later.

I was still nervous from watching the game. I couldn't get over the way Stu Jackson and Jimmy Rodgers were suffering all the way through it. I'm to the point where I get upset just watching games—I'd rather coach them. I watched the two coaches and said to no one in particular, "What person in his right mind would put himself through all that agony?" I was only half kidding.

I wondered about our players as we went onto the floor. They finally have an opponent, but how do they feel about it being New York instead of Boston?

I didn't worry long. They got right into it and were terrific. We started practicing against traps because we thought that was the way New York would play.

The problem, of course, is going to be Patrick Ewing.

We like to attack him—go right at him and try to get him into foul trouble. Insiders in the league, however, know that Patrick Ewing is one of the players who gets seven personals a game instead of six. He gets this edge because people like to see him in the game. He also gets that third step on a drive more often than most.

Ewing is a great player. I coached him briefly in the All-Star game, and I saw in that short time what kind of competitor he is. He sat there before the game working himself up. I could see the fury, the intensity, and the deter-mination build inside him, and I knew I would not have to say anything to him to get him fired up. He's a scary player.

We'll have three or four guys defend him. It's the only way to go or we'll lose people one by one on fouls. Luckily, the Knicks don't have a lot of low-post players, but we have to watch Charles Oakley, who's awfully tough in the lane. He goes right to the rim after every miss.

On offense we'll have to make that extra pass. We can't be casual with the ball because they are so quick. They go low post, inside and outside, and they make it tough because they have a lot of great three-point shooters. We are going to have to be ready.

We'll start with James Edwards on Ewing, then switch to Billy Laimbeer. We'll put John Salley on him and maybe Dennis Rodman. We'll try to deny him the ball whenever possible, but that will be tough. They have a basic offense: Ewing right, Ewing left. He can play well on both sides of the basket. But we are in good focus and ready to take them on.

We went out for dinner after practice—an Italian place in Rochester. On the way to the restaurant, I talked to Mike Fratello on the car phone. I like Mike; in fact, he's one of my favorite people in the profession.

When I got out of the car, I locked the door with the keys still in the ignition. I usually keep a second set in a metal box under the car, but I just got this car a few weeks ago and forgot about hiding the spare set. It's a Ford, so it has a code on the door to open it, but I couldn't remember the combi-nation. The valet said he had a rod that might open the door, but that didn't work either.

The heck with it, I said, let's go in and eat and worry about it later. We had a great meal, and the owner picked up the check, so I left a twenty-dollar tip to show my appreciation. Now I was faced with the task of unlocking the car. I called a locksmith who showed up in half an hour and got the car open. I gave him thirty-five dollars, so instead of getting a free meal, I spent fifty-five dollars, but I still drove home with a smile on my face.

I am excited because the playoffs are what our business is all about. I feel good about our club. Mark Aguirre is working very hard, and I'm impressed with everyone. I want to win this championship more than anything else I've wanted in life. More than last year. More than two years ago. I feel terrific. I feel—alive.

11

NEW YORK, NEW YORK

TUESDAY, MAY 8

I envy the people in Kane, Pennsylvania—the ones who are born there, live there, and die there. Most of them don't have high-profile jobs, but they live happy and productive lives. They make lifelong friends, which is hard to do when you move around as much as I've had to. I envy those who are able to sustain friendships with the same people over a long period of time. Friends to play golf with, drink with, go to dinner with, and, most important, friends who will always be there if you need them. I think about the people in my home town and sometimes wish I could have that kind of life.

I love my job and I love my life, but it can get too hectic at times. I live somewhere for five or six years, long enough for my family and me to start making friends, then we have to move and start all over again. Over the years I haven't made that many good friends. I suspect a lot of people like me not for who I am but because of what I do. Those aren't true friends, but they're part of life in basketball and I have to deal with them. It's even tougher on my family because they don't have all the things I have to keep themselves busy, yet they still have to keep uprooting themselves and starting a whole new life. That's why I care for them so much—they have been so understanding about what I have to do to be successful in this business.

Chapter Eleven

Something I wish I had the time to do more often: spending time with the important people in my life.

I sometimes wonder why professional teams don't just buy a house in a fashionable section of town and move the coaches in and out as they hire them and fire them. This could be a perk for the coaches—a nice place to live without having to go through the hassle of looking for a new home. It could even be a tax write-off.

We were getting ready for our first game against the Knicks tonight and this was what I had on my mind: Kane, Pennsylvania. It's a lovely place to live, and I'm going back there as soon as the season is over—just to walk around and say hello to my friends.

We had a shoot-around and I was pretty wired. The first game of a series always gets to me because I never know how my players will respond. They've been like two different teams lately—focused and unfocused—and I never know which team is going to show up. I think they're going to be all right, but I can't be sure until I see them play.

204

I know the Knicks are going to press us because last night I watched the halftime show of the Chicago-Philly game and Charles Oakley, the Knicks' forward, said, "We're going to uptempo the game."

That means only one thing: They are going to press more than they usually do. We spent some extra time working on their traps.

I was still fidgety after practice, so I decided to lie down in the coaches' room for a couple of hours. I used some towels for pillows, locked the doors, and put out the lights. Somebody was walking around and I heard every noise, but this was a little comfort zone for me and I started to doze off.

The phone rang. It was Matt Dobek.

"Jimmy Rodgers has been fired in Boston. The story is just coming over the wire," he said.

I sat up. So much for the nap. I was shocked, but not as shocked as some people. I'm always sizing up the coaching situations in other cities and talking about it with my assistants, so we knew Boston was a hot spot. We could see that early on. I happen to think Jimmy Rodgers is a very good coach and did a good job with the Celtics, but that doesn't mean anything anymore. It's the chemistry of the team and how many numbers you put in the W column.

The NBA is changing. Teams have achieved such parity that good ones are eliminated in the early rounds of the playoffs. Management can't tolerate losing when it's counting on the big bucks from the playoffs.

I am one coach who cares for his comrades, and it's painful because in this profession success for me means failure for somebody else. I don't like this part of the business.

In a city like Boston, where the media are a strong and influential presence, a coach can get into a lot of trouble. Everyone has a talk show and everyone has to have his or her say. I know. I lived there for two years. When they're having a quiet night in June or July, what do they bring up? Celtics' basketball. A coach is never away from the pressure, and when you lose one as the Celtics did to the Knicks, the conversation goes on and on and somebody has to take the fall. It's an unfortunate fact of life in professional coaching.

I couldn't go back to sleep, so I started getting ready for the game. I wondered if my players knew how focused I was. It's funny. People don't understand how involved you can get in these games. I got a call yesterday from a fan who said I ought to smile more on the sidelines. Some people think I'm a mean sort of guy because they see me scowling on TV. They perceive me as being too serious. Well, during a game I am serious. I had a guy ask me if I wear makeup so I'll look better on TV. That's not makeup. That's my face, and it's flushed from all the emotion and excitement.

I drank about three cups of tea and was really starting to get wired. We had a short meeting before the game, as is our normal procedure. Some teams have extensive pre-game meetings, but I don't believe in them. We've gotten it down to about ten minutes, because long meetings can cause people to lose interest. When you're in close contact with the same group for eight and a half months of the year, as we are in the NBA, it's easy to lose your people by talking to them too much. We have a meeting at every practice, but it might last only two minutes, or even twenty seconds. I try to use my assistants as much as possible so the players don't get so accustomed to hearing my voice that they tune out when I start talking.

They say repetition is the mother of learning, but how many times can you tell Joe Dumars, "You've got to follow your man around the screen"? Pretty soon it turns into nagging. You don't want to develop that kind of relationship.

We started going over the manual on the Knicks players. While the guys got dressed, we played the TV tapes, but it isn't mandatory for them to look at them. The tapes are just small reminders. We like our players in the dressing room ninety minutes before a game. Some take a sauna to get their bodies warmed up. Brendan Malone talks about the opposing players, their strengths and weaknesses. Brendan Suhr takes over the board and goes over all of their basic plays. Then I kind of sum it up, and out we go.

Some coaches try to be dictatorial, but I avoid that approach. You might get away with it in high school, and sometimes in college, but as you move up the ladder, you've got to let the players have some say in running the show. I don't want to know how Brendan Suhr thinks we should play the pick-and-roll. I don't even want to know what I know. We all know how to do it, and we can list five or six ways it can be done. I want to hear what Isiah Thomas and Joe Dumars think about it. How do they want to play it? They're the ones who have to execute it. If I let them tell me how they want to do it, they'll play harder to try to make it work.

With Mike Fratello, former coach of the Atlanta Hawks, who later accepted the NBC broadcasting job that I was offered.

Chapter Eleven

I learned this a long time ago when I was with Billy Cunningham at the Philadelphia 76ers. He let his players talk all the time.

You've got to involve your players in the decision-making process, because you'll get more out of them and you'll be more successful. This isn't always easy to do because it goes against the grain of coaching. We all want to be authoritarian; we all want to dominate. It takes great discipline to go the other way. A lot of times I'd like to erupt and say, "Screw it, we're doing it my way." But I fight that urge all the time.

I look at the other coaches in our league. The older ones seem to have the most success lately, with some exceptions, and I think that's because they've learned to listen to the players. They've learned they can't have two-hour film sessions every day, because it will bore players to death and take away their desire to play. The freshness of the mind, the desire to play—these are the important things. We play a kids' game. We can't make it too simple, but we can make it so complex that the fun goes out of it. Players love to play this game, and we can't take that joy away from them.

I don't know what to expect from the Knicks in the first game. They gave up 157 points to Boston in the first game and lost the second game, too, but then they came storming back and played like a whole new team in New York. And then they pulled off the big upset in Boston Garden.

That's why I have to be ready for everything. I'm not sure what's on the minds of my players, but I've got to think in terms of a seven-game series.

I know the Knicks are sky-high emotionally, but I also know that emotion can take them in two opposite directions. They could have a carry-over from Boston and be terrific, or they could go flat because they are so relieved to get out of their first series alive. Also, having to travel to Detroit without much time to prepare for us won't help them. When you don't have time to prepare, it's hard to focus.

I'm not exactly sure what to expect from our guys, either. I remember our long rest last season and how we came up flat and got beaten by Chicago in the first game of that series.

Fortunately, we did not repeat that performance tonight. We came out like caged animals, and my concerns about our long layoff were dispelled immediately. Our game plan and our defensive pressure were both good. We played Patrick Ewing straight up and made sure their other people didn't get easy field goals.

It was one of those magical games where almost everything went right for us and we won, 112–77.

The minute it was over, I sat back and said, "What did we do wrong?" That's coaching for you. I always look for the negatives. That's one of the down sides of this business. All the good things the players do, all the good things my assistants and I do, are dismissed almost immediately. I look for the mistakes.

I said to myself, "We made three bad passes—Billy on a long pass against their trap, Joe on a casual behind-the-back pass, and Isiah on a flip into the middle." That was it. Three bad passes in forty-eight minutes and I was dwelling on them. How could I even mention them?

In truth, I don't have to motivate this team very much. They're a veteran club, and very smart. There's no substitute for experience, and these guys have it. For some teams, the long season and the constant grind gets to be too much for them, but our team is programmed to go into the second or third week of June. We know what it takes to get to the end because we've been there before.

Handling the media, alone, is a big challenge. You get to the finals and there are 400 to 500 people you have to deal with. There are people from six or eight countries—whole camera crews from everywhere. It's hard work, and it can be emotionally draining, but once you've done it, you know what's required and it's easier the next time.

Chapter Eleven

I watched a good portion of the Lakers-Phoenix game from the locker room, but it didn't relax me. In fact, I started getting tense again. I was rooting for Phoenix because I want the Lakers to be extended. I want them to have to work as hard as possible because it might catch up with them in the finals, which I am sure will be a Detroit-L.A. rematch. I couldn't believe Phoenix was about to beat them in their first game. Cotton Fitzsimmons, the Phoenix Suns coach, has lost something like thirty-seven games in a row in the Forum. "Can this really be happening?" I asked myself.

The Suns hung on to win, and my mind switched back to a couple of exhibition games we played in Phoenix. We stayed at the Ritz Carlton, which we normally don't do, and it was very nice. I said to myself then, "I wonder if we'll come back to Phoenix in June?" I might even have said it to Cotton before one of our games. Los Angeles? Phoenix? I see there isn't going to be much sleep tonight, but I still believe the Lakers will win their series.

THURSDAY, MAY 10

For our second game with the Knicks, I tried the same routine that worked for the first: I hung out at the office and took another sauna. I've been here for seven years and never taken a sauna, but now I took two in a row. If this keeps up, I'll be the cleanest coach in the league.

I was a little apprehensive because I knew the Knicks were embarrassed the other night and would come out and give their best performance.

We got lucky, though. Patrick Ewing got into foul trouble, so when he sat down, I put Isiah Thomas on the bench because he had two fouls. Isiah was terrific, as he always is in the big games. He was making big plays all over the floor. When I took him out, our guys understood. I never have to explain to them what I'm doing, which is one advantage of being together so long.

I was really impressed with Mark Aguirre. He was playing both ends of the floor, working as hard as he had ever worked. He understands now what it takes to be a winner. You don't saunter down the court and throw up all kinds of shots.

It was close until the final six minutes, and then we started taking control and won 104–97.

As soon as the game ended, a vision of Madison Square Garden came into my mind. We will play there twice on the weekend and I know both games are going to be tough.

I love to play in New York. It's truly the Big Apple. My memories go back to the old Madison Square Garden on Eighth Avenue and 49th Street. I would get a thrill just walking into the place, and I still do, even the new one at Penn Station. It's the people; there are a lot of intelligent fans in New York.

The only problem in New York is security. That always worries me. Who's hanging around the hotel? How many crazies know where we're staying or will recognize us on a street or in a restaurant? A lot of us have received death threats, and it doesn't make us sleep any easier.

Chicago Stadium is the noisiest arena in the league and the toughest building to play in, but the fans in Madison Square Garden can make a big commotion, too. You have to guard your timeouts so you can keep control of your team, and nothing—but nothing—can keep a crowd down like going down the court and putting the ball in the basket. That's going to be our job in New York—to silence them at the right time.

SATURDAY, MAY 12

On the bus to the Garden for game three I found out that Dennis Rodman was sick, of all things. He had the flu and looked just awful.

211

"How come I didn't find out about this before?" I wanted to know.

I found out that Dennis got sick in the night and had a friend in the room with him feeding him chicken soup. We have a team trainer and a team physician with us, but Rodman eats chicken soup in his room with a friend. I'm surprised my hair isn't grayer than it is.

I had a busy day. Before the game I had to do my TV show, "One-on-One." We do extra shows during the playoffs and this was one of them. The moment we got there, I found Trent Tucker of the Knicks and did a seven-minute taped interview with him. I tried to find out as much as I could about the Knicks without being too obvious. Our show went on at noon, but before that, I did my radio show with George Blaha. Two columnists also showed up with him, so I was stretching it a little bit.

The game was intense, as I knew it would be, and early on we started missing free throws. I can understand missing a few, but when you miss fourteen of them, there's no way you're going to win a playoff game on the road, no matter what else you do.

We couldn't do anything with Ewing either. He was unstoppable. He made fourteen free throws, and we missed that many. When that happens we don't have much of a chance at all. We were lucky we were even in the game.

Near the end of the game, with the score 107–103, we made a steal, but the ball slid off Isiah Thomas' leg. If we had scored there, we could have been in a position to steal the game, even with our all our problems.

But this was the Knicks' day and they deserved to win. The final was 111–103.

When the game was over, I went into an interview area where reporters were firing questions from all sides. I did the best I could and, as I was leaving, I heard a voice from behind a curtain say, "Nice speech, coach."

I turned around and saw three guys walking away. One of them was Peter Falk.

In the locker room we told our guys how we had beaten ourselves at the foul line. I was more than a little upset, so I went back to the hotel with my coaches and we went over the whole game on tape. We had to decide what to do to combat Ewing because he got about forty points, and that's just too many to give up.

I thought about getting some potato chips and dip for the guys, but it cost twenty-five bucks on the room service menu. I decided we'd go out to eat when we finished.

We worked about three hours, until eight o'clock, when my TV producer came by and wanted to tape the next day's show.

While we went over the game in one room, he set up in the next room. I told him he'd better get some guests, so he found Don Drysdale, who was in town with the Los Angeles Dodgers, and we did about a seven-minute interview. I did another one with Brendan Suhr for about eight minutes and we had a wrap, as they say in show biz.

I'd had nothing to eat but a doughnut all day, so I guess I'm not too much smarter than Dennis and his chicken soup.

About nine o'clock we went out to an Italian restaurant on the Upper East Side. We had quite a group: Pat O'Brien, Bill Rafftery, and Bill Gray of CBS; Bill's wife, Joanie; Albert Linder, my attorney from Philadelphia; John McEnroe's father and his wife; Brendan Suhr; Matt Dobek; and Dr. Ben Paolucci, our team physician. It ended up as a big party.

Mr. McEnroe said to me, "You should have been thrown out of the game today for the way you acted."

"I just watched a tape of the game and saw your son sitting courtside and rooting for the Knicks. I got up and threw something at the TV set. Tell him I don't like him," I responded, laughing. "Tell John I know where he gets his nastiness from." That's New York for you.

213

Chapter Eleven

SUNDAY, MAY 13

I got up early today to go to church. We're staying at the Grand Hyatt in New York, but I didn't eat at the hotel because it's too expensive. Usually, George Blaha or Mike Abdenour calls, but nobody did this morning, so I went down the street to a little coffee shop, where I had a muffin and tea. I went to ten o'clock mass and had some time to kill before a 1:15 team meeting I called. I heard that Donald Trump was in the hotel, which he happens to own, and I said to myself, "Geez, I'd like to meet him."

About twenty minutes before our team meeting, I went down to the lobby to see if he was around. I started down the escalator and saw a group of people getting out of a limousine on 42nd street. Suddenly I saw "The Donald" himself. He came in the door and started up the opposite escalator.

As we passed each other, he looked at me and I kind of nodded at him. "Hi, coach!" he said. "How're you doing?"

I was surprised he recognized me, and for one of the few times in my life I was speechless. I went back up the escalator to meet him. I got a big kick out of the whole thing because he's one of the most celebrated people in the world, and there he was talking to a kid from Kane, Pennsylvania.

As I was going into the ballroom, I saw Isiah Thomas standing there. He stuck out his hand to shake mine and whispered, "Hey, don't go to NBC. Stay with us and you'll be the first coach to win three championships in a row."

Actually, Red Auerbach of the Celtics won eight in a row in the sixties, but I didn't quibble. I got his message.

The guys were waiting for me in the ballroom. I gave them a short speech and tried to say something that would really hit home. They were up against the wall because we lost the day before, and they aren't used to being in that position. I knew they would play well today because that's how they are, but I wanted to let them know how I felt.

"Hey," I said, "one of these two teams is going on vacation very soon. You can decide who it will be. I don't want to come back to New York. Maybe you do, but I don't. I'd like to come here for a vacation, spend a little time and enjoy myself, but I don't want to come back here and play again this season."

I told them they had to win this game and the next game in Detroit. I even told them what time the plane back to New York would leave—you do some terrible things as a coach.

I put a chair out on the dance floor to represent the basket and I walked them through some plays, sensing they were ready.

Vinnie Johnson was upset because he didn't get enough minutes in the previous game. He didn't say anything to me, but I knew it. Matt Dobek told me he called Vinnie's room to ask how he was doing, and Vinnie said, "I'll get over it."

He always does. That's the kind of player he is.

As the game progressed, Dennis Rodman started playing off the wall. I looked down the bench about the time I would normally substitute Mark Aguirre for Dennis, and Mark said, "He's playing good, don't worry about me."

A peculiar thing happened during the game. We were in a timeout and, just as it was breaking up, I called a play we hadn't used all through the series. We call it "Horns." It's a screen-and-roll to the top with Jimmy Edwards. I don't know why I called it—just instinct. We needed a change and I said to the guys, "They're going to make a mistake on this play coming off the screen, and Jimmy will be wide open on the left wing for a shot."

We worked it three times and Jimmy made three baskets.

That's when coaching can be fun, but you have to have the players to make these things work. And you have to have them for a long period of time so they understand what you're trying to do.

Ewing got into foul trouble and so did Charles Oakley, and we won the game, 102–90.

Stu Jackson, the Knicks' coach, really let the refs have it in his post-game press conference. I try never to criticize the officials. I'll put in my two cents sometimes, but I know it doesn't do any good.

The game was over and everyone was ecstatic. The guys were in the showers, which they always have turned on a few minutes before the end of the game, so it's like a steam bath. I was watching the end of the Lakers-Phoenix game. When it was over I went to the shower room and said, "Hey, team, the Lakers lost again."

We went out the side door to get on the bus but had to wait while Mark Aguirre and Scott Hastings stopped at a street vendor to get a couple of hot dogs. It's impossible for them to walk past the hot dog man at the side door of Madison Square Garden.

I still feel L.A. is going to win its series.

TUESDAY, MAY 15

We have a chance to close out the series against the Knicks tonight. I stayed in The Palace the whole day and did my usual routine grabbing a half-hour nap in the coaches' room, then taking a steam bath.

Both Brendans were more nervous than usual. It's hard getting the fourth win in a seven-game series. We know if we lose it will be back to New York, and then you're into a seventh game before you know it. Also, we are quite aware of how the Knicks came back against Boston. My mind never shuts down, and I'm constantly playing out worst-case scenarios. Coaches should probably be psychoanalyzed.

We were in a good frame of mind at the shoot-around, but I don't always put a lot of faith in that. I've seen some guys look lousy at eleven o'clock in the morning and then play like gangbusters that night. I've also known guys to be flying in the morning and not even show up at night. That's why the mood at the shoot-around isn't reliable. It's all I have before a game, though, so I hang onto it. I went to the press room but all I could eat was a salad. The desserts looked good, but I couldn't get any of them down. I had three or four cups of tea to get my caffeine buzz going.

Al Bianchi and Stu Jackson were very unhappy with the officiating in the last game in New York, complaining about Patrick Ewing getting into so much foul trouble. If you look at the tapes, however, you realize he could have been assessed a lot more fouls than were actually called against him. You really can't tell these things in the heat of a game, but you can see them clearly on tape later. I'm not saying they protect him, but he definitely gets the benefit of the doubt because of the great player he is. This is probably typical of the way all coaches think about their opponents.

When I complain about calls, I know that I'm wrong in a lot of cases. NBA officials are good at their jobs. They are the best in the world, without question. They know that a lot of our complaining is just theatrics, as it is in other sports, and they understand that.

I used to have an official's license in Pennsylvania to referee high school football and basketball. I loved officiating football, and some weekends I'd do as many as three games. I did this when I was coaching at Punxsutawney Area Joint High School because I wanted to gain some objectivity. I wanted to see the game from inside the striped shirt, and I found out how difficult it could be. Now, I don't complain just for the sake of complaining.

If I see something wrong, I jump up. I don't know why I do it because I know it doesn't help. It's a spontaneous reaction. Winning a game in this league is so hard that I get totally involved and work for any edge I can get. Standing up and yelling doesn't mean a hill of beans. The officials have heard it all before, and they don't care who wins. Some people say

Although I sometimes complain about the calls, NBA officials are good at their jobs.

the refs are influenced by the home crowd. Not the good ones. They just come in and call the game because that's what they are trained to do. They are true professionals, believe me.

Bianchi and Jackson complained to the newspapers, which I never do. I might say, "Well, they did a good job of getting to the line," but that's as far as I will go. It doesn't do any good to complain about the officiating because you're not going to influence the officials. These men are only human and besides they're under tremendous pressure. In fact, they've got an almost impossible job.

They've had to bring in a third official in the last few years and this has created problems, because some are inexperienced. Darrell Garrettson, the head of the NBA officials, does a great job. He tells his new men, "You have never refereed players like this in your life, so be ready to learn."

The athletic ability of the players is astonishing. I see Byron Scott throw in a three-pointer at the buzzer for the

Lakers. Then David Wingate does the same thing for the San Antonio Spurs. Impossible shots, but they make them. These are six-feet, seven-inch, giants flying acrobatically through the air, going all out, and the officials are supposed to call everything with an unerring eye.

When a coach is trying to win he has to establish his own territory, make his presence felt, and protect his players. My players expect it from me, and that's why I get on my feet and scream at the officials. Sometimes I get carried away, and I'll get a technical. It's no big deal. It costs $100, and if I'm ejected, it's $250. I have to pay it out of my own pocket because the league no longer allows teams to reimburse players or coaches for their fines.

When we got on the floor tonight we didn't have the emotion or the intensity we needed. Defensively, they were taking us off the dribble at the guard position, and they were coming off their screens and hitting their shots. We weren't getting our hands up, and the Knicks were causing us all kinds of problems.

It was a hard first half of basketball. During one of the timeouts, I was screaming at the players, trying to get their attention. I told them about getting back on that plane to New York. I carried on something fierce, but they completely ignored me. Some of them were looking into the stands, probably at a cute little blonde or redhead in the sixth row.

Our game plan was solid. We knew the ball would be entered to Ewing through one of the guard positions. If Oakley was on top, we were to stay put; if he wasn't, we double teamed Ewing. But we got confused and missed three assignments in a row. We got it cleaned up a little, but Brendan Suhr said to me, "We'd better move in some other people."

I agreed.

Chapter Eleven

I walked up and down the bench, and Vinnie was looking at me. He knew what was going on and what might be in my mind. It's sad when players look up at me with those fawn-like eyes that say, "Coach, please put me in."

Vinnie kept watching me and finally I said, "Vinnie, get in there and make something happen."

It was earlier than normal for him and he jumped up, excited about going in.

A lot of times, when you surprise a guy like that, the adrenalin will start flowing and he'll go in there and play better than he normally does.

I could see that Dennis Rodman was getting a little con-fused by our rotations on defense, so I got him out earlier than usual. I said to myself, "Let's get to Mark Aguirre and see what he's got to give tonight."

We put Vinnie and Mark on the floor and they played superbly. Mark needs to be in better shape, but he was working very hard. He tends to grab and hold on a little too much and pretty soon he had three fouls. Normally, I'd take him out, but when he looked over to me I waved him off. He was on a roll and I felt I ought to ride him. It's just a gut feeling—you see it, you do it. I didn't want to break up this group because they were at very high emotional level. As it turned out, Mark hit a tremendous shot at the buzzer and we went in with the lead at halftime.

We went into the coaches' room and Mike Abdenour came in to let us know exactly where we stood with personal fouls. If we're playing well, I give the players more time by themselves; but if we're not, or if I'm upset about something, I go right in and talk to them. I might even go in without talking to my assistants, but this is rare, because I always like to have their input. At some point, the three of us will go in and talk to the team. Brendan Suhr keeps a little board that shows our fast breaks and second shots. He puts ours next to the other team's, and he posts the figures for all the guys to see. We call these "effort points." He added up the points and we were sky high, beating them something like twenty-six to four on effort points.

It meant that even though we were struggling, we were getting a good effort. But we were settling for too many long jump shots. You get in a pattern and it's hard to break. Isiah Thomas will say, "I'll make two or three long shots and we'll be in the game," but they don't go down for him. Then Joe Dumars will say, "I'll get us going with a couple of long shots," and they don't go down either. Now you've got a problem.

We decided we needed to be more patient and force the Knicks to play our game. We wanted to make them wonder what we were going to do, create a little confusion for them.

The one thing we really wanted to do was challenge Patrick Ewing's shots. We'd been putting the wrong hand up when he went up to shoot. We should be mirroring his shot. If he is going with his right hand—which he is—we should have our left hand up there. We were using our right hand for his right-handed shots, and he was getting them off without much trouble.

Brendan Suhr and Brendan Malone are big on mirroring shots. They preach it all the time in practice. Why we forget, I really don't know.

I was moaning and groaning all over the place when we went back out, but Ewing got tired and we went on a twenty-three to nine run. He had played all-out for four games and now he was running out of strength. He went something like one for ten in the second half. That's what happens in the playoffs, and that's why you need a deep bench. You have to play the full forty-eight minutes, and it's hard for one player to do it game after game.

When I looked at the scoreboard in the fourth quarter, I saw that they had only sixty points.

"Hey, we must be doing something right," I said to myself.

The final score was 95–84.

Chapter Eleven

★ ★ ★

Now we were looking at playing a maximum of fourteen more games. That seems like a lot to some people, but not to us. We have been programmed since the beginning of October to play that many games, and our club is feeling good. Mentally, they are sharp, but that doesn't necessarily translate into good performances each night. Isiah Thomas had an off night tonight. For whatever reason, he seemed a little spaced out. They're all human, and their minds wander. We're lucky because we can get help elsewhere.

I still think L.A. is going to win its series.

I got home about 11:30 and the Lakers were down to their final few minutes with Phoenix. I couldn't believe they were on the brink of elimination. I thought back to my problem with Jack McCloskey, when he didn't want to give me a bonus for winning the first round. "You're supposed to win the first round," he'd said.

Terry and I with Senator Bill Bradley (Democrat, New Jersey), former Princeton University and New York Knicks star.

There is no "supposed to" in sports. The Lakers struggled through the first round against Houston and now it was almost over for them in the second round. They look fatigued to me. Magic Johnson—43 points in the previous game? He was trying to take his game to the heights, but maybe he was taking some of his teammates out of their game. The Lakers have so much pride. It is a shock seeing them lose. As I watched the final seconds tick away, I sensed Pat Riley's desperation.

A lot of thoughts went through my mind. Losing certainly isn't something the Lakers are used to—they haven't been eliminated from the playoffs this early since the early 1980s. I identified with Pat Riley's feelings of disbelief. His players probably thought this couldn't happen to them. Some teams begin to think they're invincible, that there will always be a miracle finish.

I sensed this in Riley after his team lost its third game. I watched his press conference, and I knew he was convinced they would come back and win three in a row. It didn't happen, though, and now it is over for him.

Everything comes to an abrupt end. You've been going since October 6, every day, either practicing, traveling, or playing, with no weekends off, and hardly any days off. You're totally immersed in basketball.

Suddenly you can't go to practice or do anything else. Bang! It ends. It is the most empty feeling in the world—you don't have a plane to catch or a game to go to. You think it will go on and on, but suddenly there is nothing left.

I can almost hear Pat Riley thinking, "I have to live in this town until next October, and I'm going to have to put up with all the harassment and all the second guessing. Do we need to break this team up? Where does the problem lie?"

These things never leave your mind. Every time a columnist needs a story, he'll write about the demise of the Lakers. The same thing happens on the talk shows, just like it happened with Jimmy Rodgers in Boston. When they've got nothing to talk about, they'll bring up the Lakers. When you're in Los Angeles, you're expected to be number one. It is more difficult performing there than any place in the country.

I understand Pat is due for a new contract—an enormous, multi-million dollar contract. I know he'll be back in coaching, but right now, on this night, I know he is dying just a little bit.

12 BAD DREAMS AND MICHAEL JORDAN

SATURDAY, MAY 19

It was hot. We were getting ready for our third-round series against Chicago, and I found out we had to practice at Oakland University for three straight days because of other scheduled events at The Palace. I know the management there has to use the building for concerts and other events whenever possible, but it bothered me that they wouldn't give us at least one day on our own floor to get ready for the Bulls.

Oakland is a nice facility, but not for something as big as the playoffs. Hundreds of people from the press are milling about, and there is no place to put them. They have to stand around in the halls until after practice, and there's no good setup for the film sessions. We could have taken the team back to The Palace to look at films, but that's not a good solution because I don't want to take sweaty players outside in the fifty-degree weather and risk having them get sick.

Today's practice was the longest of the year, and I didn't like that at all. I don't like to keep my guys too long. But we had to bring over the film equipment and get it set up the best we could.

I had to start making speeches again. I looked around the room and said to the players, "I know you guys didn't want to have to play Philadelphia in the playoffs because of the

225

tough time they gave us during the season, but I've got some news for you. Philly beat us three out of four, and now we have to play the team that just beat them in the second round of the playoffs, four games to one. Forget everything that's going on. Forget the Lakers. Forget Phoenix. Forget Philadelphia. We have only one team to think about, Chicago, and this is the team that has Michael Jordan on its side."

I was worried. The Bulls have gotten better with experience and have become a very competent basketball team. Twice I had to stop practice because I wasn't happy, and I don't like to do that. I don't like having to hear my own voice, but I didn't see any enthusiasm for what we are doing, so I told them about it.

"Hey," I said, "we haven't put any pressure on you all season long to defend the title, but we're defending it now. We're in a great position and it's not time to slow down. We've got two more series. We've got to win eight more games. It

Interviewing NBA Commissioner David Stern for my pre-game show.

would be foolish to work this long and this hard and not take advantage of it."

Naturally, I made no impression on them.

I don't know why, but the pressure was starting to get to me. I wanted to win that title more than anything I had ever wanted in my life, and it was starting to affect me. I couldn't sleep well and I was eating only sporadically. I was drinking too much tea. I tried to read, but my mind wandered. I tried to watch TV, but I kept picking up my play board, trying to work out something new—something that might get us a basket in the clutch. Every step a struggle? It was a struggle just to close my eyes at night.

SUNDAY, MAY 20

Game day. I didn't sleep last night and I really felt it. I went to 9:30 mass and got to the arena early.

I had to set up my TV show, which we were doing live again, and I wanted to have Jackie Mullen, a writer from the Boston *Globe*, as one of my guests. We wanted to do a show from a woman's viewpoint. We called her hotel but apparently she was listed under her married name and we couldn't locate her. Instead we got Andrea Kramer of ESPN, Leslie Visser of CBS, plus Johnny Kerr, the old redhead who played and coached in the league, and the show went well.

I did my pre-game radio show with George Blaha and I was more uptight than I have been during all of my seven years in Detroit. All I could do was try to hide it.

I've coached some bad games in my life. Earlier in my career, when I wasn't sure of myself or of what I was doing, I used to get on people, hard. I'd get on my coaches. I knew I shouldn't be doing it, but it was difficult to control my emotions. I felt all this coming over me again.

I was worried because I had no idea how we were going to play. The three days at Oakland University were really weighing on my mind.

Chapter Twelve

★ ★ ★

Both teams started out a little sluggish—with the exception of Mr. Jordan. Generally speaking, we did a pretty good job, but we couldn't make any shots. Buddha Edwards, Mark Aguirre, and Isiah Thomas were struggling offensively, but defensively they were doing all the things coaches love.

Dick Mayer, the cartoonist for the *Free Press* and a very creative guy, did a cartoon the other day showing a telephone booth in the parking lot of The Palace. Coming out of it in a Superman suit after a quick change of clothes was you know who: Michael Jordan. When I saw that, I thought, "Phew, our 'Jordan Rules' better work."

Rules or no rules, Jordan is a one-man wrecking crew. I was upset with Joe Dumars because I didn't think he was playing Jordan straight up as hard as he should, so I brought in Vinnie Johnson a little early.

Vinnie was giving us a problem, too. He wasn't following his man the way we wanted. I told him before the game, "Don't try to go through people—you're trying to bust your way past two or three of them. Go around them."

But Vinnie was still trying to run through people.

We got a break, though. Jordan launched a shot with three of our guys on him. He tried to change direction in mid-air, and he landed on his hip. He stayed down for a minute, and I could see he was hurt. He got up hobbling and kept on playing, but he lost about twenty percent of his effectiveness. Nevertheless, he went to the dressing room with twenty-six points.

Dumars knew I was ticked with him at halftime. I understood his problem and had to get it resolved.

"Joe, you've got to play him for one step or two before you can expect any help," I told him.

Fortunately, we had some tape so I could show Joe what was happening. We had three or four extra minutes during halftime because they were holding a lottery drawing on the floor during intermission. We looked at the tape and stressed Jordan. He loves to go right, but he was faking right, taking a bounce-step to the left, and putting up his jump shot. Very clever. He had done his homework on us. Joe wasn't coming close to bothering him. He was getting left at the gate.

Sometimes you've got to change your personality to reach people. You've got to jog them, which I try to do at halftime. I'm lucky because I have players who will accept it.

I liked the long halftime because an injury tightens up when you're not playing on it, and I thought this might happen to Jordan. That's playoff basketball. Injuries are a part of it because everyone is playing so hard.

In the second half Jordan was not the same player. He took only twelve shots and obviously was hurting. Jim Paxson hurt his ankle and he wasn't as effective, either.

The game itself was ugly, and I felt the pressure. I was hollering at my players and assistants more than I usually do, and I was all over the officials.

We won 86–77, but I don't ever remember feeling more exhausted than I did at the conclusion of the game. I can't ever remember working that hard, even in the lime pits back in Pennsylvania. I was physically and emotionally drained, and this was only game one of what I am sure is going to be a seven-game series.

MONDAY, MAY 21

I was still feeling bad about the way I yelled at Joe Dumars at halftime of the first game, so I called him into my office after practice.

"Joe, when you have a son, there will be times when you'll have to reprimand him. Do you know what I'm saying?"

He looked at me, smiled, and said he understood. He's a man's man.

Chapter Twelve

TUESDAY, MAY 22

I knew both teams would play better in the second game. The media is saying the winner of this series will go all the way, but they're usually wrong. All they have to do is look out West. How many of them predicted that Phoenix would beat Los Angeles?

There are good teams everywhere, and injuries or other unforeseen events can spoil anybody's chances.

I can't get the Lakers off my mind. When it came to crunch time, they didn't have anyone to throw it to in the low post. They really missed Kareem. Even if he didn't score a lot he was still a low-post threat, and the opponents had to set their defense accordingly. We're fortunate we have James Edwards and Mark Aguirre, who can work in there. When we throw it to Mark and they double up on him, all he has to do is kick it back out and we've got an open shot. The Lakers couldn't do that.

I stayed in The Palace the whole day. Taking a nap was out of the question; I was completely wired. I worry about game twos. We've got to win them to protect our home-court advantage.

The press room was moved to accommodate more members of the media, who seem to be coming in from everywhere. I liked it better when it was just across the hall, but this way I can waste some time walking back and forth to get my tea.

I know the Bulls worked hard to get ready for this game. I heard they had nearly a two-hour film session, then went on the floor for another hour and fifty minutes.

I've been kidding the press about our "Jordan Rules." They think they know what they are, but they aren't even close. I tell them, "Maybe they're real or maybe they're a myth. You'll never know."

Bad Dreams and Michael Jordan

Our "Jordan Rules" were in effect in the game, but I began wondering if we should back off and let Joe Dumars play Jordan fairly straight to see how active he would be. He was tentative in the first half because of his injury. None of their guys were coming forward and they were missing all kinds of shots.

We went into the locker room at halftime up by fifteen points, and that surprised me. When that happens, I expect a letdown. It's an almost automatic reaction.

Right away I could tell we were flat in the second half, and Chicago started to charge. From being down fifteen at half they went to one up, and Brendan Suhr said, "We'd better substitute."

Jordan's injury had disappeared. He was getting into the lane, hitting his shot, and finding the open man. We lost a big lead and were in trouble. I had to make a decision: do I go with my offensive guys or my defensive guys? These fifty-fifty propositions drive me crazy.

I decided on offense. We finally were able to build up a small lead, and when it got down to the four-minute mark, I put in my defensive players. Vinnie Johnson and Mark Aguirre gave us some outstanding performances, and we won game two.

I found out that Jordan had blown up at his teammates at halftime. He was in the locker room yelling and throwing things around, which isn't at all like him. It was his pride and his frustration showing. When you do that, you'd better go out there and step up and show the way. He did so, and with great purpose, but it wasn't quite enough.

Sometimes I don't understand how we win. We didn't play well in either game yet we won both of them.

Isiah Thomas wasn't on his game at all, and I wondered if he might be spending too much time practicing at home. He and Walker D. Russell, one of our former players, were shooting two hours a night in Isiah's gym. I said to Walker, "Why don't you forget that for a while—let's get him to work so he can give us a good hour and fifteen minutes a day in practice. Lay off that other stuff."

I wasn't too happy after the game. We are going to Chicago for the next two games and it's never easy to win there. Bill Laimbeer came to me after the game and said, "Don't worry about Isiah and me—all we want to do is win. Our time will come."

WEDNESDAY, MAY 23

We have the night off, so I watched Phoenix at Portland in the second game of their series. I was antsy, and decided that if we played Portland we'd stay in a hotel by the river, one that is quieter than our usual one. I've already changed hotels in Chicago. We switched from the Westin to the Ritz Carlton because the wives and families are staying at the Westin, and I don't want my guys distracted. I don't like it when their families are around, but it's playoff time and they want to be part of the excitement.

Phoenix was beating up on Portland. Although it wasn't even close, I stayed up to watch. Portland came back with a miracle finish, and the announcers started talking about a "team of destiny." The Portland fans wouldn't leave the arena after the game was over—they stayed there and cheered for an empty floor. We are definitely changing hotels in Portland.

FRIDAY, MAY 25

We flew to Chicago at 5 P.M., and wanted to watch Portland at Phoenix in game three. Not many hotels have TNT, but ours does. We went out to eat at an Italian place, but I had an upset stomach and didn't eat much. By the time we got

Timeouts: so much to say, so little time to say it.

back to the hotel, Phoenix, playing at home for the first time, was blowing out the Trail Blazers, and the game was no contest. It's what I expected, because the home floor is a wonderful weapon.

SATURDAY, MAY 26

Another sleepless night. I wondered all day what was going on in the Bulls' camp with Jordan and his relationship with his teammates and the press. He walked out on the press after the second game in Detroit, and I wonder if this is going to create a problem for the Bulls or make them even more focused.

As it turned out, Isiah Thomas came out on fire and we played well. He made his outside shots, he made three-pointers, he made everything. I liked it, but it didn't allow us to make much inside contact, which means we couldn't get them into foul trouble. A coach is never satisfied, I suppose. We led 69–55, but I could see them raising their level of

233

intensity. In almost no time at all they caught us and passed us, and we were in foul trouble.

The Bulls' run brought the crowd back into the game and we began struggling. You can't underestimate crowd noise. You can say these guys are professionals and it shouldn't bother them, but studies have proved that crowd noise can affect concentration. The Bulls had a nine-point lead with three minutes to go, but there was still time to catch up. Mark Aguirre had a chance to tie the score with a wide-open shot for three points with a few seconds to go, but it banged off the rim. He could have moved in a little closer, but that's how it goes.

I got a cab right after the game because I didn't want to wait for the team bus. I have a VCR set up in my hotel room and we went over the entire game. I could see that our rebounding killed us. We had balls in our hands that we just couldn't control. They stole the game from us. Billy Laimbeer came up with a big doughnut—zero points—and Joe Dumars was a little tentative, and we just couldn't rise above those things.

I've heard rumors that Joe's father is sick, and that might be bothering his play. His dad is diabetic and has lost a leg, and may be in serious trouble.

I went to dinner with my wife, who was staying at another hotel, then kissed her good night and told her to have a nice evening. Later I bumped into Dick Stockton, and we talked about the TV business for a couple of hours. Stockton is a professional and an insider in the television industry, and he gave me some input as to what a tough business it could be.

SUNDAY, MAY 27

We had a day off between games in Chicago. We had a light workout, went over our "Jordan Rules," and came up with some new ideas. I let the players talk because I wanted their input. Coaches do not have all the answers.

MONDAY, MAY 28

I woke up concerned, knowing we couldn't have a shoot-around today because we had another afternoon game. This was probably the most worried I've been in the last four years. First of all, we are playing against the ultimate superstar in the game, someone who can set the tempo for everyone. Jordan can drive, distribute the ball, or take his jump shot and get twenty points before you know what hit you. He can double that, or even triple it, and he has a way of preserving his energy. Second, Chicago is a better team than it was a year ago. They left our building in disarray, but winning at home has given their confidence a terrific lift. Third, their pressure on our end of the court is making it difficult for us to get into position to work our offense. They're taking seconds off the clock, which is a smart move on their part.

We're basically a methodical offensive team. When we can run our offense, we're hard to beat, but they aren't allowing us to do that. The credit should go to coach Phil Jackson, who is doing several things to stop our offense. For one thing, they are staying home with Billy Laimbeer and giving him no outside shots. For another, every time James Edwards gets the ball, four guys are running at him because he isn't used to making the extra pass, and this forces him to take tough shots. They are also doubling on both Mark Aguirre and Vinnie Johnson whenever they can, which makes it difficult for them to get the ball to someone else.

I gathered the team together in a large room for a little talk and a film session. The mood wasn't the same as in that ballroom in New York. I went over some things, but didn't feel we were clear on how to handle Jordan. I didn't sense any confidence, and I was very concerned about the mood of our team. Everyone must be thinking the same thing: if we lose this one, it's a three-game series, and that's a lot of pressure when Michael Jordan is on the other team.

I got on the bus early and so did everyone else, and I could feel the anxiety. Isiah walked to the back to be by himself. He was in one of those pensive moods, concerned about something. When we got to Chicago Stadium, I said to Brendan Suhr and Brendan Malone, "We could be in for a very tough day."

The Bulls came out on fire. They took it to us and we were struggling at every possible turn. We couldn't score, and at one point, we missed twelve straight shots. Dennis Rodman was having a sensational game, twenty points and twenty rebounds, so I couldn't go to Aguirre, and I knew it was bothering him. I could tell by Mark's body language. He can speak without saying a word.

I felt we should pick up Jordan at half court, but we didn't do it. We got behind by fifteen points, and not until we started going after him out by mid-court did we start to function. I figure we have to fight fire with fire.

Jordan was getting to the foul line almost untouched, and we had to put an end to that. We started to pressure them down court and cut the lead to four, but we still weren't taking the kind of shots we should take.

They held on to win 108–101 and I was really upset. I went into the dressing room and used some pretty strong language. I was mad and I didn't care who knew it. I had been keeping a lot of things inside myself and I let it all out, even talking about some things that happened last year. They were having things too easy. We were faced with a real test against Chicago, and I wanted them to know how I felt.

I told them they can't be selfish; not now. We have to make that extra pass. We have to play as a team. I kicked something over, which is uncharacteristic for me, but I wanted to get my point across.

"OK, I've made my statement," I yelled. "You know how I feel. This is the last time I'm going to say it. You can blow me off. You can say I am right or I am wrong. But we've got some problems and we'd better get them straightened out."

I got on the plane to head home and wondered how they would react to my blowup.

When I got home I found out about another problem.

Mike Abdenour called, very jolly, and said, "You know the ankle Rodman sprained? I think he has a chipped fracture."

That's all I needed to hear.

Then Rodman got on the phone, and what did he say? He apologized for missing two layups in Chicago.

Coaching isn't all grief.

TUESDAY, MAY 29

The phone rang at 8 A.M. and I knew it would be Stuart Sussman calling from Philadelphia. He's a friend who has been doing special stats for me since my days at Penn. He really doesn't know much about basketball, but he watches the games and is a terrific help to me. He's a lawyer, and his mind works like a computer. He keeps offensive and defensive charts with complete statistics and has always had a feel for exactly what I'm looking for.

He says he checked last season's statistics at the point when we were 2–2 against Chicago in the playoffs, and the defensive stats are virtually identical. The problem is with our offense, particularly in the matter of turnovers. We had twenty-one turnovers in the second game in Chicago and gave up twenty-one offensive rebounds in the first game. We out-rebounded them, 52–37, in the two games, and hit forty of forty-nine from the free-throw line, but lost the second because of the turnovers.

One of our crucial stats is assists. If we can get more assists than the other team, the chances are we will win. It means we're moving the ball around. As in the other offensive categories, we are weaker in that area in the two Chicago games than we were the previous year.

On the way to work I stopped at the corner of Woodward and Square Lake and called Debbie Mayfield, who works for Matt Dobek. I was only ten minutes from The Palace, but I wanted Debbie to get copies of the four box scores together so I could study them when I got there. I wanted to find out what proportion of the shots Michael Jordan was taking and how many layups he was getting. I knew the two Brendans would have that information also.

It turns out that he had only five or six layups, but I couldn't remember a single one of them. He had forty-seven field goals, and they all seemed like jump shots. We weren't getting up on him and we were putting him on the line too often.

When I went downstairs for practice, I talked to Joe Dumars and got his ideas about what we should do with Jordan. Joe's a smart guy and when he talks, I listen. I called a little meeting and told the guys that I had my say in Chicago and if anyone wants to say anything, this is the time. I am willing to listen to anybody because we are in this together.

I wasn't angry anymore—the Irish in me had taken over.

Isiah had something to say. "I think what you said yesterday was correct, but now we're in a three-game series. We're still in a position to win. We know Jordan is going to pop, and we know the Bulls are going to pop, but we've got to be ready for them and work our way through this thing."

I wanted to encourage some discussion about attacking their press. They brought up some of their own particular problems in the way we were doing it. We kicked things around, trying to come to some common ground about what to do with their press. I also stressed that we had to do a better job with the extra pass. I felt they were coming back a little bit, and their mood was improving. I put the tape on and we had what probably was our longest film session of the season.

I could tell Mark Aguirre was still mad because I held him out of the second half of our second game in Chicago. The moment practice was over, he bolted out of the building. I didn't stop him because I like it when he gets upset. He plays better.

Remember, I don't have a doghouse. If a guy has a bad game, it's over at midnight. Then it's a new day and we go on from there.

WEDNESDAY, MAY 30

The guys had a strange attitude in our shoot-around; it was like they were in another world. For the first time all season, I saw pressure in their faces.

I called Joe Dumars into my office after the shoot-around and told him we had to go back to the basic stuff against Jordan, meaning to stay all over him and make him work every moment he is on the court.

We're at home tonight for game five, and it's a must game for us. If we lose this one, Chicago can finish us off in their building on Friday night.

I spent my usual afternoon around the building. I took a brief nap but it didn't amount to much, then I did my steam act. I could see the tension in my coaches' faces. We are all feeling it. As I went into the pre-game meeting, Bill Laimbeer said to Brendan Malone that we ought to think about starting Mark Aguirre because maybe Dennis Rodman can't play. I went in to see Mike Abdenour and Dr. Ben Paolucci to find out what they thought about Rodman's status. Then I went to Dennis and asked him to try to warm up. He nodded.

"Do whatever you can," I said.

This whole thing made me nervous because without Rodman in the game, we have a major problem.

Chapter Twelve

The Bulls came out hard. Their offensive rebounding started to rear its head again. Mike Abdenour had set up a trampoline at the end of our bench so Rodman could jump on it to keep his ankle loose. It was a strange sight: I'm trying to watch the game and I can see what looks like a circus act out of the corner of my eye. Rodman goes up and down . . . up and down . . . up and down. This was Abdenour's idea.

Trainers today are light years ahead of their predecessors. They have many innovative methods to treat players, but the pressure is also on them to keep the players in the lineup. When a guy gets injured, the trainer is expected to get him back as soon as possible. I don't get involved in it. I let Mike call the shots, along with Dr. Ben. I learned a long time ago to let the bus driver drive the bus, the trainer do the training, the general manager do the general managing. I let the guy who cleans up our lockers alone. I give my coaches jobs and I let them do them. If we have problems, I step in, but I believe everyone should be allowed to operate in his own way.

The Bulls had their hard hats on under the basket and were doing a terrific job of getting the ball. One encouraging sign was that in one possession they had the ball four times but scored only once. When that happens, it doesn't hurt so much. If they stick one down every time they come up with a rebound, we're in big trouble. Joe Dumars was doing a great job on Jordan, playing him straight up, and that kept us in control. We know it's tough on Joe, but it's also tough on Jordan, who tries to save his strength. When you're playing every other night, it is hard to save much.

This was Dumars' best game. He made a commitment early in the game that he would dog Jordan all night, particularly when he brought the ball up the court. He realized he'd better do something after Jordan's two big games in Chicago.

We were making the extra pass, as I'd been pleading with them to do, and it resulted in a 97–83 victory.

I did all the media stuff after the game, and it was getting to be a load. We went up to The Palace Grill and had a couple of shooters and some nachos.

Sleep? I fell off about 3:30 A.M.

THURSDAY, MAY 31

We flew to Chicago at five o'clock in the afternoon and went to a restaurant where we knew they'd show game six between Portland and Phoenix. I watched it until the third quarter, then got fidgety and went back to my room to watch the rest of it.

Phoenix lost its best player, Kevin Johnson, with a hamstring pull. Right away I thought of Adrian Dantley and Vinnie Johnson cracking heads in Boston Garden. I thought of Isiah Thomas spraining his ankle in Los Angeles. I thought of the Lakers losing Byron Scott and Earvin Johnson in last year's finals. Now I was looking at Cotton Fitzsimmons, the Phoenix coach, who was so close, but so far. He was trying to do something he had never done before—win an NBA title—and when he lost Johnson, he was through.

Portland won and the Trail Blazers deserved it because they played well, especially in winning away from home. But I had eyes only for Fitzsimmons, who handled himself well. He congratulated the other club and made no excuses. I put the light out in my room but still saw his face in the darkness. I felt sorry for him, another "lifer."

I thought about Portland. People said that whoever won our series would win the NBA Championship. Wrong. Wrong. Wrong. Our record was exactly the same as Portland's. They're big. They're strong. They're quick. They can get out on the break and rebound with anyone in the league. Clyde Drexler . . .

Go to sleep. Sure.

Chapter Twelve

FRIDAY, JUNE 1

I got up at 8 A.M. Not bad—I had only twelve hours to kill until game time.

We had our shoot-around in Chicago Stadium and everyone seemed confident. When I got back to the hotel, I decided to go for a walk. My knee was killing me. I had it operated on a few years ago and I thought that had taken care of it, but the pain came back two weeks ago. I'd been taking Emperin 3 and my head was a little light. I wondered if the pain was really from my leg or from the pressure. I knew I shouldn't be walking on it, but I couldn't stay in the room, so I put on my brace and away I went.

But I made a mistake. I forgot my hat.

I'm no Hollywood star, but I guess in Chicago people recognize my face. I wasn't out of the hotel two minutes when people began stopping me. They wanted to talk basketball, or ask for my autograph. It was embarrassing because other people walked by who didn't know who I was, and they stared as though they had just seen me swoop in out of the sky.

I stopped at a place where men were doing some construction work. The guys recognized me and gave me the "Hey, Chuck!" routine. I stopped and talked to them about the game. When I left they shook my hand. This proves what a powerful and influential medium television really is.

I was looking for some Chinese food and there was a place nearby, but the construction workers gave it a thumbs-down. I went in anyway. I sat down but decided I didn't want Chinese food after all, so I left. I went to an Italian deli where they make marvelous sandwiches. They looked delicious, but they're fattening, so I walked out. Finally I went down Oak Street and walked into a restaurant and ordered Eggs Benedict. It was awful. I kept on walking and wound up in Bloomingdale's. I decided to go back and try to take a nap, and by the time I got back to my room, I was dead tired. It was already 2:30, and thank God, I fell asleep. Just for a half hour, but it was enough.

I felt good when I got up. Refreshed. Confident. I felt as if we had a chance to win and close out the series.

Before we left the hotel, however, I was told that Bill Laimbeer had received a death threat. This was not a new phenomenon, but it was still unsettling. I've had them, Isiah Thomas has had them, a lot of guys have had them. Some creep calls up and threatens you, then hangs up the phone. I decided not to address it because there wasn't anything I could do about it.

When I got to the building and the game started, the noise and the intensity of the Bulls' play caused me to unravel. We were horrendous on offense. Michael Jordan hit his first three shots, then kind of disappeared. This was a break for us, but we couldn't do anything with it. We were only three down at halftime, but we couldn't get anything going in the second half. Isiah Thomas threw up three air balls—two clean misses and a double-pump that came up short.

We lost 109–91 and I told my guys only one thing in the dressing room: "It's down to a one-game season, guys. Let's get out of here as quickly as possible."

I didn't think it was time for a Knute Rockne speech.

We got on the bus and started for the airport. Mike Abdenour has a portable phone he uses to call our crew to let them know we are on our way, and I heard him cursing. God forbid Mike should curse. I asked him what was going on and he said there was an accident with the plane—a fuel truck backed into it and damaged the nose cone, putting it out of commission. They ordered another plane but didn't know when it would be available.

Wonderful. Our plans to get home early and get some rest went out the window.

We went to the lobby of the terminal. They had some pizza for us and the guys ate it and went to the soda pop machines. I studied their faces. I was a little concerned and wanted to see how they were taking our loss. I saw small groups talking, and the conversations seemed serious.

They finally found us a plane. Our flight home was uneventful, but we couldn't watch any of our tapes, which annoyed me. The players looked knocked out on the plane.

When we landed, I saw a little life in them, a little animation. These are pro athletes and they're resilient. They can put losses behind them. Part of the reason is that they are not held responsible for winning and losing. When a player ends his career, whether it's an Isiah Thomas or a Magic Johnson, there are no W's or L's after his name. There is a shooting percentage, how many points he scored, how many assists, how many rebounds. The record books don't show his win-loss record. But what do the coaches have after their names? Only one statistic. Wins and losses. We have to live with it, and that's one of the reasons we carry the games with us a little longer than the players.

We got in about 2:30. I worry about the guys driving home at that hour of the night. We had no booze on the plane—never do—but they were tired, and there are some strange drivers out at this hour.

I got to my house about 3:30 and read the papers and looked at a few magazines. I thought of Michael Jordan. He is going to get the ball all through the final game. How can we stop him? I went to my desk and started scribbling, trying to work a few new designs.

I fell asleep at 4:30, but not before leaving a note for my wife: "No phone calls, please."

SATURDAY, JUNE 2

When I got to the arena, my coaches had the tape of Friday night's fiasco ready to roll.

"Throw that damned thing in the garbage can," I said. "We're not going to learn anything from that performance."

I wanted to talk to Isiah Thomas. I sensed he was upset about something, and when he gets that way the players are sensitive to it. I hung around the hall outside the dressing room, and when he came out, I took him into the players' lounge.

"What's up, Zeke?"

He said he was a little upset about some people not giving up the ball, not going for that extra pass. We talked it out and got it settled. I told him I would take care of it.

I talked to Joe Dumars. I was concerned because referee Darrell Garretson told him in the middle of the last game to keep his hands off Michael Jordan. "No hand-checking," he said to Joe. Great. Everyone has been hand-checking all through the series. Thomas and Dumars are getting it from the Bulls and now the chief referee is telling my man it is suddenly off. I wish Garretson had said something to me so we could work it out.

SUNDAY, JUNE 3

The moment I woke up, I saw Michael Jordan's face. It was like the continuation of a bad dream, because I know what this guy is capable of doing in a big game. On the other hand, I felt good about the way our players reacted yesterday after our blowout in Chicago. They appeared to be calm and confident.

Still, I worry about all the potential problems. What if Joe Dumars picks up three quick fouls? What if Dennis Rodman's ankle doesn't hold up?

I got up early, read the papers, drank some tea, and went to Prince of Peace Church on Walnut Lake Road for the 9:30 mass.

After church, I headed straight for the arena because I had to do a TV show before the game.

Boxer Tommy Hearns had said he would be one of my guests, and the Gianopolis brothers, John and Peter, had told me Muhammad Ali was coming to the game and that maybe I could get him on the show. I didn't know if he'd be up for an interview, but it was a possibility—an intriguing possibility.

I got to the arena, grabbed a bagel with cream cheese and another tea, and went looking for my guests. None of them were around. We wanted to tape the show at 11:45 to go on at 12:30, but we didn't have any guests. I got Jack McCloskey and Jerry Krause, the general manager of the Bulls, and I put them together and played off the "Are you nervous?" factor. I had a lot of fun with them. The whole thing was a little crazy, but it helped fill the time. Thank God I have something to do other than sit in that office and go crazy.

I did one interview with John Wetzel, the former coach at Phoenix who is now an assistant with Portland. So instead of no guests, I wound up with three of them. We finished with just four minutes to air time. I was happy to get it over because I was anxious to get into the real preparations for the game.

We had our usual pre-game meeting, and I decided there would be no new speeches. Instead, I talked about taking care of little things—setting screens, boxing out, following your man around a pick. Little things win big games—not big things.

The meeting was brief, but it seemed pretty upbeat. A couple of guys really seemed to be in focus, and there was a lot of energy in the room. We went out on the court and the moment had arrived: the dreaded seventh game.

In a way, this is what you dream about when you're a kid: one game for all the marbles. But when you actually face it, it's different, because the fear of failure becomes a knot in your stomach.

Both teams started out as if they were playing a seventh game. Neither club could make a basket. Both sides were struggling, and it didn't look like NBA basketball. Isiah Thomas was playing great and, overall, we weren't doing too badly. I decided to go with a smaller lineup in the second quarter, so I left Isiah in there. I felt good about the way he was playing. He was getting defensive rebounds—something like seven or eight in the first half. We usually think of him as a penetrating point guard, getting to the basket, but now here he was rebounding with guys seven feet tall. We started to get an uptempo game and that surprised Chicago. After a terrific run we pulled out to a fifteen-point lead, and were in a good float, but I knew Chicago still had that other guy in their dressing room at halftime. His face never leaves my mind.

At halftime I told the guys it was an even game. Forget the score. It's all tied up and we've got to go back out there and beat them in the second half. We've had so many letdowns in third quarters. We call it the third-quarter blahs, and I didn't want it to happen this time. I sped up the halftime and tried to get them back on the floor earlier than usual so they wouldn't be sitting around too long.

The players kept saying, "No letdown! . . . No letdown!" Mark Aguirre was as verbal as anyone. He had a terrific second quarter and was still flying.

We maintained our lead for a while, then they cut it to ten. That's when I got nervous. I began thinking, "Hell, Jordan can wipe that out in three or four trips down the floor."

But he was getting tired. I could see it. He was making passes to open guys and they weren't doing anything with the ball.

I'd heard that Scotty Pippen was bothered by migraine headaches and has vision problems. I've been through that before. It comes from tension. Maurice Cheeks used to have those kinds of headaches and so did Kareem Abdul-Jabbar.

Chapter Twelve

"What do you mean, a mohawk? No way!"

The damned clock wasn't moving. I kept looking at it, but it was standing still.

We finally put them away, 93–74, and Phil Jackson, the Chicago coach, congratulated me and said, "Nice situation."

I guess he thought we were going to beat up on Portland.

Jordan came up just beyond half court, shook my hand, and wished us well in the playoffs. He's the perfect gentleman, almost too good to be true. He handles success as well as anyone. He has it all. I have nothing but admiration for him (and for his golf game!).

The celebration started in the locker room, but it wasn't much of a party. The guys quieted down very quickly. There was only going to be one celebration for them—if and when we won the title.

I ran into Magic Johnson outside our dressing room.

"If you want to win the next series, you've got to keep them off the offensive boards," he whispered to me.

"Thanks," I said. I only wish he'd told me how to do it.

So now I had a new problem: Portland. They are big, strong, and aggressive. When do we get a chance to relax and enjoy some of this stuff?

Not yet. Here comes Brendan Suhr with tapes in his hand.

"Here's your tape of Portland," he said to me. I wanted to put it in the drawer until the next day, but I knew I'd look at it before going to bed.

I went to John Ginopolis' place, had a few drinks and something to eat, and went home and crashed in bed. But I slept only an hour because I had to go on Mitch Albom's radio show at 9 P.M.

Later, I put on the Portland tape and lost myself in it until two o'clock in the morning. Don't ask me what day of the month it is. All I know is that this is June, and everything counts.

MONDAY, JUNE 4

I knew everyone would be dragging, so even though we've got just one day to prepare for Portland, I went easy on them. We sat down on the floor of the arena and had a little meeting. We walked through some stuff and barely touched a ball because I felt they needed rest more than anything else.

The whole thing had become a media circus. I had to deal with scores of journalists and it wasn't easy. They had a job to do, so I tried to help as much as possible, but the questions were always the same, and I had to stand there and answer them over and over and try to give decent answers. Just standing there tired me out, so I drifted over to the table at sidecourt so I could sit down.

Later on I sat down with Mike Abdenour and went over our travel plans. We were going to be staying at the Benson Hotel because everyone else—including the media—was staying at the Marriott, and I wanted to get a little privacy for my guys.

Chapter Twelve

We haven't won in Portland in our last seventeen games, but I told the press, "Hey, you can only blame seven of those on me." They didn't know that I won there when I was a coach at Cleveland. I was about to be fired—in fact, they had already told me I was gone—and we went up there and beat the Trail Blazers. I don't know if it ever counted as an official victory on my record, but I'll take it. And now I'd like one more like it.

We should be able to win one out of three there. Don't you think?

13

Blazing The Trail in Portland

TUESDAY, JUNE 5

The finals. Right away, I know I have a problem. We went to our morning shoot-around and I sensed that my guys were looking at this as a regular season game instead of as game one for the championship. They are physically and emotionally drained from the Chicago series and haven't had enough time to recover. Portland is coming in free, rested, and ready to go. They've had four days to recover from their series against Phoenix. That's just right—long enough to get some rest, but not so long that you lose your touch.

But this is their first time in the finals and they'll have their problems handling everything — coming across the country into our building, adjusting to the time change, dealing with the media. It's not just playing basketball; it's everything else that goes along with it.

Brendan Suhr saw how our guys were acting at the shoot-around and said, "Let's just get through it; let's not make it fancy. Let's try to win some way, somehow, and then we'll have a whole day to collect ourselves."

I went through the usual TV stuff, interviewing Dick Vitale, which is fun because I can kid him a little, and then I got Rick Adelman, the Portland coach, to come on with me. This may have been a first in the NBA finals—one coach interviewing the other coach. But Rick is a nice man, a long-time coach, and he did a nice job.

At last, it was game time.

We came out like we were running in mud. We couldn't make a shot to save our lives, and Portland hit seven of eight. We tried, but our minds just weren't with it, and I knew the whole evening was going to be a battle.

"I've got to find the right buttons to push tonight," I said to myself. "Maybe something will work out for us."

Luckily, Portland started to struggle and allowed us to hang around, even though we were still shooting horrendously. I give credit to our guys. They were playing defense, and they were rebounding, but I knew we were in trouble when we came off our screens and settled for long-range jump shots.

I started hollering at them. We hit one of fourteen, and I was hot. We weren't going to the basket. We weren't going inside. I looked at the time and it was eleven o'clock. Time to think about going to bed. But we still had a game to finish, with the toughest part coming up.

Bill Laimbeer played a great game for us. He competed all night long and had the most drive of anyone on the floor. He kept rebounding the ball, keeping them from second shots. Bill doesn't get a lot of credit for how he plays. He gets a bad rap because people are always pointing out his lack of skills. But that's an incorrect assessment, because he is a winner, and he can make a winner out of other guys. When we're all down, he keeps on driving, putting his fatigue aside, and takes the other players with him. He is a unique individual.

Clyde Drexler had four personals and I kept shouting at Joe Dumars to go at him to give him his fifth, but nothing happened. Joe was just too fatigued. It was easier for him to settle for a twenty-foot shot. Besides, if a star player has four fouls, it doesn't mean the refs are going to be quick to call number five on him. Nobody wants to see the great ones sitting on the bench. How many times did Wilt Chamberlain foul out in his career? Zee-ro.

But it's strange. If you go at one man and try to draw him into a foul, it can mess up your whole offense. You have to keep taking what the defense gives you. You hear them say that in football, and it is also true in basketball.

In Portland, it was only eight o'clock, so maybe the time change was working in their favor. I don't know if all of this is important, but that's the sort of stuff that goes through my head when we're struggling.

That's when we went to the ammonia capsules.

When I was a high school coach, and even a college coach, and once in a while as a pro coach, I'd go to my trainer and get some ammonia capsules, which ordinarily are used to keep people from fainting. My guys weren't about to faint, but they needed something to wake them up. I decided to try the ammonia capsules because my button-pushing wasn't working and time was running out on us. Mike Abdenour has them in his kit. I broke one open and got Isiah Thomas to try it. Then Joe Dumars tried one, then Billy Laimbeer, and then John Salley. I thought about taking one myself but decided against it. I am hyper enough. Actually, I was becoming a nut case.

We absolutely have to win on our home floor, particularly in the 2-3-2 setup they have for the finals. If we lose one of the first two at home, Portland will have a chance to end the series in their own building, where we haven't won since 1974. I was so scared I'd try anything, including ammonia capsules.

Nor was I above trying a psychological ploy with Isiah. I saw Magic Johnson sitting up in the stands and I called it to Isiah's attention late in the game.

"Don't let Magic see you lose this game," I shouted.

I was ready to sell my soul to win that game.

253

Isiah got hot. He started throwing in everything, from everywhere. The place was bedlam and our players on the bench were going crazy. Isiah was throwing up unbelievable shots and everything was dropping. We took the lead and went on to win, 105–99.

I had seen Isiah do this before, like the night he scored sixteen points in a minute and a half, and the night he got twenty-five in one quarter against the Lakers. And now tonight. I don't know how he pushes himself the way he does, but he does. He's got a heart bigger than his chest.

Isiah saved the night because I couldn't get anything done.

But what was I going to do with Vinnie Johnson? I had been with this man for a long time, and this had been a difficult season for him. I had stuck with him through some tough situations, and all of a sudden he would come through and start making big baskets all over the place, but it hadn't happened this time. I needed somebody like him in the playoffs. He had been in a slump, but I couldn't give up on him. I had to trust him, just as I trusted all my players.

The game was over, and at midnight it would be a whole new day. We'll start out even because, hey, he is still my player. He is still V.J. He means a lot to this team and I'm not quitting on him.

THURSDAY, JUNE 7

I saw the same attitude at our shoot-around that I saw before our first game. The guys were still dragging. Even though we won the first game, I didn't see the same kind of emotion that we showed in the regular season. They just weren't into it. They were still tired.

Game two is scheduled to start at 9:20 and that bothers me. We have been getting to The Palace at six o'clock. Now we have an extra two hours to kill, and that can make the days seem interminable. This is what happens to teams in the East. I talk about getting more caffeine into our systems—coffee, tea, Diet Coke. They need a wake-up call.

James Edwards had a lot of bounce at the start of the game, so we went right to him and he scored big in the first quarter. I brought in Mark Aguirre and Vinnie Johnson, but both were struggling. We depend on them to give us an offensive lift, and when they struggle, we struggle. Vinnie looks like he is in a bad mood, too. When he gets that way, there's not much that's going to shake him out of it. He isn't playing badly; he just isn't scoring, and when he doesn't score, he gets down. I can see he is not a "happy camper." Mark is having his problems, too, so we weren't going anywhere in the first half.

"Hey, we can't wait for heroics," I told the guys in the dressing room. "You can't lay back and expect your teammates to save you at the end, the way Isiah did in the first game." I told them they all had to do a better all-around job if we were going to win this game.

We kept struggling after intermission, but the Portland team wasn't playing great, either.

I could see Billy Laimbeer was especially tired, but he kept working. Suddenly near the end of the game, he came alive and started making three-point shots from everywhere. With four seconds left, in a scramble on an in-bounds pass, he got the ball, threw it up, and it went in from out on the highway. Amazing.

We had a one-point lead, and what was I thinking? I was wishing he had done it with two seconds left, because four seconds can be an eternity in the NBA.

We set up a good defense. I yelled, "Don't foul! Don't foul! Make them hit a tough basket!" I put Dennis Rodman on Clyde Drexler, their biggest threat. I knew everyone was wondering why I was putting Rodman in with his sore ankle. The reason was, Dennis Rodman on one leg is a better defensive player than anybody else we have, or maybe anybody else in the league.

Drexler drove on him and there was some contact. The call could go either way, or it could be a no-call, but they called a foul on Dennis.

That bothered me. When Isiah Thomas goes to the basket like Drexler just did, he gets bodied up but the refs don't call it. I didn't argue, though. When an official makes his call, good or bad, there is nothing I can do that's going to change it. I can complain, but it doesn't matter. Anyway, we missed four out of five free throws down the stretch and that's why we were in this predicament. So blame us, not the referees.

Drexler hit both shots as easy as can be and we called time out with 2.1 seconds left.

You may not believe it, but we have a play for such a situation—a throw-in to James Edwards, who turns and tries to get off a halfway decent shot. The problem was, they still had a foul to give, which meant they could bang into Edwards the minute he got the ball and we would lose a second or more on the clock. There was nothing we could do about it.

We threw it in, two guys grabbed Edwards, and the foul was called. Now we had 1.2 seconds left and decided to try it again, because Edwards is a good shooter and might be able to get one off. It's a good play, and we practice it a lot, but we never get to practice it with the other team on the floor. The intensity isn't there with your own guys, no matter how much we make believe it is. Also, the other team can change up on you, putting different guys on different players, so you're not sure how they are going to defend you. The sight of five guys coming at you at once makes the whole thing very uncertain.

Edwards got off a pretty good shot, but it didn't go in and we lost by one point. I had to give credit to the Portland team. They hung in until the end.

Everyone understood then why the Trail Blazers were in the finals instead of the Lakers. They played tough all year, and now they had played tough in one of the biggest games of the season.

We had lost our home-floor advantage, but as I went to the dressing room I didn't feel all that bad. We had a good club and could win one on their floor. We were a good road team, maybe the best around. I knew our guys would be back. I just worried about Rodman's condition because he was so important to us.

A thought suddenly came to my mind: Why not start Mark Aguirre and hold Rodman out in the third game? We didn't play Friday or Saturday. Game three wasn't until Sunday, then we were off Monday and didn't play again until Tuesday night. If I held Rodman out that long, his ankle might get better.

I was glad we were going on the road. We needed to come together as a team, and we could do that better on the road than at home.

We'll see.

FRIDAY, JUNE 8

I liked what I saw on the plane—the guys were having some fun. It was a long flight and we had a chance to look at the tape very carefully. We stopped in Billings, Montana, for gas and the CBS affiliate showed up at the airport. There's no escape.

I talked to Dr. Ben Paolucci about Rodman's condition.

"The way The Worm is walking, I don't think he can go on Sunday," he said.

"What does that mean in terms of recovery?" I wanted to know.

"I think it will help him."

"But won't he go back to square one the first time he twists it?"

"Probably."

I knew I had no choice. We'd dress Dennis, tape him tightly, but I wouldn't use him except in the most dire circumstances. It would take a lot on my part to keep him out, but that's what I had to do.

I went through the cabin once and leaned over and whispered to Mark Aguirre, "Be ready to start on Sunday afternoon."

We went to Jake's, in Portland, one of the great seafood places in the country. There were a lot of people around and I started feeling pretty good about the whole trip and the game on Sunday. Amazing what two pops and a piece of fresh salmon can do for your spirits.

SATURDAY, JUNE 9

We had to practice at a community college about twenty minutes from town. I told the writers I was planning to start Mark Aguirre. It's strange how it works. When you lose one of your key players, sometimes the other team tends to relax, and your guys take it up a notch. I was hoping this would be the case. I talked things over with Dennis and he said, "Let's see how I feel tomorrow."

The big question I have is, "Why haven't we won in Portland in twenty years?"

I think I know the answer. Most people don't understand how tough it is on one of those West Coast trips where you play four to seven games in a week to ten days. After being away that long, the players want to get the last game over with and get home. They say they'll give it their best shot, but by then "best" isn't all that good. They have traveled enough and want to get home to their families and their own beds. Believe me, last games on any trip are very hard to win.

I knew the Portland fans were going to be psyched. I kept thinking of the night they beat Phoenix and wouldn't go home after the game. A guy asked me what I thought of the

Detroit fans walking out of the building before the end of our game against Portland the other night. I didn't like it, but when games go to 12:30 in the morning, fans have other priorities in their lives, like work the next morning and babysitters who have to get home. If they don't beat the traffic, they can add another forty-five minutes to the time it takes to get home. I left the building at least forty-five minutes after the game ended and traffic was still jammed up. I tried to get on I-75 but couldn't. I tried to go down Lapeer Road and couldn't, so I went north to get on I-75 and couldn't do that. I finally wove my way through Pontiac and got home at 2 A.M.

Terry and Cydney were staying in other rooms because I needed my room for meetings. Normally, I had a two-room suite, but here I had only one large room and it got a little crowded. If they had their own rooms it gave everybody a little more space.

I usually met Terry for breakfast, but I forgot this morning and she was a little mad.

I was apprehensive about the game, because without Dennis Rodman, we would have a hard time. We couldn't afford to lose a player like him. But I liked our attitude at the shoot-around. I felt they are back into it. Some guys went out to a movie and then came back together. That was a very good sign.

Dennis asked me if it was all right if he went to the dog track. He loves to go to the dog track. I didn't see anything wrong with it, so I told him I'd check with Jack McCloskey. I figured it would be a diversion for him.

"Here's $100," I said. "If you lose it, you lose it. I understand."

Chapter Thirteen

I didn't see him again until we got back to the locker room. The coaches, for once, have a little office. Dennis came in, reached into his shoe, and handed me eighty-one dollars.

"What's this for?" I asked.

He didn't say it, but I knew he lost nineteen dollars.

William Bedford and Scott Hastings were staring at the money in my hand.

"What's that for?" Bedford asked.

"William, don't you understand? That's how this guy gets all his minutes. He pays me before every game."

Bedford looked at me with a strange expression on his face, trying to decide if I was putting him on or not.

"Just think, out of all the hundreds of thousands of dollars you have, you could have given me some of it and you'd be a big star in the NBA today."

I got a little nuts before some of those games; that was my diversion. I had to get through the hours as best as I could.

Mike Abdenour came in and said, "The Worm feels pretty good, the swelling is down."

"I'm not starting him. I have already decided." But the question I had not yet answered was, "Do I play him at all?"

I met Terry and Cydney in the hotel lobby at seven o'clock to go to dinner, just the three of us.

There were about a dozen people milling around the lobby and suddenly I got the idea that it would be nice to do something special. There's a Trader Vic's in the hotel, and the manager had done me a favor in Kansas City five or six years ago. I went to him and asked, "Do you remember the team dinner you gave us in Kansas City?"

"Sure," he said. "If you need a private room here, I'll fix you up."

The restaurant was booked solid, but he got us a room in ten minutes and kept adding chairs as more and more friends joined us. They fixed us a terrific Polynesian dinner and we had a great time.

The Benson is an old-fashioned hotel, European in style. If you want glitz and glitter, you go someplace else, but I love it here. There is a bar right off the lobby, which you don't see much anymore. It's very elegant with a mahogany bar and fixtures. You can really "lobbyize," as I like to call it. No matter where people go for the evening, they congregate back at the lobby. It's wonderful.

The players didn't like it because old-world atmosphere is not their style. Their biggest complaint was that there were no hand-held remote controls for the televisions. They had king-sized beds, but the rooms were small, and with no clickers at their side, I knew they were not happy. Everybody should have such monumental problems.

The pianist entertaining the lobbyizers knew I liked jazz. She kept looking over to see if I was pleased with what she was playing.

The rooms at the Benson faced the street. I didn't think that would be a problem, but when I went upstairs at 11:30, I could hear noise outside my window. There were about six drunks standing across the street yelling at us. I was on the third floor and could hear them very clearly: "Detroit sucks!" "Isiah sucks!" "Laimbeer sucks!"

Someone from upstairs stuck his head out the window and yelled at them, but that only made it worse. They went on and on. Finally they retreated into a parking garage and then walked around the block. But they came back. They did this several times. I wanted to call the police, but I didn't know what good it would do because they were across the street and not on hotel property.

This went on until 2:30, and then I finally dozed off.

Chapter Thirteen

SUNDAY, JUNE 10

I kept my phone off the hook until 9:30. If I didn't, I'd be answering it every two minutes. Somebody always wants something—long-lost friends looking for tickets, reporters asking questions, or even good friends, wanting to send their best wishes. A lot of nice people want to talk, but there are just too many for me to deal with if I'm going to accomplish what I came here to do.

At 9:30 I felt good, really good. This encouraged me, because the way I feel is usually the way our team feels. I went down to breakfast and saw a few of our players. They were bright-eyed and bushy-tailed, which made me feel even better.

I went around the corner and got a cup of tea at a small café, because the hotel was too busy. I like to check the price of tea around the country. Sometimes it's seventy-five cents, sometimes eighty-five cents. In New York it's $1.23. In Chicago it's $1.27. Here it's one dollar. The young woman handed me the cup. As I was taking off the top, she looked at me again and said, "Are you the coach of the Pistons?"

"Yeah," I said.

"Then here's your dollar back."

That was pretty much the way Portland reacted to us. These people were some of the nicest sports fans in the country. They loved their team. Blazermania raged all over town, but they were always polite and congratulated us when we did well. You didn't find any bitterness in this town, and that was refreshing.

They were very social. If you went to a restaurant, the owner would buy you a bottle of wine and make the whole thing a very pleasurable experience. It was good for the Detroiters who were there to see that kind of conduct. As money-oriented as these games can get, there still has to be some sportsmanship to them as well.

262

Everybody got on the bus on time; nobody was dragging. But I was beginning to feel apprehensive. "The last time we were here, we got beaten by twenty points," I reminded myself. I looked around. The guys seemed very confident.

"The Worm feels great," Mike Abdenour said to me.

We called our meeting and I told the guys, "Look, I'm going to start Mark. I'm keeping Dennis on the bench. If we need him in the last seven or eight minutes, if we have a chance to win, I may go to him."

I was sitting in the tiny coaches' room when Matt Dobek walked in. "Joe Dumars' father just died," he said quietly.

Matt had gotten a call from Joe's wife with the news. Now we had to decide whether or not to tell Joe. My inclination was to tell him. "Some things are bigger than basketball," I said. "I'm not sure I wouldn't want to know if it was my father. However he handles it, he handles it. If he has to leave, it's okay."

"Maybe you should talk to Debbie Dumars before you do anything," Matt suggested. The guys sensed something was up. We tried to find a private area and I called Debbie in Detroit.

"Please don't tell him," she said. "Let him play the game."

I told her how I felt, but agreed to respect her wishes. I learned later that they had agreed that if Joe's dad died, he wouldn't be told until after the game.

I called Isiah Thomas into our office. He's our captain and I wanted him to know what was going on. Joe would need some support and Isiah could give it to him.

Isiah went through the same thing when his father died a few years back just as we were going into training camp.

As we went out onto the floor, I pleaded with myself, "Please don't holler at Joe today."

Chapter Thirteen

Portland hit ten of their first twelve shots, and I was saying, "Oh, oh . . . we've got problems." But we kept hanging around.

Both sides were complaining about the fouls, but I knew we couldn't change the way it was. We had to keep pushing. Bill Laimbeer was playing like a man possessed. On my TV show yesterday he said that not only were we going to win one game in Portland, we were going to win two of them. I said to myself, "I'll take one. Just get us back in our own building."

I saw a completely different team out there. We were perked to attention. Our guys were a little scared, but that's okay—they play better that way.

I wanted to bring Vinnie Johnson in early, but our guards were playing so well I rode it out with them for a while. When Vinnie went in, Isiah came to me and said, "No plays for Vinnie, he just came into the game."

"We're going to Vinnie right away," I said. "We do it sixty to seventy times a year, and this is no time to stop."

Vinnie hit his first shot, an open jumper, and then got slammed the second time. I started screaming at the officials. If I got a "T," I got a "T." I wanted Vinnie to know I was trying to help him. He hadn't been scoring, but he's a crucial part of our offense, and I wanted to get him going. The next thing I knew he was really into it and became a major, major force in the game.

We got into some foul trouble and I said, "The hell with it, let's go with David Greenwood and Scott Hastings." We had three games to play in this building and I decided to throw all caution to the wind. If somebody could help us, then let them help us. I like to bring in guys who don't think they're going to play. Sometimes it gets their attention and they give a little more than they normally are capable of giving.

I was thinking of leaving them out there for one, two, or three minutes, but at four and five minutes, both guys were playing well, so I kept riding them.

Greenwood took three hard fouls, got some big rebounds, and also tipped in a basket. He is a very physical player and he made a great contribution by giving our men some time on the bench. It allowed us to get through the half in pretty good shape.

In these situations, the first five minutes of the second half are crucial. Many times one team or another comes out lackadaisical and the other team gets a burst, which puts them in a good position.

Dumars and Laimbeer were having a sensational game and we had a strong second half. Overall we played a superb game and beat them, 121–106.

I was feeling pretty proud of our guys as we left the floor.

I heard Laimbeer saying, "Maybe we can play better here than in our own building. The time change isn't against us. Maybe we should think of taking all three."

All three? I was glad to get one.

The minute we got into the locker room, I went to Joe. Jack McCloskey had arranged a limo and a plane, Bill Davidson's private jet, to get him back to Detroit. I assumed Joe would go to Detroit, pick up his wife, and fly to Louisiana.

I took him into the office with Jack, Isiah, and Matt Dobek. I kind of squeezed Joe's arm and told him his wife was on the phone. I could see him start to break up as he listened to her.

A lot of us have gone through this ourselves, but no one is ever ready for it. I saw a few tears in the room as Isiah led Joe back to his locker.

When we were done with the media, I got on the bus back to the hotel, and when I got there, I had a very solid vodka on the rocks with a twist.

Chapter Thirteen

I went up to Brendan Suhr's room because we had agreed to meet there to watch a tape of the game. I knocked on the door but there was no answer, so I sat on the floor to wait for them. Down the hall, some security people were looking at me. They were delivering Detroit newspapers to the players' rooms. "I'll bet they think I'm a drunk," I said to myself, so I waved and they waved back. I guess they thought a friendly drunk is harmless.

We watched the tape, got our "bitching" out of the way, then got ready for a party at Nike headquarters.

They had a great setup for us: drinks, food, music, the whole works. John Salley did a five-minute comedy routine. When we got back on the bus, John took my seat. Normally the coach sits in the front seat, on the right side, but this was a party bus, not a team bus, and I have no status, so I sat in the back. John started into his Chuck Daly imitation. He pretended he was looking at the stat sheet and glaring back at the players. He had the whole bus in stitches. By the time he went into my "love affair" with Mark Aguirre, everyone was dying with laughter. I think John should go into another line of business.

MONDAY, JUNE 11

I woke up early and learned that Joe Dumars hadn't gone home. He went out to dinner with Isiah Thomas and decided to stay with the team since his father wasn't being buried until Saturday.

It would be tough for him. He'd get a thousand calls. Every person had to handle it in his own way. If he had said to me, "I'm going home," I would have respected that decision, because I knew how much Joe loved his father.

TUESDAY, JUNE 12

It takes seven minutes to get from our hotel to the arena in Portland. I timed it so I could make sure we left in plenty of time. Traffic would be heading north when we went to the game, and I wanted to make sure we left in plenty of time so we wouldn't get caught in it. Now I was even worrying about the traffic.

We got to the arena at 4:30 and had a team meeting scheduled for 5:30. That meant I had to get my TV show done in an hour. I like doing it; I feel very comfortable before a camera, and I never prepare. I just let the interview flow. I guess it's delicate when I interview my own players, but I put on my journalist's hat and ask things like, "How come your coach doesn't play you more?" They always come back with something like, "Because he's dumb, that's why." We have a lot of fun with it. I had Mike Fratello on and we talked about all the coaching changes in the league. I also talked to David Greenwood.

The guys in the dressing room were saying we could win this game if we play through all of Portland's emotion.

The Trail Blazers started out hot again. We were settling for too many long shots and got behind, and then we got into foul trouble. Isiah Thomas picked up his third and James Edwards got two very quickly. I was still trying to work out the Dennis Rodman equation. He said he could play, the doctor said he could play, but I wasn't so sure.

Joe Dumars got hot and we went into the dressing room ahead at halftime, and then I was excited because I sensed we could win this game.

I told the guys we weren't doing a good job of trapping on Clyde Drexler and Terry Porter off the screen-and-roll.

Suddenly Bill Laimbeer piped up, "Listen, listen to what he's saying! He knows we can win too!"

Laimbeer put a spark in me, and I started to get fiery.

"Look," I said, "we can take their hearts. We can do it right now. They're beginning to wonder about things. You can see their confidence going down. If we play smart, we can win this one!"

All of a sudden, in the second half, we had Mr. Fire on our hands. Isiah Thomas started throwing them in from all over and we got a big lead. I couldn't believe our good fortune. I looked at the scoreboard and wondered, "How can we get the clock to move faster?" I don't trust clocks. Never have, never will. When you're ahead, the damned things won't budge; and when you're behind, every tick takes off a minute instead of a second.

We inbounded the ball, took it down the court, set up, and the clock didn't move. They started pressuring us and we came apart.

We had most of our good people in the game, but Portland completely disrupted us, and suddenly we looked like a junior high school team in disarray. They were trapping all over the floor and we had trouble getting out of our own end. They went to a 1-2-1-1 and 2-2-1, but they were just chasing after the ball, ganging up on our players, and that threw us out of whack. Isiah alone gave up the ball three times. There went our sixteen-point lead.

I saw our heads dropping. Somehow we kept making baskets, so we were able to hang in there. Our three guards were doing a fine job. Both teams used up all their timeouts, which is rare for us. I hoard timeouts like the few pennies I can save. I never want to go into the final two minutes unless I've got two or three timeouts. We used them out of necessity tonight. They had a one-point lead with a little more than thirty seconds to go, and the place was a madhouse. I couldn't even think, the crowd was making so much noise.

Isiah was in the corner. He was dancing around, dribbling the ball, looking for an opening, and they had two guys on him. He lofted one up, and all those hours of working at the gym in his Bloomfield Hills home paid off. The ball went through and we had a one-point lead.

There was dead silence throughout the building—Isiah had done it to them again. It might have been the most important shot of the series.

There were still twenty seconds left, and as Terry Porter was driving through the middle for the go-ahead basket, Isiah knocked the ball away from him. We had Gerald Henderson in the game and he broke clear, taking the pass from Isiah. Nobody was near Henderson, and the clock was almost out. I was going to yell at him to dribble out the time, but instead I said to myself, "Leave him alone. He's going to put the ball in for an easy basket. When it goes through there will be no time left and we'll have ourselves a three-point victory."

But he scored a little too quickly.

They had three seconds left and put the ball right back into play. James Edwards and Mark Aguirre both went to the ball instead of going back to protect. Danny Young had the ball, taking it up the sideline. Joe Dumars had him at mid-court and should have fouled him, but Young danced around Joe and put up a thirty-five-footer which split the cords.

Chaos!

I was watching everything at once. I went to the officials screaming, "No good! No good!"

One of the refs was signaling, "Good! Good! Good!"

Dumars was yelling, "Zero-Zero-Zero," meaning the clock had run out.

They waved us away and into a huddle.

I'm not sure what happened—if the shot was good or not—but right away I started to organize my thinking.

Who's going to the jump ball if we go into overtime? Who's rested? Who's tired? Who's ready? Who isn't?

Suddenly, I saw Dennis Rodman jumping in the air, bad ankle and all. Our other guys were jumping around.

"I can't believe it! I can't believe it!" I blurted. "We got a break!" They called the shot no good and we left the floor with a stunning 112–109 victory. Earl Strom had made a great ruling.

I wondered if they had failed to start the clock again. We checked it back in our room when we looked at the tape. It clearly showed that we were cheated out of 5.8 seconds earlier in the game, just before we fell apart and almost blew it. But the refs called the last one right. Time had run out by the time Young got the ball off. I was glad because I didn't want to win on a fluke, and I was also glad for the officials. They didn't need that kind of grief.

Feeling hyper, I went for a walk after watching the tape. I had to be by myself, and I ended up walking around downtown for about forty minutes. Some people recognized me, since I'd forgotten my hat again. Some of them congratulated me on winning two in a row. They're such nice people. In Chicago, they want to throw bricks at you. They get seriously mad at you in New York. Other cities are just as bad, just as bitter. But here in Portland the people walk up to you and shake your hand and say, "Nice game." It's almost like the college game. It was like that when we won a year ago. People saw Detroit in a different light—they saw that it isn't all crime and corruption downtown.

WEDNESDAY, JUNE 13

An off day, but a busy day. I got up at 6:30, after only four hours of sleep, and went over to the CBS studios for a couple of TV shows. We have to decide what to do about Joe Dumars and his father's funeral. Some guys are talking about flying to Louisiana. I went to Isiah to get their feelings, and told him he'd better talk to Joe before they decide anything. The thing could turn into a media circus. Isiah asked Joe how he felt, and Joe decided he didn't want the whole team to go. I think it is the right thing because it should be a very personal time for him and his family.

We went to our shoot-around and discovered we had a new problem. So many reporters were there that they'd walked all over the floor and made it slippery. It was so slippery we couldn't run. All we could do was some minor shooting and a few walk-throughs.

After practice, I asked Isiah if he'd go on my TV show, and he agreed. We planned to do five minutes, but I liked the flow. He answered everything intelligently. I asked him what it was like to be a leader and what that entailed, then what it felt like to have to be the man every night and how much pressure this put on him. How long could he keep doing it, I asked. He was doing so well that I inquired if he might be a political figure in the future. The whole thing ran ten minutes and our producer, Clark Atterbury, loved it all.

When we were done, Isiah whispered to me, "If you stay, we'll win three in a row," the same thing he had said in New York.

THURSDAY, JUNE 14

We could wrap it up tonight, but I was dead tired, as tired as I had ever been. The biggest problem was the phone, which seemed to ring incessantly. As soon as I put it down the red light went on and I had to call the operator for more messages.

We had to win the next game because I didn't think I could coach one more game. I couldn't even eat. All I wanted was a hot dog or a peanut butter sandwich. That's how I get on the road. After going out night after night, I start yearning for something simple. I had a sandwich last night with John Gianapolis, as good a friend as I've ever had in Detroit, and thought about what to do after the game if we won. Do we stay or go home? If we lose, it's easy—we go home immediately.

I decided that if we won we would stay and have our celebration in Portland. But I was superstitious, and I didn't want to bring our bags to the arena because that was like saying we were going to lose. Still, we couldn't go back to the hotel and do all our packing because that would delay us by at least three hours.

So I decided we would half pack—get some of our stuff ready but leave it in the room. And I didn't want to hear anything about champagne in our dressing room. The first year I was with the Pistons we went to Atlanta for the final game and had a chance to win our division. They put champagne in the room, but we lost. Ever since then, I haven't even wanted to hear the word *champagne*.

I was optimistic about winning the game. If we could stay even until the half, we could take it. The other team would be thinking, "We don't want to go back to Detroit. That's a hard trip for us," but that thinking would start to work against them. I've seen it happen before. If we could keep it close we would be in good shape to win it at the end.

I half packed and told everyone else to do the same. We could come back to the hotel and be gone in thirty minutes if necessary.

The Dennis Rodman debate continued. Do I use him? Do I keep him on the bench?

"If we don't play him, we're going to lose him," Brendan Suhr told me.

I talked to the doctor, then I talked to Dennis. I found out he was getting down. He felt as if he wasn't part of the team, and that was a new problem. He felt as if he wasn't wanted. I was concerned because he hadn't been doing anything, not even in practice. He said he felt better than he had in a week, so I made up my mind to put him in under our normal rotation. I would start Mark Aguirre and then go to Dennis. He was one guy who could play through pain.

Portland started out strong again, but we played well too. Isiah Thomas was great, but our other two guards—Joe Dumars and Vinnie Johnson—were struggling, and when that happens, we often lose the game. It's almost a sure thing. We need two of our guards to play well, and when three of them play well, we are almost unbeatable.

At halftime, I went to the blackboard and wrote two/four, with a line underneath it. "You have two quarters to play or you can go back to Detroit and play four more quarters," I explained. "The choice is yours."

They knew exactly what I meant.

"Every time you make a mistake on defense, or don't hustle, it might cost us the game, and then we'll have to play more in Detroit. Is that what you want?"

We went into the second half, and not only was the fatigue factor taking over with our guys, but they started getting bumped and bruised out there. Isiah came out of the game and I thought he had broken his nose. He sat down and it bled and bled. They couldn't get it stopped. I had trouble deciding who should play and who should sit—Joe couldn't make a shot; Vinnie couldn't make a shot; Isiah was on fire, but we couldn't get him back into the game.

Portland scored a couple of times down the floor and took a 90–83 lead with a little over two minutes to go. I called time out and looked at the huddle. I knew they were thinking, "We don't have enough time to come back."

I put Isiah, Aguirre, and Bill Laimbeer back into the game. We needed some offense. We needed Billy's rebounding and Isiah's leadership. "All we need is a basket on this possession, and then a stop, and we're back in it," I said to them.

"We have a lot of time. We're a championship club. We know how to handle our timeouts."

Brendan Malone pointed to his ring and his heart. He was telling them that's what it would take to get through the next two minutes.

Vinnie threw in a whirl-around jumper and got fouled, which cut their lead to four points with about 1:50 to go. We got a stop and we were back in it. Laimbeer got the rebound—thank God he was back in the game—and Isiah hit a tough shot with the twenty-four-second clock running out. Portland missed again and Vinnie hit another one. The score was tied, 90–90.

We went back on defense, and I was surprised Portland didn't call a timeout.

Terry Porter threw the ball away under our basket and now we had it with about twenty seconds to go. We called time, which meant the ball would go up to half court, and this is the nightmare of all coaches—getting the ball into play.

We could have taken it in from back court, but I never like to do that because if you lose it, they can go in for an easy layup. We found this out in the Boston series four years ago, when Larry Bird stole the ball on Isiah's in-bounds pass and flipped it to Dennis Johnson for the winning basket. It's harder to throw it in from half court, but I'd rather do it that way. Besides, we've had pretty good success at it.

We called our "X" play, which means two players come off on either side of Billy, and Isiah catches the ball in the clear. We wanted to get the ball into Isiah's hands.

"Let me have it at the top by myself," he said. "If they double team, I'll kick it to a shooter on either wing. If not, I'll go in myself."

He took the ball and was at the top of the circle. The clock was running down. They didn't double up on him and he started to penetrate. Jerome Kersey came off Vinnie on what was Isiah's right wing, but he came over only a few steps and Isiah flipped the ball to Vinnie. Vinnie caught it but wasn't ready to shoot. It looked as though he was in trouble and might have to pass it back to Isiah.

Vinnie looked at the clock, then took it into the lane, right to left, dribbling the ball. All I remembered was his unbelievable ability to rise over his opponents. All year long we've had this kind of situation without much luck. All I could do was hope.

I saw Jerome Kersey go up in the air, but I knew Vinnie was going to elevate over him because of his tremendous leaping ability. He got in almost to the circle, went up over Kersey, and damned if the shot didn't go in.

It was not a play, just a great individual effort by Vinnie Johnson. I still can't believe it went in. I looked at the clock and there were seven-tenths of a second to play. I ran to my coaches because I knew Portland could still get a shot at the buzzer, and probably would.

We put in all our key people on defense. Normally, we put a guy on the ball, but because we had three guards in the game, we told Vinnie to get off the ball and go wherever the ball is thrown. But he went too far down and that allowed them to throw the ball into the corner. We usually stop that pass, but this time it got through. Terry Porter got the ball and Dennis Rodman was late in switching and Porter got the shot off. I'm pretty sure it was a three-pointer, but it banged off the rim and the game was ours, 92-90.

I don't know when I ever felt more relief. Everybody was running off the court, and I've never felt happier over a victory in my life.

We went through all the stuff in the dressing room and I kept thinking how much more this one meant than the last one. We were expected to win a year ago, but to come back and do it again—to stay healthy—you have to be very lucky. We were very lucky. I started thinking about winning three in a row in Portland, where we hadn't won in twenty years, and clinching our second championship on the road. It was a great feeling.

Things were getting pretty wild in the dressing room when someone came to me and said, "OK, it's time for your TV show."

I'd completely forgotten about it. They were doing a post-game show as well as a pre-game show, but TV was the farthest thing from my mind. But I had all the guys around and it was the easiest show I ever did.

It felt so wonderful. It felt that way because all the arguments, all the problems, all the grief, every bad word I had with any of the players, all the contract problems were completely forgotten. None of it meant a thing anymore. It was a terrific feeling to see everyone so happy.

There's no feeling like it!

We got back to the hotel and they had a huge party organized. Madelon Ward, our box office manager, arranged the whole thing. She is one of the great people in our organization. If I had to trust only four or five people in my life, she would be one of them. She does it all for the Pistons. She had to put out something like six or seven thousand dollars for the party and wouldn't get any of it back if we had lost.

"Madelon, how could you do such a thing?" I asked.

"It was okay," she said, "until you were down seven points with two minutes to go, and then I told myself, 'Those jerks better get going.'"

It was one of those spectacular moments in life when everything is right. I tried to get as many of my friends as possible into the party, and everyone was singing and dancing the night away. I was happy to see Joe Dumars there. He came into my office after the game and shook my hand and hugged me. "Thank you for staying with me," he said. He wasn't making any shots but, God forgive me for saying this, I didn't care about his scoring. I needed him for defense and he played the hell out of Clyde Drexler.

FRIDAY, JUNE 15

I got up, finished packing, and for the first time I realized I am going to have to decide about my future very soon. Up to this point, thinking about nothing but the playoffs, I have put off my decision, but I can't do that any longer. TV, general managing, or coaching?

I felt relieved as we left the hotel. I didn't have to worry about our next game, and the one thing we are not going to do on our plane ride home is watch a tape of the game. We've watched hundreds of tapes, hundreds of games. I didn't want to see one more minute of any of them.

The flight was very relaxed. A lot of guys tried to catch up on their sleep. It was "let the air out of the balloon" time. The party went on for much of the night. I got five hours of sleep, so I was feeling pretty good. Some of the players looked as if they only got five minutes.

After we took off we heard about the riot in Detroit: several people killed in a post-game celebration. I couldn't believe it. Why can't people be happy without going crazy?

Jack McCloskey and I talked about going to Joe's father's funeral. We announced that the plane would leave at 8:30 Saturday morning. Nine of us are going, including Jack, me, our coaches, and the front office people. We'll take Round-ball I.

We landed at Willow Run Airport so we wouldn't block traffic at Detroit Metro. I was first off the plane, and there were hundreds of people there with tight security. I got out and high-fived everyone in sight. We stayed about forty-five minutes, got back on the plane, and flew to Metro, about ten miles away, where we have our own private spot.

I was looking for my baggage when Jack McCloskey ran me down and said there was a report on the news about Isiah Thomas and a gambling probe.

"Oh, no," I thought. "I can't believe the timing. Just like the Rick Mahorn mess last year. I wonder if our victory is going to be spoiled again."

Jack assured me that it was not a probe of Isiah, but had to do with a friend of Isiah's, a neighbor. Matt Dobek knows him and I've seen him around.

I talked to Matt about it because I knew the phone would be ringing off the hook. I didn't know what to do about Isiah because I wasn't sure what was going on. I thought about calling him, but I knew he wouldn't be answering his phone. I would just dismiss it as nonsense because I know Isiah so well, but when these things come out in the press they can be very touchy, even when you're completely innocent.

I saw him on the Bill Bonds show in the evening and I felt a lot better after hearing him explain that he had done nothing wrong. Isiah handles himself very well. I have no doubts about him.

SATURDAY, JUNE 16

We flew straight to Natchitoches, Louisiana, Joe's home town, a place of about 20,000 people. Roundball I was unavailable, so Bill Davidson let us use the new G-4 jet from his own private fleet.

Two cars were waiting for us when we arrived. They took us into town, across from Joe's house, and we stood around, not wanting to intrude.

Across from Joe's house is a large liquor store. There is a fenced-off lot on the corner with a satellite dish in it. I figured it must be the one Joe bought for his family so his father could see all the games.

When Joe was a kid his father built him a basket and a backboard, and Joe used to play basketball late into the night by the light from the liquor store. I was intrigued by the store, so I went inside. It is immense. I met the owner and found out that he has been there for forty-one years.

Back outside, Brendan Suhr said that Joe came out of the house and waved to us. We went into the funeral parlor, where they had an old-fashioned southern ceremony with some gospel singers from Detroit. It was very simple and tasteful.

I didn't get to talk to Joe because we wanted to stay out of the way as much as possible. Joe stayed with his family. There were photographers and TV cameras all over the place.

On the flight home the plane climbed to 42,000 feet, and at 500 miles an hour, we were back in Detroit by 3:45 in the afternoon.

It was another long day, but I am glad we went. I think it meant something to Joe to have us there.

SUNDAY, JUNE 17

I wanted to hit a few golf balls today, but I didn't know where to go. I am worn out and needed to get away by myself, so I drove north of The Palace, found a small golf course, and knocked around a few.

My back hurt a little when I got home.

I watched a couple of movies on TV—a spy film and *Red River* with James Arness. I used to love him in "Gunsmoke." I tried to relax, but my mind was still going: the funeral; the Isiah story; my future.

MONDAY, JUNE 18

The celebration was fantastic. They had brunch for us at The Palace from ten until half past eleven, then they took us downtown in five buses for the parade. The police are getting good at this. They gave us a motorcycle escort and kept

Addressing the crowd in downtown Detroit, June 18, 1990.

going ahead of us and closing off the ramps to make it an easy trip.

There were 200,000 fans along the parade route. It was really great seeing so many people enjoying themselves, especially after the tragedies that occurred the night we won. This was what the country should see: Detroit at its best. As we got to the riverfront I looked across and saw the Hilton Hotel in Windsor, Ontario. That's where we have training camp. I got a giant lump in my throat. "Am I really not going to be there when camp opens the first week of October?"

Everyone thought I was going to TV, but I hadn't made up my mind yet. This was not going to be an easy decision. The Hilton looked pretty good on the horizon, even after all we've just been through.

When we got back to The Palace we were given ear plugs. Thank God. I didn't know people could make so much noise. They had to close the doors and leave some people outside because of fire regulations. Our organization did it right— complete with laser lights and smoke on the floor. It was like a rock concert. The three TV channels gave up their six o'clock newscasts to carry the celebration, which is unheard of in broadcasting.

As I sat on the stage for our second celebration at The Palace, I thought of all the things I wanted to say about this team. I wanted to tell the fans about the sacrifices these players had made to win. They gave up personal glory, points, assists, rebounds, minutes played. All the things most players live for. Our guys gave up these things so we could develop other players and become a team. We won because our players were secure enough within themselves and unselfish enough to give up their personal stats and glory.

We also won because we were willing to change. I see our team as kind of an amoeba, a form that has a nucleus but is

Speaking to the crowd at The Palace celebration.

always changing. We have twelve players on our roster, and we keep trying to improve each position. Can we trade our number ten guy for someone who might work into our system as number eight or nine? Would Edwards be more effective as a starter rather than coming off the bench? Can Aguirre and Rodman switch places and adapt to their new roles? We're constantly asking ourselves questions like this, testing the changes we suggest, and always trying to improve.

I'm still not sure how we managed to win the championship twice in a row. But having coached at all the levels I have, I know one thing: teams win championships, not individuals. The players must have ability, but it's essential that they perform as a team. They have to be unselfish, and it's hard to find unselfish players.

Much of our success revolves around Isiah Thomas. He has been our unquestioned leader—physically, emotionally, and spiritually. He sets the tone for everyone, including me.

When he realized that the greatest rewards come from winning games, not averaging thirty-five points a night, we began developing as a team. If he comes to practice and doesn't want to work hard, our team goes down. That is one of the most difficult things for me to deal with as the coach. When he is into his game and shows up sky-high, the team goes along with him, and we are very hard to beat.

I talk a lot about teamwork, but even now I'm not sure we've achieved the true team concept. Our guys accept a lot of this philosophy simply because we've won. But if we were to become erratic in winning, we would lose some of the qualities we've acquired. That has nothing to do with me, with coaching, or even with the players themselves. It is just how things go in life.

The big step was to get our players to believe in playing defense, which is nothing but hard work. It's difficult to keep running around screens and chasing your man, night after night, week after week, month after month. They did it, though, and when they found out it could make them successful, they kept on doing it.

When things go wrong, it's human nature to point the finger at someone else. If we lose, it's somebody else's fault. It happens in all sports, and it happens with some of the greatest players, managers, and coaches. It's a lot more difficult to point the finger at ourselves and to accept our share of the blame. Our players weren't perfect about this, but they overcame a lot of the temptation to blame teammates, officials, or coaches. This attitude made us even stronger. If one guy faltered, another one stepped up, and nobody made an issue out of it.

To make this work, you have to take some big chances. You have to have something of the riverboat gambler in you, and it's usually the general manager and/or the coach who has to roll the dice. If you elect to play it safe, your days in the NBA are numbered.

Chapter Thirteen

I didn't get a chance to say any of what I was thinking about our players, our team, our philosophy. When it was my turn to speak, the fans began chanting so loudly I couldn't be heard. "One more year. One more year," they roared.

When Jack McCloskey held up two fingers, the place went wild. Then he knocked them out by holding up three fingers. Then four, then five.

If he keeps it up I'll be a hundred years old, I was thinking.

Oh well, what's wrong with being a hundred years old?

And I heard the old riverboat gambler inside me whispering, "Come on, let's roll the dice one more time."

THURSDAY, JUNE 21

How many people get to meet the president of the United States even once in their lives? We've done it two years in a row, and the second time was as exciting as the first. For us, maybe the second time was even better because we had a shroud over the first experience. We had just lost teammate Rick Mahorn in the expansion draft, and he would be leaving us as soon as our White House visit ended.

Still, last year's occasion was memorable.

We landed in Washington in 1989, about forty-five minutes late because of rainstorms, but the people were ready for us the moment we touched down. They put us on a bus headed for the White House. About three blocks away some FBI men got on and started checking to make sure only the proper personnel were on board, then they took us to the side of the White House.

They ushered us in and started taking us to "holding areas." We went to one area and waited, then to another. This happened three times before they finally took us into a small auditorium.

Inside, a young, good-looking kid with a security badge came up to me. "Do you remember me?" he asked.

His face was familiar, but I wasn't sure where I had seen him. I was about to say something when he answered for me.

"I'm the guy you cut twice at Penn, but now I'm in control of you, so you get to the back of the line."

We both broke up laughing.

They seated our wives in the audience and led us to the platform. Pretty soon the president came out. I marveled at the whole situation because I wondered how many times he has to do this sort of thing. He knew who we were, but he had file cards in front of him so he would say all the right things.

He handled it well, very well.

He asked Isiah Thomas to say something, and Isiah went to the microphone. Right out of the blue, Isiah announced that we no longer were "The Bad Boys" because we had lost

House of Representatives, Washington, D.C., 1990. I'm not sure what Bill Laimbeer was praying for. I hope it wasn't that I'd take the NBC job!

285

Rick Mahorn in the draft. He did it before a national TV audience and I thought of Dr. Ron Berris, our team dentist. He had the patent on the name "The Bad Boys" and was making a lot of money out of it. I could see him gulping and gasping all over the place. Isiah's off-the-cuff comment was going to cost him a lot of dough.

As soon as we got on the bus back to the airport, Oscar Feldman called out to everyone, "You know, guys, in the business world we expect a ten percent improvement from one year to the next. So we're going to expect more out of you next season."

Thinking back on that comment makes me smile.

Our second visit to the White House was as much fun or more. This time Mr. Bush didn't need a file card when he introduced me. He simply said, "And now, the coach of the year as selected by *Gentleman's Quarterly*, Chuck Daly of the Detroit Pistons."

If only my mom could have heard him.